D0290207

Time to Be in Earnest

Also by P. D. James

Non-fiction

P. D. JAMES

Time to Be in Earnest
A Fragment
of Autobiography

'At seventy-seven it is time to be in earnest'
– SAMUEL JOHNSON

FABER & FABER

First published in 1999
by Faber and Faber Limited
Bloomsbury House,
74–77 Great Russell Street, London, WC1B 3DA
This paperback edition first published in 2015

Typeset in Palatino by Discript, London
Printed and bound by CPI Group (UK) Ltd, Croydon, CR0 4YY

All rights reserved

© P. D. James, 1999

The right of P. D. James to be identified as author
of this work has been asserted in accordance with Section 77
of the Copyright, Designs and Patents Act 1988

*This book is sold subject to the condition that it shall not,
by way of trade or otherwise, be lent, resold, hired out or
otherwise circulated without the publisher's prior consent in
any form of binding or cover other than that in which it is
published and without a similar condition including this
condition being imposed on the subsequent purchaser.*

A CIP record for this book
is available from the British Library

ISBN 978-0-571-32569-6

2 4 6 8 10 9 7 5 3 1

To the Memory of my Parents

Sidney Victor James
1895–1979
Dorothy May James
1893–1966

remembered with gratitude and love.

CONTENTS

CONTENTS

ILLUSTRATIONS

PROLOGUE

A diary, if intended for publication (and how many written by a novelist are not?), is the most egotistical form of writing. The assumption is inevitably that what the writer thinks, does, sees, eats and drinks on a daily basis is as interesting to others as it is to himself or herself. And what motive could possibly induce people to undertake the tedium of this daily task – for surely at times it must be tedious – not just for one year, which seems formidable enough, but sometimes for a lifetime? As a lover of diaries, I am glad that so many have found time and energy and still do. How much of interest, excitement, information, history and fascinating participation in another's life would be lost without the diaries of John Evelyn, Samuel Pepys, Virginia Woolf, Evelyn Waugh, Fanny Burney and Francis Kilvert. Even the diary of a fictional Victorian, Cecily Cardew in *The Importance of Being Earnest*, 'simply a very young girl's record of her own thoughts and impressions, and consequently meant for publication', would have its appeal.

I have never up until now kept a diary, largely because of indolence. During my career as a bureaucrat, a working day spent mainly in drafting reports or speeches and writing letters or minutes left little incentive for further writing, particularly the recording of trivia.

And any writing, if it is worth doing, requires care, and I have preferred to spend that care on my fiction. My motive now is to record just one year that otherwise might be lost, not only to children and grandchildren who might have an interest but, with the advance of age and perhaps the onset of the dreaded Alzheimer's, lost also to me. It will inevitably catch on the threads of memory as burrs stick to a coat, so that this will be a partial autobiography and a defence against those who, with increasing frequency, in person or by letter, announce that they have been commissioned to write my biography and invite my co-operation. Always after my refusal there is the response, 'Of course, once you have died there will be biographies. Surely it's better to have one now when you can participate.' Nothing is more disagreeable than the idea of having one now and of participation. Fortunately I am an appallingly bad letter-writer and both my children are reticent, but at least if they and others who enjoy my work are interested in what it was like to be born two years after the end of the First World War and to live for seventy-eight years in this tumultuous century, there will be some record, however inadequate.

I have a friend who assiduously keeps a diary, recording merely the facts of each day, and seems to find satisfaction in looking back over, say, five years and proclaiming that 'This was the day I went to Southend-on-Sea with my sister'. Perhaps the reading of those words brings back a whole day in its entirety – sound, sense, atmosphere, thought – as the smell of decaying seaweed can bring in a rush the essence of long-forgotten summers. The diaries capturing adolescence, I suspect, are mainly therapeutic, containing thoughts that cannot be spoken aloud, particularly in the family, and a relief to overpowering emotions, whether of joy or sorrow. A diary, too, can be a defence against loneliness. It is significant that many adolescent diaries begin 'Dear Diary'. The book, carefully hidden, is both friend and confidant, one from whom neither criticism nor treachery need be feared. The daily words comfort, justify, absolve. Politicians are great keepers of diaries, apparently dictating them daily for eventual use in the inevitable autobiography, laying down ammunition as they might lay down port. But politicians' diaries are invariably dull, Alan Clark's being a notable exception. Perhaps all these motives are subordinate to the need to capture time, to have some small mastery over that which so masters us, to assure ourselves that, as the past can be real, so the future may hold the promise of reality. I write, therefore I am.

Perhaps some compulsive diarists write to validate this experience. Life for them is experienced with more intensity when recollected in tranquillity than it is at the living moment. After all, this happens in fiction. When I am writing a novel, the setting, the characters, the action are clear in my mind before I start work – or so I believe. But it is only when these imaginings are written down, passing, it seems almost physically, from my brain down the arm to my moving hand that they begin to live and move and have their being and assume a different kind of truth.

A diary, by definition, is a daily record. I very much doubt whether this proposed record of one year in my life will be a diary within the proper meaning of that word; certainly I can't see myself recording the events of every day. I feel, too, that many social events can't properly be mentioned since I have no intention of betraying confidences and some of the most interesting things I learn are said to me in confidence. I love gossip in other people's diaries, while recognizing that its interest is in inverse proportion to its truth, but I suspect that this record will have little to offer in the way of titillating revelations. And to look back on one's life is to experience the capriciousness of memory. When I was very young and leaving church with my mother, she told me that the hymn we had sung, 'Blessed are the Pure in Heart', was sung at the funeral of a friend of hers who had died in childbirth with her baby during the great flu pandemic which followed the First World War. Now I can never hear it without thinking of that young mother and her child, both dead before I was born. No effort of will can banish a vague unfocused sadness from my thoughts every time that hymn is sung. And the past is not static. It can be relived only in memory, and memory is a device for forgetting as well as remembering. It, too, is not immutable. It rediscovers, reinvents, reorganizes. Like a passage of prose it can be revised and repunctuated. To that extent, every autobiography is a work of fiction and every work of fiction an autobiography.

So tomorrow, on 3rd August, I shall write the first entry in a record which I propose to keep for one year, from my seventy-seventh to my seventy-eighth birthday. Will I persist with this effort? Only time will tell. And will I be here at the end of the year? At seventy-seven that is not an irrational question. But then is it irrational at any age? In youth we go forward caparisoned in immortality; it is only, I think, in age that we fully realize the transitoriness of life.

There is much that I remember but which is painful to dwell upon. I see no need to write about these things. They are over and must be accepted, made sense of and forgiven, afforded no more than their proper place in a long life in which I have always known that happiness is a gift, not a right. And there are other matters over which memory has exercised its self-defensive censorship. Like dangerous and unpredictable beasts they lie curled in the pit of the subconscious. This seems a merciful dispensation; I have no intention of lying on a psychiatrist's couch in an attempt to hear their waking growls. But then I am a writer. We fortunate ones seldom have need for such an expedient. If, as one psychiatrist wrote – was it Anthony Storr? – 'creativity is the successful resolution of internal conflict', then I, a purveyor of popular genre fiction, and that great genius Jane Austen, have the same expedient for taming our sleeping tigers.

DIARY 1997

SUNDAY, 3RD AUGUST

I am writing this sitting in an almost empty first-class compartment of the 3.32 train from Newton Abbot to Paddington, and staring out at the red Devon countryside, now blurred and seeming to dissolve in rain; even the eagerly awaited stretch of coast at Dawlish and Teignmouth failed in its usual magic.

But it has been a happy weekend despite the continual rain today. I have been at Paignton to help celebrate the Golden Wedding of Dick and Mary Francis. Their son Felix arranged it, at the hotel where they have stayed annually with their family for over forty years, and about sixty relations and friends gathered to rejoice with Dick and Mary on their wonderfully happy and productive partnership of half a century. Fortunately the rain stopped yesterday for the main event, the evening dinner-and-dance, and we were able to wander out from the dining-room to the terrace and drink our champagne looking out over Tor Bay.

The hotel is typical of the kind I relish, a mock castle designed by a Victorian colonel in an excess of either alcoholic or imperial zeal, but with comfortable rooms and a staff, most of whom have been at the hotel for years, who give the impression of enjoying their work and actually liking the guests. The portrait in oils of the founder-architect hangs on the stairs, painted, I suspect, by himself. I was given a room with a balcony overlooking the sea and was able to sleep with the windows open, listening to the surf and the call of the gulls.

On Saturday morning, sitting in the lounge, Mary passed round her photograph album with the wedding pictures, and how they brought back memories of wartime weddings! The cleverly contrived dresses – butter muslin was a popular expedient – since coupons could not be spared, nor was material available for a more traditional dress; the huge bouquets, the small hats of the women guests with the eye-veils, the suits we wore with their over-tailored shoulders, the groom and

3

best man in uniform. It was interesting trying to identify the guests from their photographs of fifty years earlier, the smooth, eager young faces untouched by the depredations of war or the vicissitudes of peace. Only Dick and Mary, smiling into the camera, seem hardly altered.

On Saturday afternoon I took advantage of a break in the weather and walked alone into the little town, its main street jostling with residents doing their weekly shopping, holiday-makers crowding the shops selling the usual holiday and beach ephemera. But I did find one antique shop and bought a small Doulton jug and bowl as mementos of the weekend.

As a writer I like small seaside towns best in autumn or winter. There is something nostalgic and slightly melancholy as well as depressing about the slow death of the season that makes the seaside at the end of summer a suitable setting for a crime novel; the windswept esplanade, the last tight shrivelled buds on the rosebushes in carefully planted municipal gardens, the amusement arcades locked and deserted, the peeling paintwork and deserted shelters. I used such a town in one scene in *Devices and Desires* when the serial killer, the Whistler, kills himself in a seedy hotel, the decline of the year symbolizing his pathetic unlamented end. For me, setting, character, narrative are always interdependent.

I seldom have a birthday without thinking back to that date which none of us can remember, at least not consciously; the moment of birth. Mine took place at home, as most births did in those days, at 164 Walton Street, Oxford. I was a much wanted first child, arriving three years after my parents married when my mother had had medical treatment to make conception possible. My father would have much preferred a boy but was, I think, grateful to have a child, and to hope for a son in the future. It was a long and difficult labour and the doctor was present – unusual in those days when the family wasn't rich. I must at some time have been told the time of my birth, but I have forgotten it and, as those present are now dead, it is one of those facts which I shall never know. I can, however, recall my mother saying that a friend had baked and iced a cake for my christening but that the doctor and my father had between them eaten it all during the long night hours of waiting. This suggests that I was probably born in the early morning. I occasionally find myself wishing that I knew the actual hour, an irrelevance which can only be a form of egotism.

Memory casts a capricious and undiscriminating light. The high peaks may stand brightly illuminated – love, marriage, childbirth, bereavement – but the beam ranges with a fitful radiance over the dark and lost plateaux between. My first memory is of an incident when I was just learning to walk. Perhaps it is this which caused the beam to rest, otherwise there is nothing remarkable about it. I must have been under eighteen months old and my mother had taken me to Winchester to stay with her parents. My grandfather, Edward Hone, was Headmaster of the Choir School, later to become the Pilgrims' School, and the boys were taught in a special classroom block in the garden. Having broken free of my mother, I toddled into the classroom to be met by a burst of laughter from the boys. I remember that my grandfather was sitting at a high desk in front of them and came over at once to take me by the hand and pass me over to my mother, who came fluttering through the door full of apologies. Mother always spoke of her childhood as a happy time, but I'm not sure how far this expressed reality. She was a woman who believed in appropriate emotions and I don't think it would have occurred to her to criticize either of her parents or the lives that they led.

The only information I have about the Choir School comes from *A History of the Pilgrims' School* written by John Crook, published in 1981, which was sent to me a few years ago by one of my uncles. I find it interesting, not only because of the light it sheds on my mother's early life, but because the school must have been typical of not very distinguished boarding schools of its time. My grandfather took over the position of Schoolmaster of the Choristers in 1887. His predecessor was a William Southcott, who was required to resign following a dispute about the voice trials during which he and the organist came to blows. Colebrook House was certainly a beautiful place in which to be brought up. It was, and is, a large sixteenth-century building facing the east end of the Cathedral with a mill stream flowing through its gardens. My grandfather taught the Choristers, virtually unaided except for one assistant, and on occasion also sang solos in the Choir – he had a beautiful tenor voice. My grandmother ran the boarding school. Edward Hone received £15 for each Chorister and £50 as a housemaster's allowance, to be reduced by £5 for every non-Chorister boarder he received over the number of ten. It seems to have been a complex and far from satisfactory arrangement and money was certainly in short supply. However, things became a little easier in 1905 when Colebrook House was made an all-boarding school and my grandfather's allowance was considerably increased.

Even so, life at Colebrook House seems to have been tough. The boys were woken at 7 o'clock in the morning throughout the year and were required to wash in cold water. Breakfast at 8 o'clock consisted of thick slices of bread and dripping, known as 'toke', though occasionally there was fish paste or marmalade. The only morning on which a cooked breakfast was provided was on the last day of term when the boys would be given a boiled egg before their journey home. My grandfather was obviously anxious that the school should emulate more famous preparatory schools and the boys wore Eton suits, mortar-boards and carefully blacked boots. They would make their way in a crocodile to the Cathedral, first of all for practice and then for Mattins, which lasted for three-quarters of an hour and was followed by morning school until 1 o'clock.

Lunch was apparently more satisfying than breakfast. It was taken in the elegant dining-room at the back of the house. My grandfather would carve, my grandmother and their two daughters would hand round the vegetables. Perhaps because it was a meal shared with the family, Mr Crook describes it as 'tolerable'. Lunch was followed by afternoon school until 3.45, unless the weather was fine when games would be played instead. Evensong was at 4 o'clock and there was then a further choir practice for the boys until teatime. This, like breakfast, was a miserable affair, consisting of tea and 'toke' with black treacle, which had spread all over the plate on which it was served before the boys arrived. (This was the practice my mother continued during our childhood. Breakfast was always bread, butter, treacle and tea, and the treacle would be spooned on to our plates the night before so that by the morning it had completely covered the plate up to the rim. In childhood we only had an egg occasionally, sometimes on a Sunday morning.)

Bedtime was early for the boys at Colebrook House. My mother or her sister, my Aunt Marjorie, would take a dish of 'toke' and a jug of cocoa to the schoolroom, after which insubstantial supper the boys would go up to the dormitories. As one might expect, Sunday was a particularly busy day for the Choristers. The first service would be 11 o'clock Mattins occasionally followed by a Choral Communion. The most important of the Sunday services, however, was Evensong at 3.30, and this included a lengthy anthem. It was to be many years before Holy Communion became the main service at the Cathedral.

The boys were inevitably educationally disadvantaged by the demands of the Cathedral services, but my grandfather was a conscientious schoolmaster and did his best. I don't know whether I actually remember what he looked like, or whether the image firmly fixed in my mind comes from a single photograph. In this he looks very like Edward VII: heavily built, bearded, bespectacled. He was a good teacher of English and was genuinely musical, but he was a severe schoolmaster and it was good for the boys that this severity was tempered by his assistant, Percy Spillett. I remember my mother speaking of him with great affection. He seems to have been one of those gentle and erratic schoolmasters, typical of his period: a bachelor, tall, thin, moustached, scholarly, soft-voiced and with a passion for palaeolithic artefacts. Sunday afternoon walks over St Catherine's Hill were a hunt for the prehistoric treasures which never came to light. Between them Edward Hone and Percy Spillett seem to have given the boys as good a general education as was possible under the circumstances.

Both my grandfathers were schoolmasters and both were fond of music. My paternal grandfather, Walter James, was also a good linguist who for some years worked for the British and Foreign Bible Society. I know little about him, but I do remember visiting him and his wife when I was about ten and they lived in a small terraced house in Southsea. He had by then retired, but was an organist at the Garrison Church. Some of the anthems he wrote for the choir were published, but none, as far as I know, has survived. I think he was largely self-educated; certainly I can remember a framed diploma in the hall which I think was awarded by London University after he had taken an external degree. I have always believed that he was Welsh, although I have never been told so. Certainly I see his, and indeed my father's, face very clearly when I am in the Principality. My father was born in Reading, but I have no idea what my grandfather was doing there at the time. Some of his brothers and one sister were certainly born overseas, and I am told that for some years Walter James acted as tutor to the children of the Rajah of Sarawak.

My father never spoke of his childhood but I don't think it was easy. Money seems to have always been short. Certainly he left school

7

at the first possible time and entered the Patent Office, I think at the age of sixteen. He is an example of the waste of intelligence which was tolerated during the first half of this century. Just before the First World War he must have had a job at Winchester, either in the Patent Office, which seems unlikely, or in the local office of the Inland Revenue. It was in Winchester that he met my mother. This isn't surprising as he was exceptionally fond of music and would naturally have attended the Cathedral services. They became engaged during the war and married, I think in 1917 when he was a young officer in the Machine-gun Corps. Mother was twenty-five, an age at which, in those days, a girl was beginning to feel that she might miss her chance of marriage.

I think the days of the engagement must have been some of their happiest. A few years ago I found a photograph of my father sitting with his troop, a slight, good-looking young man with his hair parted down the middle as was then customary, the three stripes of a sergeant on his sleeve. On the back is written, 'To my darling girl, a better one next time'. There must at one time have been love, or what both of them believed to be love; but they were ill-suited. My mother was sentimental, warm-hearted, vivacious, impulsive and not intelligent and, although she had a rich contralto voice and loved the church music which had been part of her childhood, she neither understood nor loved music as deeply as did my father. He was intelligent, reserved, sarcastic, deeply distrustful of sentimentality, fastidious and with little ability to show affection. I don't think he had known much demonstrative love in his childhood and what a child doesn't receive he can seldom later give. I think the first years were happy and became more so when I arrived, the first longed-for child. I was followed eighteen months later by my sister Monica and, eighteen months after her birth, the hoped-for son arrived. He was christened Edward, after Edward Hone.

Children live in occupied territory. The brave and the foolhardy openly rebel against authority, whether harsh or benign. But most tread warily, outwardly accommodating themselves to alien mores and edicts while living in secret their iconoclastic and subversive lives.

I think that all three of us realized quite early in life that we were the children of an unhappy marriage. Of course it lasted; marriages, however unhappy, did last in those days. Divorce was still regarded not only as a disgrace, but as a social failure, and for my mother, deeply religious, it would have been a sin. But there were more material considerations. It was just not possible for my father to support two households, and my mother – untrained except for her nursing experience in the First World War which was, of course, voluntary – had absolutely no means of earning a living for herself and three children. These were inhibitions which applied to all except the rich and those powerful enough to defy convention.

For the whole of my schooldays, both in primary school and at the High School in Cambridge, I never knew a child whose parents were either separated or divorced. No doubt this fact hid many wretchedly unhappy marriages and some that for the wife were little more than institutionalized slavery. But for the stoically enduring there were compensations. Couples, knowing that they were yoked together for life, frequently made the best of what they had. Those who were able to survive the more turbulent years of youth and middle age often found in each other a reassuring and comforting companionship in old age. They had a far smaller expectation of happiness, admittedly, and a far lesser tendency to regard happiness as a right. All our brightly minted social reforms, the sexual liberation since the war, the guilt-free divorce, the ending of the stigma of illegitimacy, have had their shadow side. Today we have a generation of children more disturbed, more unhappy, more criminal, indeed more suicidal than in any previous era. The sexual liberation of adults has been bought at a high price and it is not the adults who have paid it.

MONDAY, 4TH AUGUST

The beginning of a new year, whether the calendar year or the day after a birthday, produces in me a desire to get rid of rubbish, rearrange my books and drag into the light of day old boxes of long-forgotten papers. This morning I discovered a book of press cuttings which I started keeping after the publication of my first novel, *Cover Her Face*, published in the autumn of 1962. It is a hardback analysis book which I imagine I picked up as a bargain, finding the ruled blue and red lines helpful to the careful placing of my cuttings. I can't be the only writer who, in the flush of triumph and excitement after publication of her first novel, decided to keep reviews and articles. For me the enthusiasm lasted only until publication of the second novel. But I was glad to find this first press-cuttings book although it has survived more by chance than by careful hoarding.

Some of the reviews were laudatory, and most encouraging. All assumed that P. D. James was a man except Leo Harris in *Books and Bookmen*, who wrote: 'This is a very fine first, and I can't help feeling that the author is a woman.' E. D. O'Brien in *The Illustrated London News* wrote: 'It is always pleasant, though not always possible, to praise a first novel. *Cover Her Face*, by P. D. James, justifies just such an enthusiastic encomium.' It ended: 'Insofar as this is a mystery, I failed to solve it. Mr James will, I hope, give us many more such treats.' Francis Iles in *The Guardian* wrote: '*Cover Her Face* by P. D. James is one of those extraordinary first novels which seem to step straight into the sophisticated preserves of the experienced writer, yet retain the newcomer's freshness of approach.' The reviewer in the *Oldham Evening Chronicle & Standard* wrote that the book was 'the kind of novel which suggests that the author is planning a lengthy career in the business – particularly with the introduction of a colourful character in Chief Inspector Adam Dalgliesh'. But he or she much deplored the cost of the book – 18 shillings. By present book-price standards a hardback at less than a pound was not exceptionally dear, but it was certainly not cheap for what the reviewer a little unkindly described as 'this kind of material'. An established writer, he suggested, could perhaps get away with this overpricing, but not a newcomer.

There is even the cutting of an interview with photograph by a reporter from the *Surrey Comet* who came to talk to my younger daughter, Jane. We were then living at 127 Richmond Park Road, Kingston. I was working as a Principal Administrative Assistant at the North West Regional Hospital Board. Both Jane and her elder sister, Clare, were at home, and my husband Connor was with us, rarely, between bouts of hospitalization. Obviously he hadn't been at home at the time of the interview but, due to Jane's discretion, the article is blessedly free of details about his illness or suggestions of the brave little woman writing to support her family. Jane said that her mother had always been keen on writing, was highly delighted to have this first novel published, and that most of her evenings and weekends were spent working on her books. It is an apt comment on what life at the time was actually like. The article ends: 'In Inspector Dalgliesh, she has a character who will benefit from greater attention and who no doubt will be called upon to solve future P. D. James mysteries.' There is a photograph in which I sit, arms folded, gazing at the camera, hair obviously newly set, and with an air of slightly quizzical self-satisfaction.

It is interesting how many reviewers assumed that I was a man. One of the questions I am often asked after signings is whether I deliberately chose to write under the name P. D. James in order to conceal my sex. Some questioners actually assume that I thought it an advantage to be mistaken for a man. This certainly never entered my mind and I am grateful to have been born a woman, perhaps more from an innate positiveness rather than from any careful weighing-up of the relative advantages and disadvantages. But I would certainly never dream of pretending to be other than a woman. Not only would this be pointless, since the truth becomes known fairly quickly, but women are generally well regarded as crime writers and only a minority of readers would reject a book because they disliked the sex of the author, although I have to admit I have known cases. My memory is that when the manuscript was ready to be sent off to an agent or publisher, I wrote down Phyllis James, Phyllis D. James, P. D. James, and decided that the last and shortest was enigmatic and would look best on the book spine. It never occurred to me to write other than under my maiden name. I have never regretted my choice, particularly now, when I may have to sign as many as three hundred books at an American signing. That is seldom a problem here; the British are much less addicted to standing in long lines to meet an author.

I began writing *Cover Her Face* when I was in my mid-thirties. It was a late beginning for someone who knew from early childhood that she wanted to be a novelist and, looking back, I can't help regretting what I now see as some wasted years. In the war there was always the uncertainty of survival and one needed more determination and dedication than I possessed to embark on an 80,000-word work when the bombs were falling and lack of paper made it difficult for anyone new to get published. There is also in my nature that streak of indolence which made it more agreeable to contemplate the first book than actually to begin writing it. It was easier, too, to see the war years as a preparation for future endeavour rather than an appropriate time to begin. I can remember the moment, but not the date, when I finally realized that there would never be a convenient time to write my first book and that, unless I did make a start, I would eventually be saying

11

to my grandchildren that what I had wanted to be was a novelist. Even to think of speaking these words was a realization of potential failure.

I can't now remember how long it took to write *Cover Her Face*, but I suspect it was years rather than months. When I began the book I was working at Paddington Hospital Management Committee, and the book was largely planned on the Central Line as I travelled from Redbridge to Liverpool Street, then on by the Metropolitan Line to Paddington. The writing, always by hand, was done in the early mornings when I would get up in time to spend about an hour writing before I needed to leave for work, occasionally at weekends between visits to Connor in hospital, and sometimes on the journey. The work was hindered by family emergencies, by pressure of my job and by the need to spend some evenings at the City of London College in Moorgate, studying for the qualification in hospital administration which I hoped might eventually result in a job sufficiently well paid to support my family. I don't think it occurred to me then that writing novels would be either lucrative enough or dependable enough to rely on.

It didn't occur to me either to begin with anything other than a detective story. They had formed my own recreational reading in adolescence and I was influenced in particular by the women writers: Dorothy L. Sayers, Margery Allingham, Ngaio Marsh and Josephine Tey. I had no wish to write a strongly autobiographical novel about the war or Connor's illness. I suppose, too, I have a streak of scepticism, even of morbidity, which attracted me to the exploration of character and motive under the trauma of a police investigation of a violent death. I could always imagine myself writing a novel which wasn't a detective story – indeed, I have written two, *Innocent Blood* and *The Children of Men* – but I can't imagine myself writing a book which doesn't include death. Death has always fascinated me and even in childhood I was always aware of the fragility of life.

And there were other reasons for my choice. I love structure in a novel and the detective story is probably the most structured of popular fiction. Some would say that it is the most artificial, but then all fiction is artificial, a careful rearrangement by selection of the writer's internal life in a form designed to make it accessible and attractive to a reader. The construction of a detective story might be formulaic; the writing need not be. And I was setting out, I remember, with high artistic ambitions. I didn't expect to make a fortune, but I did hope one day to be regarded as a good and serious novelist. It seemed to me, as it has to others, that there can be no better apprenticeship for an aspiring novelist than a classical detective story with its technical problems of balancing a credible mystery with believable characters and a setting which both complements and integrates the action. And I may have needed to write detective fiction for the same reasons as aficionados enjoy the genre: the catharsis of carefully controlled terror, the bringing of order out of disorder, the reassurance that we live in a comprehensible and moral universe and that, although we may not achieve justice, we can at least achieve an explanation and a solution.

Glancing now through *Cover Her Face*, I am struck by how conventional it is. This is very much a detective story in the mode of Agatha Christie even if it aspires to probe more deeply into the minds and motives of its characters. Here is the English village, the stock characters of priest and doctor, the anxious virgin who runs the home for unmarried mothers. The book is very much of its time. Today the victim, Sally Jupp, would not have found it necessary either to seek refuge in Miss Liddell's home, or to take a job as a house parlourmaid with the Maxie family. The local authority would have provided her and her child with a flat and the local social workers would have helped her to furnish it, and welfare payments, although not generous, would have enabled her to survive. But I'm surprised how many readers say that they like *Cover Her Face*. It seems that the cosy, domestic, English village murder has never quite lost its appeal.

After the book was finally finished and typed I had a stroke of luck. I was selected for a three-month residential course at the King's Fund College for Hospital Administrators, then situated in the Bayswater Road. The head of the college was an ex-headmaster of Brighton School. He was a good administrator and I suspect had been a good teacher, but not immune to that particular brand of social snobbery which I have encountered more than once in the headmasters of minor public schools. But he liked me and was helpful to me, and I was invited by his wife to spend a weekend at their oasthouse in Kent. A fellow guest was the actor Miles Malleson, for me always associated with his incomparable portrayal of Dr Chasuble in the film of *The Importance of Being Earnest*. He had written books about the theatre and I confided to him that I had just finished my first novel. He

13

suggested that I send it to his agent, Elaine Greene at MCA, and gave me an introduction. My memory is that I took the manuscript in person. I can recall an imposing building in Piccadilly, the large letters on the brass nameplate, and meeting this dark-haired, rather intimidating American woman who accepted the manuscript but was not, as I remember, either particularly effusive or encouraging.

Elaine was at that time married to Hugh Carleton Greene, Director General of the BBC, and after reading my manuscript she had gone with him to have lunch or dinner – I forget which – at All Souls College, Oxford. There she had sat next to Charles Monteith, a Director of Faber and Faber. Elaine, an enthusiast for detective fiction, had said how sad she was at the death of the crime writer Cyril Hare, whose novels, mostly set in the world of law, are some of the most elegantly written in the genre. One, *Tragedy At Law*, is in my view among the most enjoyable classical detective stories. Charles Monteith said that Faber would now start looking for a replacement for Cyril Hare, and Elaine told him that she thought she had found one. She sent the manuscript to him next day and Charles accepted it. I think this success produced some unease among my daughters, who had read that any writer of real talent could paper his or her walls with rejection slips. They tactfully pointed this out, anxious to arm me against future disappointment. I retorted with some tartness that children with no faith in Mummy's talent would not get new bicycles out of the proceeds. A couple of extremely good bicycles as well as other small treats constituted for me financial success.

I have remained with Faber and Faber ever since, and remained also with Elaine until her death. After that her younger partner, Carol Heaton, took over and I am more than happy to be in her hands.

I can remember the moment of that telephone call with great clarity. I was late home from work and returned as usual to an empty house. My husband was in Goodmayes Hospital, the children both away and my parents-in-law had retired to Suffolk. The telephone rang almost as soon as I unlocked the door. Elaine had been trying to get me earlier and had made one last attempt. Receiving the news that I was at last to be a published author was one of the most exciting moments of my life, far more exciting, in retrospect, than receiving the first six free copies of the novel. It would have been good to have someone with whom to share the news, but I don't recall that this mattered at the time. It was sufficient to know that I was going to be a novelist. I knew that evening, as I pranced up and down the hall, that people do literally jump for joy.

There was one disappointment. The book was due to be published in 1961, the following year, but I received a letter to say that Faber's fiction list was too large and that my novel was being deferred for twelve months. At the time the wait seemed insupportable, but at least it gave me an added incentive to make a beginning on my second novel with quiet confidence that it would stand a chance of acceptance.

TUESDAY, 5TH AUGUST

This morning I caught the 11.30 train from Liverpool Street to come to Southwold where this evening I was engaged to speak to the Southwold Archaeological and Natural History Society. The venue was a room on the pier. I was met at Darsham station by Steve, who normally drives me when I come to Southwold. I have been familiar with the East Coast since childhood. After the First World War my father purchased one of the large army bell tents and this would be erected on the cliff at Pakefield, just south of Lowestoft. Here under brown flapping canvas we would spend two weeks each summer, the five of us sleeping with our feet towards the pole like the spokes of a wheel. It was fun for us children but hardly a holiday for our mother. But then I can't remember her having a proper holiday during all her married life.

Suffolk is not the loveliest of English counties, its beauties less accessible, less dramatically beautiful than more famous parts of England, but I early grew to love the great skies, the sense of space, the bird-loud estuaries and the churches.

I have used East Anglia as a setting for a number of my novels, the last example being *Devices and Desires*. The book had its genesis when I was exploring Suffolk with an elderly long-standing friend, Joyce Flack, who drove me in her ancient Mini. I stood for a few minutes alone on a deserted stretch of shingle and looked over the cold and dangerous North Sea. I remember that there were two wooden fishing boats scrunched into the shingle and some brown nets strung between poles, drying in the wind. Closing my eyes, I could hear nothing but the tinny rattle of the shingle drawn back by the waves and the low hissing of the wind, and I thought that I could have been standing on the self-same spot a thousand years ago, hearing the same sounds, looking out over the same sea. And then I opened my eyes and, looking south, saw the silent and stark outline of Sizewell nuclear power station dominating the coastline. I thought of all the lives that have been lived on this shore, of the windmills, once providers of power, now prosperous homes, of the ruined abbeys at Leiston and South Cove which seemed like monuments to a decaying faith, of the detritus of my generation, the great lumps of concrete half embedded in the shingle, and the concrete pillboxes, part of the defences against the expected German invasion on this coast. And immediately I knew with an almost physical surge of excitement that I had a novel. The next book would be set on a lonely stretch of East Anglian coast under the shadow of a nuclear power station. The book, at present no more than a nebulous idea born of a moment in time and a specific place, might take more than a year to research and plan and the writing even longer, but already it has life.

The Southwold house which I bought in July 1995 enclosed me as I entered it with a sense of welcoming peace. Brian Duncan, the builder, has removed the cumbersome and difficult-to-operate gas fire in the sitting-room and opened the fireplace. It now looks much as it must have done when the house was built in the seventeenth century. He managed to find old bricks to line it and an oak beam for the lintel, which matches the beams in the ceiling.

The lecture this evening was appropriately on the use of place in fiction, a title which seemed to me to relate only remotely to the concerns of the Society although this, they had told me, was not a problem. The atmosphere of indulgent holiday expectancy was helped by the constant sound of the sea splurging against the pier. I illustrated the talk with examples of the way setting is used in fiction: to create mood and atmosphere; as an aid to characterization; to root the action in the firm soil of a recognized place, thus aiding credibility, and to provide that contrast which, in crime fiction, can enhance horror as well as providing a relief from it. Setting can also have a symbolic importance, as does the black tower in my novel of that name and the nuclear power station in *Devices and Desires*.

The talk was followed by twenty minutes of questions and discussion. One question which I can be sure of getting, and did so this evening, is: Why are women writers pre-eminent in the field of crime fiction? I reply that if we are surveying the whole field of crime writing, then it's hardly accurate to say that we are. Even if we consider only the detective story, I think it is still arguable that the sexes may be more equal than is sometimes alleged. Even so, many people, asked to name writers of detective fiction, would begin with Agatha Christie and probably go on to Dorothy L. Sayers, Margery Allingham, Ngaio Marsh and, today, Ruth Rendell and a score of other well-known women crime writers here and in the United States. Some of the greatest novelists writing in English have been women: Jane Austen, the Brontës, George Eliot, Virginia Woolf. As women's creativity seems to find a natural outlet in fiction, it's not surprising that women should be attracted to fiction's most popular form.

And women have, I think, natural advantages, particularly that eye for detail, for the minutiae of everyday living, which is so important in clue-making. George Orwell has said that murder, the unique crime, should arise only from strong emotions, and here too women can be pre-eminent since they have a greater interest in those strong emotions than they have in violence or weaponry. I expect, too, that women find the conventions and the form both satisfying and supportive. Thus psychologically buttressed, we can deal with violent events and emotions with greater security than we could in any other form of fiction. The detective story is, after all, one way in which we can cope with violent death, fictionalize it, give it a recognizable shape and, at the end of the book, show that even the most intractable mystery is capable of solution, not by supernatural means or by good fortune, but by human intelligence, human perseverance, and human courage.

I've been considering the question since my return home. According to Julian Symons in his book *Bloody Murder*, the first authentic note of the detective story proper was struck as early as 1794 in the novel *Caleb Williams*. Not surprisingly this is by a man, William Godwin, Shelley's father-in-law. Certainly this novel has many of the elements of classical detection: a central mystery, physical clues, an amateur detective, a pursuit and disguise. It even fore-shadows the use of this formulaic genre to say something about society which the author regards as important. As the intellectual leader of the English radical movement, Godwin believed in an ideal anarchy in which there would be no crime, no administration and no government. Hazlitt said that, once begun, it was a novel impossible to put down. Personally I find it unreadable.

I suppose most readers would award the distinction of being the first modern detective story to *The Moonstone* by Wilkie Collins, published in 1868, and again by a man. In my view no other single novel more clearly adumbrates the later development of the genre. Wilkie Collins created one of the earliest fictional police detectives, Sergeant Cuff, eccentric but professional, shrewdly knowledgeable about human nature, and based on the real-life Scotland Yard detective Jonathan Whicher. Collins is meticulously accurate in his treatment of medical and forensic details, there is an emphasis on the importance of physical clues, and all the clues – a paint-stained nightdress, a smeared door, a metal chain – are made available to the reader, foreshadowing the tradition of the fair-play rule whereby the detective must never be in possession of more information than is the reader. The clever shifting of suspicion from one character to another is done with great adroitness, and this emphasis on physical evidence and the cunning manipulation of the reader were both to become common. But the novel has other more important virtues as a detective story. Wilkie Collins is excellent at describing the physical appearance and the atmosphere of the setting and makes good use of the contrast between the secure and prosperous Verinder household and the eerie loneliness of the shivering sands, between the exotic and accursed jewel which is stolen, and the outwardly respectable privileged lives of upper-class Victorians.

But *The Moonstone* is a single book; I suppose that the credit for having, as it were, invented the detective story and laying down its main conventions has to be shared between two writers, and again both of them are male. It can be argued that, in five tales alone, Edgar Allan Poe anticipated virtually every type of succeeding detective story. The sensational thriller in *The Murders in the Rue Morgue* (1841), the treatment of a real-life crime combined with meticulous deduction in *The Mystery of Marie Roget* (1842), the tale of a secret agent in *The Purloined Letter* (1844), a puzzle revolving round the breaking of a code in *The Gold Bug* (1842) and a murder mystery solved by the narrator in *Thou Art the Man* (1844). Poe's detective, Chevalier C. Auguste Dupin, is an early example of the cerebral detective, a man who solves crimes not by acts of egregious bravery or spectacular cunning, but by observation and reason.

But if the detective story was born in the United States, one could argue that it came of age in Victorian England. Conan Doyle is the creator of the most famous detective in literature. He bequeathed to the genre a respect for reason, a reliance on ratiocination rather than on physical force, an abhorrence of sentimentality and the power to create an atmosphere of mystery and Gothic horror which is yet firmly rooted in physical reality. Above all, of course, and more than any other writer, he established the tradition of the great detective, the omniscient amateur whose personal, sometimes bizarre eccentricity is contrasted with the rationality of his methods and who provides for the reader the comforting reassurance that, despite our apparent powerlessness, we yet inhabit an intelligible universe.

Then there are the more modern American writers, Raymond Chandler and Dashiell Hammett, both fine novelists, who have had an influence beyond the genre. Chandler was born in America but brought up in England and was much influenced by Hammett. Most aficionados of detective fiction would agree with Chandler that his books should be read and judged, not as escapist literature, but as works of art. I would only add that I don't see why escapist literature shouldn't also be a work of art. Chandler would undoubtedly have deplored many of the detective stories written by women. He wrote that the English might not be the best writers in the world, but they were the best dull writers, and he inveighed against what he saw as the artificiality of the detective story, proclaiming his wish to give murder back to the people who committed it. This, of course, is to reiterate an old criticism, but in his case, I think, with little force. Chandler's lone romantic hero striding down the mean streets, imperfect but still superior to the viciousness and savagery which surrounds him, is in his way as much a figure of fantasy as is Lord Peter Wimsey, Roderick Alleyn or Albert Campion. Women too, in the American hard-boiled novel, seem often devoid of reality. They are either patient little helpmeets tapping away at the typewriter in the office, or seductive villainesses, as irrelevant to the hero's integrity as they are to his life.

Then there are the novelists of espionage, the best of those surely being men: Graham Greene, Eric Ambler and John le Carré, with his fascination with treachery and betrayal and his marvellously persuasive evocation of the sad bureaucracy of spying. No woman has written about international espionage with quite the same authority.

But I don't think it is rewarding to argue over which sex is pre-eminent in the genre. And perhaps the balance is shifting. Too many male crime writers, obsessed with violence and with the search for

19

what they, a uniquely privileged generation, see as the gritty reality which they have never personally experienced, are portraying a world as nihilistic as it is bloody. Perhaps it is to the women we must look for psychological subtlety and the exploration of moral choice, which for me are at the heart of even the most grittily realistic of crime fiction.

Tom and Mary Norman arrive tomorrow – they say shortly after five – to stay until Saturday. Tom is one of my oldest friends and one of the few who knew Connor. They met during the war when both went to Cambridge for some preliminary entrance examination before taking their B.A. courses. They were due to have a practical examination the next day and Tom suggested that they should go down to the laboratories to see if the incubators were working. If they were, at a time when energy had to be carefully conserved, it would be possible to draw up a list of probable questions. The incubators *were* working and Tom gave Connor a list of subjects for last-minute revision. Connor told himself, 'This man is a genius and I will stay close to him all my life', which, with a few difficult years' intermission during the worst of Connor's illness and when they were serving in different theatres of war, he effectively did.

I can't remember my first meeting with Connor, but I know that it was when I was working at the Festival Theatre in Cambridge. I was assistant box office manager, assistant stage manager, and indeed assistant to anyone who needed a willing if inexperienced factotum. I had finally said goodbye to my first disastrous job in the tax office at Ely and, in taking the job at the theatre, probably had some idea that I would like to be a playwright and that this would be good experience. It was certainly experience of a kind. Connor and Tom came together to one of the performances and we met. I had no intention of asking my parents for permission to marry – parental consent was then necessary if bride or groom were under twenty-one – but we married on 8th August 1941, five days after I came of age.

I shan't write about my marriage in this incomplete diary except to say that I have never found, or indeed looked for, anyone else with whom I have wanted to spend the rest of my life. I think of Connor with love and with grief for all he has missed: the grandchildren in whom he would have taken such joy, my success, which would have made the burden of mental illness easier to bear – as money always does – the journeys, the laughter, the small triumphs and the day-to-day living we haven't shared. Tom Norman is one of only two friends now living who experienced with us those Cambridge days and, later, our move to London, the small one-bedroom flat we rented in Manchester Square which was later destroyed in the bombing, Connor's life as a medical student. I don't see him often enough. It is one of the penalties of fame and its concomitant over-busyness, and a matter for shame as well as regret, that our lives become ill-directed and we spend so little time with the people we love and most wish to be with.

SATURDAY, 9TH AUGUST

Tom and Mary dropped me at Darsham station this morning to catch the train before themselves driving back to Winterborne Houghton in Dorset. The visit was a happy one for the three of us.

Mary was anxious to see Somerleyton, so we drove there on Thursday. It is an extravagantly splendid example of early Victorian country-house architecture, built round a Tudor-Jacobean shell but retaining few of the original features of the old house. The particulars of sale prepared in 1861, when Sir Morton Peto was forced to sell the estate, described the Hall as 'a specimen of the architecture of the Elizabethan period, transformed by the purist taste into a rich and noble example of Anglo-Italian, a rich, harmonious style pervades the whole building'. It is very much a family home, which I liked.

We had lunch there in a small agreeable café with a view of the gardens, and then went on to see the Church of St Mary the Virgin at Blundeston, notable for its round thin tower constructed in about 988. Two women from the village appeared while we were there. They took pleasure in telling us about the church. I said how glad we were that it wasn't shut, and one of them replied that the police had advised that it should be and that one of their previous vicars had, indeed, closed it for a time but the congregation had insisted that it remain open. She said: 'Why should we let vandals close our church when Hitler couldn't do it?'

I love visiting country churches although, not being a motorist, the opportunity to do so is limited. Usually now there is someone from the village keeping watch and ready and willing to talk about the church and its history. The pride and the love shown are appealing. The custodians are seldom young and I wonder how long this close personal interest will continue.

On Friday we drove south to Thorpeness, that extraordinary black and white mock-Tudor holiday village created between the wars, a bastion of middle-class respectability and conformity incongruously facing the bleak wind-scoured beach and the untameable North Sea. For me it is peopled with the ghosts of 1930s nursemaids and small children in their floppy-brimmed hats. A good place to set a detective story? Certainly it provides an intriguing contrast between claustrophobic security and the contaminating disruption of violent crime, but the architecture is too uniform to stimulate the creative imagination. Then from Thorpeness to Aldeburgh, where we ate a picnic lunch at one of the wooden tables with benches outside the Moot Hall. It was warm and sunny, as it was for the whole of the visit.

One of the delights of being with Tom and Mary is their knowledge of natural history. There isn't a bird, butterfly, flower or tree which they can't name. They spend much time travelling, often in some discomfort, in remote areas of Asia, searching for and photographing rare orchids. One, which Tom was the first to discover and describe, is named after him. At Covehithe we saw a butterfly that Tom said was called the Holly Blue and which he recognized as female because of the darker hue round its wings. It lives for just three days, and I wondered whether ours were the only human eyes that had actually seen it during that brief span. As Tom and Mary moved through the gate leading to the abbey ruin, the butterfly fluttered to a leaf close to me and rested motionless. It was one of those rare moments in which a fugitive beauty, briefly contemplated, untouchable, is experienced with a peculiar intensity, the sense of being a privileged spectator of a life which, however brief, is part of a mysterious whole.

MONDAY, 11TH AUGUST

I'm back again in London. Last night was swelteringly hot and I awoke this morning to find myself lying in a pool of sweat. The house is again being underpinned and the mess outside is appalling. The two young men on the job, who seem to work cheerfully in this awful heat, have dug deep holes at the front, side and back. Despite my offer of unlimited tea, surely necessary in this heat, they won't come into the house – I imagine because the firm have a policy that they never do – but bring their own drinks with them. The house today looks particularly depressing and dilapidated. The cracks seem to have widened during the last few days as if the house has resigned itself to decrepitude. I shall have to wait several months after the under-pinning is finished before any repairs and redecoration can be carried out. I long to see it restored to what it once was.

I had lunch with Frances Fyfield at the Belvedere in Holland Park. It is always good to see Frances, whom I admire as a crime writer and value as a friend. Arriving early, I spent some time quietly walking round what must be one of London's loveliest parks. I have been fortunate all my life to live only in beautiful and historic places, first Oxford, then Ludlow, then Cambridge, and finally London. I can't remember when my parents moved from Oxford to Ludlow, but it was certainly before I went to school. I don't think young children respond to natural beauty; people are more important than flowers and trees; but to live in Ludlow from the age of four to eleven meant that my eyes saw little of the world outside home which was without beauty, and this constant exposure to the delights of one of England's loveliest towns must surely have left its legacy.

Looking back on my early schooldays, they seem closer to the Victorian age than they do to the life of a primary school child today, and indeed they were closer, in time as well as in attitudes to teaching. I was taken to my first school, which I must have attended from the age of five, not by my mother, but by a boy little older than myself who lived nearby. My memory is of being lugged along at a furious pace by this reluctant but not unkind attendant. The schoolroom was large and square with a huge coal fire burning in winter, the fire surrounded by a high fire-guard. It was a room which came alive in memory when I read an account of the schoolroom at Lowood in *Jane Eyre*, although I am sure the two establishments had absolutely nothing else in common. There were no inside lavatories and I can distinctly recall the day in which I was sitting on one of the wooden seats in the outside shed when part of the plaster ceiling fell on my head. I was temporarily stunned by surprise – although certainly not hurt, since no one at home was ever told of the misadventure – but I sat there, my head covered in plaster, until one of the children, alerted by the noise, summoned a teacher. I can remember her gazing at me with an expression half-shocked, half-amused.

We seldom went straight home after school. My small minder had a fertile and slightly morbid imagination (but who am I to complain?) and would lug me down to the river in the hope of seeing drowned bodies of which he seemed in daily expectation. We were disappointed, but I do remember being taken to see a man who had broken his arm. He was sitting in the back garden on a kitchen chair, nursing his arm and moaning, and we children gazed at him through the chink in the wooden fence in fascinated anticipation, although he was a very poor substitute for a drowned corpse.

The two medical problems of the school were nits and ringworm, the second the more serious. Those afflicted would have their heads shaved and subsequently wore small cotton caps, a badge of shame, in which they looked like diminutive clowns. One compensation, however, was that girls with straight hair – regarded as an affliction in those days – frequently grew it with curls after the shaving.

My second school, which I remember much more clearly, was the British School, a red-brick building on Old Street, fronted by an asphalt playground and iron railings. The school was named British, not from patriotism or any necessity to distinguish it from alien establishments, of which in Ludlow there were none, but because it was one of the schools founded by the British Society, a voluntary and charitable organization established in 1840 to provide elementary education for the children of the poor. The children of the early nineteenth century would still have felt perfectly at home in it. And the name was not inappropriate. A map, permanently displayed in the largest double classroom, with its splurges of red – Canada, India, Australia, New Zealand – its small islands like splashes of blood in all the oceans of the world, enabled our teacher to point out that this was, in truth as well as legend, an empire on which the sun never set. Empire Day was a notable event celebrated with a march round the playground and a salute to the flag. The teaching was not jingoistic but we were imbued with a belief that the empire was beneficent, and the rulers well-intentioned, a view which may have been simplistic but was probably no more damaging than the present belief of some young people I meet that everything that has gone wrong with the world in the past century is the fault of Britain.

My generation's early years were dominated by the 1914–18 war, a catastrophe which none of us were old enough to remember but which had scarred the lives of our parents' generation and cast over our own a shadow of uncomprehended vicarious sadness, a universal grieving which reached its apogee on Armistice Day when, on the eleventh hour of the eleventh day of the eleventh month, the country would virtually come to a stop as we stood for the silence.

I learned to read very young, certainly well before I started school, and I can remember the day when it happened. My mother would buy a comic each week, *Tiger Tim* or *The Rainbow*, and would find time to read it to me. From the moment the comic was handed over, the waiting to hear it read was intolerable. And then, one morning, to my astonished delight, the curved and angular shapes under the pictures suddenly came together and made sense. From now on I would need no help. I could read. I must have been helped by the pictures and it was probably a matter of relating words to image. But it is one of my earliest memories of great happiness.

The school had no library and I can remember few books except Piers Plowman's *History of England*. History lessons were my joy. In memory they are a jumble of marvellous tales: myths, legends and facts, continents, centuries and characters blissfully muddled together so that I came to see them as a series of vivid pictures. Alfred brooding by the fire as the cakes blackened, a white pall of snow falling on the coffin of Charles I, Hannibal urging his elephants across the Alps, Julius Caesar falling in a welter of blood, Wolfe storming the heights of Quebec. There must have been some attempt at chronology since I clearly recall the Blue River of History which stretched along one wall on which we would stick cut-out figures of kings and queens, insert dates and draw pictures of the main events.

I was happy at the British School. The Headmaster, Mr Wynn (I think that is how the name was spelt), seems in retrospect to have been a remarkable teacher. He loved poetry and his choice was eclectic. We learned the poems by heart and I can still remember the poems of the Shropshire countryside, particularly A. E. Housman. We enjoyed the vigour and patriotic fervour of poems which today would, I fear, be regarded as politically incorrect: 'Horatio Keeping the Bridge', 'Vitae Lampada', 'Drake's Drum'. The first poem I was asked to read aloud to the class – I must have been about eight at the time – was 'The Burial of Sir John Moore at Corunna'. I was torn between pride and embarrassment caused by my awareness when scanning the verses that the word 'bayonet' was new to me and I could neither understand nor pronounce it.

All the poems have remained favourites and I am sorry that children, no longer required to learn poetry by heart, are denied this storehouse of pleasure. The day began always with an act of worship and a hymn, although I have no memory of hymn books. I think the hymns were those we frequently sang in church so that the same ones recurred with somewhat monotonous frequency, sung in the sing-song childish voices of the Welsh border. Every morning throughout my school life I heard a reading from the King James Bible. There was, thank God, no *Good News Bible*, a version which is very bad news for anyone who cares either for religion or literature.

My parents, ever restless, moved house four times during the few years we lived in Ludlow. The third house, well outside the town, was too large and expensive for my father's income and we didn't stay very long. It was called The Woodlands and stood alone in a beautiful garden which ran down to the River Teme. My sister and I walked to school each day carrying our lunch between us in a wicker basket. It was a long walk and I can remember one winter day when we both trudged, weeping rather desolately with the cold.

I saw great poverty when I was a young child; poverty is not ameliorated by the beauty of its surroundings. There seems to be a belief that urban poverty is worse than rural poverty; I believe the reverse may be true. In cities there are more public places, more libraries, more refuges from the cold. A few of the children I went to school with were almost in rags. I can remember clearly one small boy – his name was George – with the pinched face of an adult, a similarity enhanced by a blob of white foam near his ear which reminded me of my father's shaving soap. Little else but the child's face was washed, and he came to school ill-shod and, I suspect, hungry. At one lesson he was very severely caned (the use of the cane, brought sharply across the palm of the hand, was fairly common) and howled with pain and perhaps a less focused misery. For the remainder of the lesson the male teacher was particularly kind to him, colluding with him in small jokes against the rest of us. Even as an eight-year-old I knew that this was because he was ashamed of his severity. From an early age I had this insight into adult motives and sometimes spoke uncomfortable truths aloud, a habit which caused my mother to describe me as a cynical child. I can't have been an easy one, perhaps, nor a pleasant one. I sometimes regret that my insight into my own motives has been less acute.

Despite deprivation we never saw a policeman at the school; there was no violence, nothing was ever stolen. What, indeed, was there to steal? It is difficult for people of my generation totally to accept the theory fashionable in the 1960s and still popular with some optimists that the main cause of criminality is deprivation. Deprivation is, of course, relative. The poor then had so much less, expected so much less, were satisfied with less. The inequalities and injustices of society were too readily accepted by the victims as well as by the more prosperous, but they were not constantly emphasized by television advertisements with their cunningly contrived celebrations of material success, nor were we children taught directly or by implication that because we had less, less was expected of us. But I remember George at the British School if I am ever tempted to believe that all was well with England in those years between the wars.

A Victorian child of the same class – the Pooters' daughter perhaps – received into our family would have felt immediately at home; a modern child, transported to a house without electricity, central heating, television, telephone or the use of a car, would feel himself banished to a dark age.

The sitting-room of our first Ludlow house, in a small terrace near the river, was lit by an oil lamp which dominated the square central table. As the shadows lengthened I would watch my mother turn up the wick, draw the match along its narrow oil-soaked edge and gently lower the glass funnel. It was like an evening benison to see my siblings' expectant faces glowing gently and warmly in the light. Our final house in Linney View was lit by gas. The wall-mounted lights were fitted with short chains which, when pulled, would activate the gas supply or turn it off. The gas-mantles were delicate thimble-shaped domes of what looked like starched muslin, and so fragile that they could be fractured even by the careless thrust of a taper. Most of my childhood errands were to buy new mantels for the gas lights.

And the Victorian child would have felt familiar with our weekly rituals; the coke boiler lit every Saturday to provide hot water for the weekly bath, the clean clothes laid out for church on Sunday, the weekly administration of a purgative without regard to evidence of need, a prophylactic rather than a remedy; familiar, too, with the oddly named liberty bodice and with the itchy, wash-hardened discomfort of winter combinations.

We only very rarely saw a doctor. Doctors in the 1920s had little more in their armoury than had their Victorian predecessors, but what they couldn't offer in scientific medicine was balanced by the patient's almost superstitious belief in the doctor's authority over the disease. To call in the doctor was an admission that the illness was serious, family and folklore remedies **had failed** and the secular deity must be summoned; his fee, found with difficulty, was both a propitiation and a talisman. A child admitted to hospital never saw his mother until he was discharged, there being a belief that the presence of parents only upset child patients unnecessarily and disturbed hospital routine. My brother was admitted to hospital – I think because of a fistula – soon after we arrived in Ludlow, and on his return home called Mother 'nurse' for weeks. There was a belief that intractable illness or vague ill-health were due to a focus of infection. Many adults spat out all their perfectly sound teeth into the receiving kidney-shaped bowl, while few middle-class children reached adolescence with tonsils and adenoids intact.

Children need to play as they need air, and Ludlow was the ideal town for an imaginative child. If we had been given expensive toys or had been brought up with television, video recorders and computer games, I'm sure we would have spent as much time tapping away in front of a screen as does the modern child, but without these excitements we had to make our own amusements. The street, almost entirely free of cars, was open to us, as were the water meadows sloping to the Teme, the river and Whitcliffe above, the paths hewn into the rock which surrounds the castle and which, with an outcrop of shrubs and the occasional cave, provided the setting for imaginative play and the acting out of innumerable roles. We had no bicycles and, although I longed for a scooter, my father avoided this expense by his theory that a scooter was a dangerous indulgence since it resulted in one leg being permanently shorter than the other. Similarly bedside lamps were not provided on the grounds that reading in bed damaged the eyesight.

At school, boys and girls were separated in the asphalt playground and the games we played there were less imaginative, more ritualistic and hierarchical. The two chief ones were skipping, usually accompanied by chanting, and hopscotch. A chalky stone would be used to mark out the hopscotch rectangle of six squares and we played by kicking a flat stone from square to square, sometimes diagonally, sometimes missing a square, or with other variations to test skill. It was important to find the right stone and, once found, it was jealously guarded. It needed to be flat but with rounded edges, smooth enough to slide easily but not so smooth that it skidded out of control.

On Saturdays in summer we would be taken, or more often sent alone, to paddle in the Teme. Minnows were caught and brought home in jam-jars and their early, much-lamented deaths were followed by ceremonial burying in matchboxes with full choral service. I remember that playing church was one of our enthusiasms. As the eldest I was invariably the parson, draped in one of my mother's old nightdresses, and indeed seniority established my right to the best role in any of our make-believe games.

We enjoyed a freedom unknown to most children today, freedom of the streets, the walks round the castle, the river. Some of the lessons we learned in the streets would have horrified our parents but the two worlds didn't communicate. With few toys, we constructed a richly imaginative world. Our parents could turn us loose, apparently without anxiety. I can remember only one untoward incident. We were playing in the shallow cave off one of the castle walks when a young man carrying a cane invited us to follow him to a more secluded place and spank his bottom. To children who spent some ingenuity in avoiding having our bottoms spanked the request was bizarre. When we declined he walked away without pressing us.

Children must have been sexually abused when I was a child; they always have been. But because the fear of sexual abuse hadn't become a national obsession we were never taught to be afraid of strangers. The criminal statistics for England and Wales show that seven to eight children are murdered each year by strangers and this figure has not greatly altered over the years. The figures are insignificant compared with the dangers to children on the roads, but they can never be comparatively insignificant in the minds of parents. The possible abduction, rape or murder of a child is the horror which we hardly dare allow into our thoughts. Because of those seven to eight tragic deaths children today, particularly middle-class children, live under a form of house arrest.

And for our external fantasy life we had the cinema. I am not sure whether the price of admission to the Saturday afternoon matinee at Ludlow was one penny or twopence, I rather think the former. I can remember joining the long queue of children, pressing our backs against the staircase wall, waiting for the doors to the auditorium to open. I suppose there must have been some form of censorship of films, but the ones which remain in memory certainly weren't made for children. Perhaps I saw some of them with my parents. I can remember the silent films, particularly *Birth of a Nation*, remember, too, the first talkie, *Broadway Melody* of 1929. The arrival of the talkies aroused immense interest and the manager of the cinema announced that, in contrast to the inferior sound systems in the picture palaces of Shrewsbury or London, Ludlow was to have 'the talkies not the squawkies'. As we had no baby-sitter the whole family went together to participate in this modern miracle. The auditorium darkened, the screen glowed, music swelled out in glorious bursts of melody and – almost unbelievably – the gods and goddesses spoke.

On Sunday afternoons there was usually the family walk. It can't have been much pleasure for my parents since I remember that we trailed after them, bored, tired and oblivious to everything but the need for this compulsory exercise to end. But paradoxically it left me with a love of walking which has remained all my life, and childhood walks through the Shropshire meadows return every time I smell clover or the pungent scent of Queen Anne's lace or feel wet grass against my ankles.

And then came the day of the scholarship examination, the equivalent of the later Eleven Plus. I can't recall that we were given any particular coaching for this, but we did all realize its supreme importance. If I passed I would go to the high school, an almost unimaginable privilege. I would learn French and Latin, the school would have a library, there would be all the less academic excitement of the stories in the *Schoolgirls' Own* which were my weekly reading. Those of us who passed the first written part of the examination then went to the high school for the oral, and I can remember waiting to be called into the interview room, sitting on a very low chair in the kindergarten classroom. I had no problem with the first part of the interview but mental arithmetic, as always, was sheer horror as the metal grille of incomprehension clanged down. And then some four weeks later came the letter to say that I had been successful and was to take the enclosed form with me to the medical centre for my physical examination. I can remember walking round the castle to the familiar office where we used to go to have cuts bound up, chests listened to and minor injuries treated by the school nurse. I was dizzy with happiness, an iridescence of joy which embraced not only me, but all the world around me. The stones on the path gleamed with a supernatural light, the grasses shivered and silvered, the Teme ran sparkling under a clear sky, even the ramparts of the castle reared over me like some celestial city. Alas, the triumph and the joy were both premature. Apparently the money didn't run to the number of pupils offered places and the last on the list fell off. I was undone by that dreaded mental arithmetic.

So I went instead to the National School, previously one of the charitable institutions established by the National School Society between 1808 and 1811, dedicated to the propagation of the doctrine of the Church of England. Here every week a local parish priest would arrive to teach us the Collect for the week and to instruct us in the faith. So those memorable prayers, so short and yet so pregnant with meaning, entered early into my consciousness at school as well as in church and became part of my literary inheritance.

But I wasn't long at the National School. My father, who worked in the local Income Tax office, had applied again for a transfer and, at the age of eleven, I moved with my family to Cambridge and began the last and happiest stage of my formal education at the Cambridge County High School for Girls. There was no scholarship entitlement to be transferred but my father found the £4 which was the termly fee. For this I shall always be grateful.

TUESDAY, 12TH AUGUST

Last night was the hottest yet, and I again awoke to find myself lying damply in a layer of sweat between skin and nightdress.

My secretary Joyce McLennan arrived very hot after her journey. When her number 94 bus (which was following close behind another number 94 which she had just missed) reached Holland Park and she tried to get off, the conductor shouted angrily to the passengers, 'Jesus Christ! You see what it's like? Every time you try to overtake the bus in front, someone wants to get off or on at a bus stop.' Joyce has worked for me part-time since the publication of my seventh novel. Intelligent, efficient, kind and unfailingly good-tempered, she is high among the small group of friends on whom I can rely to keep me sane.

An interesting item in today's post. A lady living in Lincoln's Inn, knowing of my interest in old diaries, sent me one from her collection, a W. Straker pocket diary for 1914. There is no mention of the original owner and all the entries are in pencil. I think from the handwriting that it was probably written by a man, and he begins every day with a note of the temperature, the weather and the wind. And then, on 30th January, he notes that 'Ethel retired as usual about 10 o'clock and must have hung herself soon afterwards', followed by the note,

'Ethel's last kiss and last goodnight'. There is no clue as to who Ethel was: she could have been wife, sister or daughter, no grief is expressed, no explanation given.

WEDNESDAY, 13TH AUGUST

A rather dull morning catching up with outstanding bills and the duller kind of post. Clare and her husband Lyn arrived in the afternoon, Lyn bearing my birthday present of a camera. It seems to me odd that I have lived for seventy-seven years without ever having owned a camera. It is, perhaps, a little late to begin photography. Lyn, patient as ever, spent some time explaining the camera's sophistications and then we went outside and, among all the dust and rubble, found a relatively clean corner and I took my first photograph of Clare. Later, after Lyn had left to have a haircut, Clare and I walked in the park and I photographed her again in the Japanese garden.

In the afternoon I completed and sent to *The Independent* a review of *The Doctor, The Detective and Arthur Conan Doyle*, Martin Booth's biography of the writer. He was a far more complex, indeed enigmatic and in some respects contradictory, character than a recital of his qualities would suggest. But those qualities were formidable. He fought vigorously against injustice, whether in the Belgian Congo or at home, advocated reform of the divorce laws which he saw as prejudiced in favour of men, and campaigned vigorously and successfully on behalf of prisoners who he considered had been wrongly convicted. But he was surprisingly naïve, even gullible. Admittedly he came to his belief in spiritualism after careful weighing of the evidence, but that didn't prevent him from being the victim of charlatans, and at the end of his life he forfeited money, goodwill and admiration by his belief in fairies, being taken in by a photograph which was a very obvious childish hoax.

But neither virtue nor eccentricity would have justified this or his previous biographies if he hadn't created Sherlock Holmes, the best-known of all fictional detectives. The world appeal of the stories is extraordinary. I remember some years ago being in Tokyo to open an exhibition of crime writing. I was visited in my hotel by members of the Tokyo chapter of the Sherlock Holmes Society. They came in beaming, all wearing deerstalker hats and shooting jackets and smoking meerschaum pipes. What, I wondered, could they possibly have in common with this fictional Victorian archetypal hero. Martin

Booth points out that the plots of the Sherlock Holmes stories may be ingenious, but they are hardly credible. Conan Doyle didn't care very much about details. The dog that didn't bark in the night is less mysterious than Dr Watson's dog, which disappeared completely. The chronology is sometimes confused, parts of London are inaccurately described and the writing is occasionally slapdash. None of this worried either Conan Doyle or his readers. A modern crime writer could wish that readers today were so accommodating. As the author himself wrote: 'Accuracy of detail matters little. I have never striven for it and have made some bad mistakes in consequence. What matters is that I hold my readers.' He certainly did hold them, and he does so still.

The readers of detective fiction in the so-called Golden Age seemed equally unconcerned about accuracy, particularly scientific or forensic accuracy. The methods of murder were ingenious indeed. Webster tells us that death has ten thousand doors to let out life, and the detective story has made use of most of them. It was not sufficient in the 1930s that the victim was murdered; he or she must be mysteriously, ingeniously, bizarrely murdered. Realism in the setting, psychological subtlety in characterization, social concern, credibility; only too often all were subjugated to the dominant need of the plot.

The writers of the thirties had very little knowledge and even less apparent interest in forensic medicine or legal procedure. Many of the most eminent – some would say the best: Dorothy L. Sayers, Ngaio Marsh, Margery Allingham – were women with no scientific training and their interest was far more in character, motive and plot than it was in forensic realism. Police methods were less well organized, less sophisticated and less scientific than they are today, and readers far less knowledgeable. Even so, we re-read some of these books with a mixture of amusement and incredulity. Post mortems were invariably carried out by the local general practitioner, presumably on the surgery couch after the evening surgery, following which he would invariably be able to provide the brilliant amateur detective with more information about precisely how the victim died than a modern forensic pathologist would be able to provide in a fortnight. The policemen, honest if ineffectual, were frequently mere foils to the talented amateur, or a species of country bumpkin, cycling to the scene of crime while deferentially tugging their forelocks to the gentry.

Typical of the books of the time is Dorothy L. Sayers's *Busman's Honeymoon*, where the newly married Lord Peter Wimsey and his wife find a corpse with a smashed skull in the cellar of their honeymoon farmhouse. Needless to say no equivalent of the present-day scene-of-crime officer arrives to inspect the scene, no photographs are thought necessary, no one in the household suffers the indignity of having fingerprints taken, and we are told that the table-top in the kitchen is scrubbed ready to receive the corpse, although I am not sure whether this implies that the police surgeon, Dr Craven, proposed to carry out the autopsy on the kitchen table. He certainly wrote a report for the Coroner before leaving the house, which seems quick work. Meanwhile the detective settles down to enlist the help of Lord Peter while exchanging appropriate quotations from *The Oxford Book of English Verse*.

In some of Dorothy L. Sayers's novels specimens are indeed placed in jars and sent to Sir James Lubbock, at the Home Office. Sir James seems to be a general-purpose forensic scientist, biologist, chemist, document examiner and pathologist. I picture him in his room at the Home Office undertaking post-mortems and examining specimens from all over the country; a Napoleon of crime investigation.

Many of the books of the Golden Age are still being read with pleasure today, an indulgence, perhaps, in nostalgia, fascination with the ingenuity of the puzzle, or a hankering for Mayhem Parva, for a more homogeneous and peaceable world, a more assured and confident morality. But they are not being written today. The modern crime writer cannot afford to ignore forensic medicine, nor does he or she wish to. One reason for this change is, of course, the popularity of television police and crime series. Readers today know the difference between the uniformed branch and the CID and are well aware of the function and the importance of the forensic science service, if only because characters in these series so frequently ask 'Heard anything yet from Forensic, Sarge?' Realism, including scientific realism, has also been encouraged by the modern fashion for professional detectives as opposed to the old reliance on the omni-talented, eccentric and romanticized amateur.

And those of us who aspire to create a credible professional detective must take trouble over our research, not only into police procedure but into modern scientific methods of investigating crime, including forensic medicine. The crime novel, like its readers, has changed fundamentally since the last war. Today the detective story is more realistic about murder, more violent, more sexually explicit, less assured in its affirmation of official law and order, moving ever closer to the sensibilities and moral ambiguities of the so-called 'straight' novel. Crime writers today know only too well that corruption can lie at the very heart of law, that not all policemen are invariably honest, that murder is a contaminating crime which changes all those who come into touch with it, in fiction as in real life, and that although there may be – indeed must be – a solution at the end of the detective novel and a kind of justice, it can only be the fallible justice of men.

I enjoy doing my own research and am lucky in that my experience at the Home Office and the friends I made at New Scotland Yard and in the Forensic Science Service mean that expert advice is always available to me, and I am grateful. That doesn't mean the books are without error. I am most likely to make mistakes where I don't check because I am confident that I already know. An example is in *A Taste for Death* where the bodies are discovered in the vestry of a church by Miss Wharton, a gentle spinster who arrives early to dust the church and arrange fresh flowers, accompanied by Darren, the young truant she has befriended. The discovery of the bodies is so horrific (an example of the power of contrast in detective fiction) that the parish priest sends her to take a recuperative holiday with his predecessor and his wife in Nottingham.

I can't think why I chose Nottingham; Brighton, Bournemouth or Scarborough would seem more appropriate. Worse, I made her travel from King's Cross, not St Pancras. I received two letters, both from women readers. The first asked rather plaintively why Miss Wharton had chosen to travel from King's Cross when she would have had to change twice and the journey would have taken an extra hour. The second wrote that she fully understood Miss Wharton's dislike of St Pancras station and would never travel from it if she could avoid it.

Tonight I had dinner with Valerie Eliot in the Grill Room of the Café Royal. I love this room, which I think is one of the most beautiful dining-rooms in London. There were few people there, partly because it's August, partly, I suspect, because of the heat. Valerie talked about T. S. Eliot and their life together and I listened, ate and felt relaxed and cool. Valerie dropped me home at about eleven.

THURSDAY, 14TH AUGUST

I woke at six with a feeling of vague unease, as if my mind were struggling free from the last clinging threads of a bad dream. It was another very hot night and I had slept fitfully. Perhaps there had been a bad dream, but I had no conscious memory of it.

I found myself thinking of my first and disastrous job in the income tax office at Ely. The examination for entry to the Clerical Class of the Civil Service was taken at sixteen and I travelled up to London with a school friend to take the examination, staying at the YWCA in Bloomsbury. It was my first trip to London without an adult and I can remember the excitement and enchantment of the city. I suppose I must have been seventeen by the time all the bureaucratic procedures had been gone through and I was allocated to the Ely tax office. I remember, when I was successful in the examination, being sent a list of government departments to which I could be sent, and the wonder now is why I chose the Inland Revenue when the whole of the Civil Service was open to me. I could have gone to London (always my ambition) and would have been happy in any job which wasn't entirely concerned with figures. The Inland Revenue was the worst possible choice. I can't remember that any other possibilities were ever discussed with me by anyone. I had left school, so my usual mentors weren't available and my father obviously wanted me to follow him into the same job. I can't think why; he was never, I believe, really happy and would rather have been a teacher if he had ever had a chance of further education after the age of fifteen.

I can't remember how long I stayed at Ely – no more than eighteen months, I think, before I resigned – but it seems in memory a time of misery. I began by finding a room in a boarding house where the cost, although reasonable, left me nothing over but my weekly fare home. There was one other new entrant, a boy with whom I had nothing in common. Even if we had liked each other, the friendship wouldn't have been helped by the head of the office, who continually held him up to me as an example. The rest of the staff seemed to be old men, although they couldn't have been much older than my father. The Cathedral was my one solace, but the little town seemed dreary and depressing. Finally I left the boarding house and started travelling from Cambridge to Ely each day. This necessitated a very early start, a long cycle ride to the station, the half-hour train journey and then a depressing trudge to the tax office.

Ely has changed now, and seems attractive, even lively, particularly the development on the waterfront. When Jane, Peter and the grand-children were at Cambridge, we would motor over and have lunch at the Old Fire Engine House. I have been back to give a talk at the Arts Centre and last year to give the first Ely Lecture in the Cathedral. Occasionally, too, the Liturgical Commission of the Church of England meets at Ely in the pleasant diocesan conference centre. On none of these visits have I ever been burdened by this morning's weight of vague irritation and regret. I suppose I regret Ely because the decision to take that particular job was so stupid. And the fault was mine. Even at seventeen and with no one to talk over the possibilities, I should have known better. Those months of servitude were such a waste of youth, enthusiasm and idealism. But my time in the Ely tax office wasn't entirely wasted. Nothing that happens to a novelist ever is.

By the time I had made my first pot of tea and fed my cat Polly-Hodge, the unease had faded. There is no point in regretting any part of the past. The past can't now be altered, the future has yet to be lived, and consciously to experience every moment of the present is the only way to gain at least the illusion of immortality.

FRIDAY, 15TH AUGUST

Has anyone discovered a really satisfactory way of reading comfor-tably in bed? For some of us this is virtually our only free time except when on holiday. Reading is so important, so necessary to the nourishment of mind and spirit that I feel that it should be as seriously ceremonial as a church service. Ideally we need a comfortable chair with back and arm support and good, well-directed light, a rest for the book if it is too heavy to hold comfortably, a small table with our favourite drink to hand, and silence and solitude. It is an ideal that few of us are able to obtain. I find in recent years that I read far less new fiction and more non-fiction, particularly letters, biography and autobiography, history and diaries. This is nothing to be proud of; I ought to tackle more new fiction – and the word 'tackle' is appropriate – but there are still so many classics unread, so many old favourites to comfort and entertain, and indeed to find new pleasures in. I like to have one old favourite and one new by the bedside. At present the old favourite is *The Small House at Allington* and the new book – new to me only – is *Sowing* by Leonard Woolf, an autobiography of the years 1880–1904.

37

I came to Anthony Trollope comparatively late, certainly in my mid-thirties, but he has provided me since then with enormous pleasure. But I wonder if he knew what a monster he had created in Lily Dale? Admittedly Crosbie is a cad, but I can't help congratulating him on his escape. And I pity poor Mrs Dale, destined to spend her old age with a resolutely single and masochistic Lily. Similarly with *The Golden Bowl*. I wonder if Henry James expected us to sympathize with Maggie Verver and her father, the millionaire American who first uses his money to buy a suitable husband for his daughter in the person of the Prince, and then, when her marriage results in his loneliness, buys a suitable wife for himself in the person of her husband's ex-lover. This is to suggest that writers occasionally don't know what or whom they have created, which is surely a nonsense.

Leonard Woolf's *Sowing*, which in this edition is only 176 pages long and which I finished in an evening, is only the first volume of his autobiography and covers his childhood and the five years at Trinity College, Cambridge, where he was a friend of Thoby Stephen, Lytton Strachey, and a group of young men who were to become the Apostles and the founders of the Bloomsbury Group. He first saw Thoby's two sisters, Vanessa and Virginia Stephen, one summer afternoon in Thoby's rooms. They were wearing white dresses and large hats and carrying parasols, and he writes that their beauty literally took his breath away. They were staying with their cousin, Miss Catherine Stephen, who was Principal of Newnham, and who was with them, not in her capacity as cousin, but as chaperone, since in 1901 a sister was not allowed to see her brother in his rooms in a male college except in the presence of a chaperone.

The rules of chaperonage were certainly much less severe when Connor was at St Catharine's College, but there were still restrictions. The porter took a lively interest in any women who came and went in the evenings and we were supposed to be out of the gate by ten at the latest. An edict was issued that ladies in college when the air-raid alarm sounded must go immediately to the Master's Lodge where they would sit with the Master's wife in her drawing-room until the All-Clear. I am not sure whether this was because college authorities feared that the excitement of a possible air raid would induce lascivious emotions, or to prevent us staying past the allotted time on the excuse that it was far too dangerous to venture out on the streets. The first siren note was the signal for a hurried mass exodus of women. Today sex for students seems to be almost compulsory. Their lives may be more liberated, but I doubt whether they have as much fun.

I have never felt comfortable with the Bloomsbury Group, strongly disliking their snobbery, their intellectual arrogance, their selfishness and their rudeness. So why, I wonder, do they exert such a fascination for me? In the years when Woolf and his contemporaries were at Trinity, Henry James was writing at the height of his powers. As students they read *The Sacred Fount*, *The Wings of the Dove* and *The Golden Bowl* as they came out. They thought there was an element of ridiculousness in the novels which made it impossible to rank them with the greatest, but they were entranced and almost hypnotized by the strange Jamesian convoluted beauty and subtlety which act upon those who yield to them like drink or drugs.

Leonard Woolf describes how, after he and Virginia Stephen were married in 1912, Virginia acted for a short time as secretary for Roger Fry's second post-impressionist exhibition at the Grafton Galleries, and Henry James came to tea, which was served in the basement. As he talked he tilted back his chair till it was balanced on the two back legs and maintained this equilibrium by holding on to the edge of the table. Henry James did this whenever he came to tea with the Stephen family and as his long sentences untwined themselves the chair would slowly tilt backwards and the children's eyes would be fixed on it, hoping that it would finally overbalance and deposit James on the floor. Time after time he managed to recover himself, but indeed one day it did happen. The chair went over and the novelist, undismayed, was flung on the floor. He was unhurt and, after a moment, completed his characteristically ceremonious and flowery sentence.

SUNDAY, 17TH AUGUST

To Oxford yesterday to be Guest of Honour at a crime weekend at St Hilda's College, of which I am an Honorary Fellow.

I was to have seen a friend for lunch at the Old Parsonage, but she rang to say that she has a virus so I kept the table booking and went with Alixe Buckerfield de la Roche, a friend who lives in my house in Oxford.

She was deeply concerned about two recent student suicides at Oxford. A postgraduate student hanged herself at the end of term and Alixe witnessed the terrible distress of her parents and young brother

39

at the Somerville College memorial service. The suicide of the young is more common now than it was in my youth. I can't recall the suicide of a single friend or acquaintance during my childhood or adolescence. Perhaps today we all take happiness as our right and unhappiness is seen as shameful and insupportable. Or is it that some people have an imperfect appreciation of linear time? For them, the present moment is immeasurable, fixed in an eternal agony. There can be no hope that things will be better tomorrow, because the idea of a tomorrow has no reality.

Sitting in the garden in St John Street I thought of the words of William Blake which I quoted in *An Unsuitable Job for a Woman*:

Down the winding cavern we groped our tedious way, till a void boundless as the nether sky appeared beneath us, and we held by the roots of trees and hung over this immensity; but I said: if you please we will commit ourselves to this void and see whether providence is here also.

It is wonderful prose, but hardly helpful in the context of self-destruction. If providence is not there we shan't be aware even of disillusionment.

I returned to London by the 7.10 bus this morning, a good time to travel before the heat of the day. The sun was a smudged silver ball and the sheep seemed to move sluggishly through that early morning mist. Polly-Hodge wasn't waiting for me at the door as she usually is, but came through the cat-flap into the kitchen as soon as I put on the kettle for the tea I didn't wait to make in Oxford. She must have been sleeping in someone's coal-house, if such a thing now exists, as the top of her head was black. She looked diminished and a little uncared-for, which she always manages to do if left for more than a day, even though provided with fresh food and water.

I read the Sunday papers with little enthusiasm. Do the public really care about the antics of the Princess of Wales and her lover? Then to 11 o'clock Mass at All Saints, Margaret Street, where Prebendary Gaskill preached on death, an unusual choice of subject. He touched on the last rites. The thought that the last physical sensation of a Christian would be the touch of holy oil on the forehead is seemly, but I wonder how often that happens in practice. Death, after all, seldom comes when invited or by appointment. We are likely to take our last breath, whether peaceful, gasping, in pain, or mercifully unconscious, in a place we wouldn't have chosen. And even if our loved ones have managed to manoeuvre their way through the traffic and have avoided hold-ups on the motorway to arrive at the hospital in time, essentially we all die alone. They will see us but we shall not see them. The most I hope for is a sight of the sky. The last person I watched as she lay dying had had nothing to look at during those last few days of consciousness but the wall of her hospital room and, beyond it, a claustrophobically close wall of grey London stone.

I slept in the afternoon. There were letters unwritten and papers unsorted. Not a productive day, but not an unhappy one, despite the thoughts about death.

MONDAY, 18TH AUGUST

Today I left for Cambridge by the 10.30 train from King's Cross which took less than an hour. The service to Cambridge is now remarkably quick and comfortable. In my childhood the fast trains went always to Liverpool Street and the slower to King's Cross, but the opposite is now true. The old Liverpool Street station was, for me, the gateway to London, a terminus of excitement and romance. I had arranged for a car to meet me at Cambridge, which took me to Swavesey to visit an elderly sick friend, Doris Wheatley, now chair-bound, and her friend and carer, Kay Harper.

After lunch to Clare's cottage in Orchard Street where I rested during the afternoon for an hour before a car called for me to take me to the BBC studios in Hills Road for the recording of a radio autobiography. The producer, Mandy Morton, had devised a programme in which I should talk about my life and work, interspersing those segments with illustrative readings from the novels. It was a long evening's work, lasting from a quarter to seven to a quarter past ten, and I was grateful that the air conditioning meant that the studio was very cool.

Mandy had brought with her a ration book and an identity card from the war to refresh my memory. They had been lent to her by a lady over eighty who frequently broadcasts about her life and the war years, and who had also written a note reminding me of the rations during the time of the worst shortages: two ounces of butter a week, six ounces of other fats – usually four of lard and two of margarine, a quarter of a pound of tea. The system was that we all registered with a butcher and a grocer. This meant, of course, that the registrations and the address on the books had to be changed when people moved. This was one of the jobs I did during my time with a local office of the Ministry of Food in Christ's College and I can remember a succession of extremely young, pretty girls, the new wives of Air Force fighter and bomber pilots, who came in with their ration books to be changed. I wondered how many of them were very shortly to be widows.

Our lives in war-time, particularly those of us with young children, seemed to be dominated by food; where to get it, how to cook it, how to make the most of what was available. It was possible to register as a vegetarian, and those who did so received an extra weekly allowance of cheese. In large families, I remember, one or more members would register as vegetarians with general advantage to the family diet. There was a points system for tinned and other goods and things came on or off points as they were available. We would queue for fish, or for anything else which was not on the ration and which occasionally would be delivered to a particular shop. The news would soon get round and the queue would lengthen.

From 1943 until the end of the war in Europe, I lived in a beautiful, now demolished, house at Chigwell Row in Essex, called White Hall. The owners, Dr and Mrs Price-Watts, had made a flat for their daughter-in-law which she now no longer needed and which I took over. There were tall elms in the garden, noisy with rooks, and the local butcher had the idea of shooting them, then selling the carcases back to Mrs Price-Watts. Her cook did, indeed, make rook pie on one occasion, which I was invited to share. I can remember a tangle of extremely sharp and small bones and virtually no meat, but the gravy was excellent.

And I can remember – which of my generation can't? – the particular culinary horrors of war: Woolton pie, composed of vegetables and sausage meat more crumb than sausage, and brown Windsor soup which tasted of gravy browning. And we got very tired of carrots. At one time there was a glut of them and we were showered with a plethora of Ministry of Food leaflets extolling the virtues of carrot soup, carrot casserole and carrot cake. Carrots, we were told, were particularly good for our eyes. It was because of the carrots they ate that our gallant airmen were successful in shooting down so many enemy planes. Woolton pie and brown Windsor soup featured largely on the menu of the British Restaurants set up under the aegis of the Ministry of Food to provide inexpensive and healthy meals. In this I think they largely succeeded. Despite shortages and occasional real hunger the country was remarkably healthy.

A red-letter day for us was the arrival of a parcel from India, where my husband, by now a qualified doctor, was serving with the Royal Army Medical Corps. It contained tea and some tins of unspecified meat, but the great joy was a round tin of butter. It was very pale, saltless, and tasted rather like newly made farm butter. I suppose I should have doled it out over the days, but I couldn't resist one glorious splurge. I would sit Jane in her high chair and we would feast on toast liberally soaked with butter.

It was on one such day when I was feeding fingers of toast into Jane's buttery mouth that I heard on the radio (which we then called the wireless) the news of the dropping of the atomic bomb. I can still recall the mixture of awe and triumph in the announcer's voice when he said, 'We have unleashed against the enemy the power of the sun itself.' I knew that the dropping of the bomb would almost certainly bring Connor home earlier and probably safely. But it was still, for me, a moment of horror and, looking almost aghast at my two happy, buttery daughters, innocently unconscious of the meaning of what we were hearing, I knew that for all of us the world had changed for ever.

TUESDAY, 19TH AUGUST
Back from Cambridge to a very heavy weight of post which Joyce and I tackled this afternoon. This is one of the penalties, or at least disadvantages, of fame. I receive numerous requests for photographs, signatures, signed books to sell at auctions in aid of local worthy causes (this is becoming so popular that my stock of hardbacks is now depleted), advice on work in progress or help with a personal problem. There is an expectation that I am an expert on law, real-life murder, civil liberties and the constitution. Then there are requests to present prizes at school speech days, talk to writers' groups or take part in a proliferation of literary festivals, here and overseas. Bulky packages arrive with depressing frequency, containing the manuscript of a novel with a request that I should either advise how to get it published, write a foreword or provide a quote for publicity.

Some afternoons, like today, we tackle the dreaded 'pending' file to which inevitably we consign the most difficult time-consuming letters in the hope that they will somehow answer themselves. Very occasionally they do. It seems churlish not to reply to kind and enthusiastic letters from readers or to refuse to help people trying to repair the church spire or provide books for their primary school, but it all takes up time I should be devoting to this memoir and I haven't the ruthlessness – or perhaps I lack the courage – to follow the example of Nancy Mitford, who sent out postcards simply stating 'Nancy Mitford is unable to do what you ask.' Meanwhile the fax machine slowly spews out its messages and the telephone rings.

I pondered this evening that I couldn't have foreseen all this busyness when *Cover Her Face* was published in 1962. But then I remembered that my first appearance in print was much earlier, in 1935 or 1936 when I won a short story prize at the Cambridge High School for Girls and my winning entry was published in the school magazine. I wish I still had a copy. As far as I remember the action took place on a South Sea island where a group of characters were marooned. How? Why? When? Memory is mercifully blank. One of the party was desperately ill and required a rare drug which fortuitously arrived when a small biplane crashed on the island. I suspect that my story was low in credibility but high on drama and atmosphere.

The announcement of the prize was one of the highlights of the five very happy years from eleven to sixteen which I spent at the school. The school uniform was a dark green gym slip, square yoked, with three large box pleats fore and aft to allow for adolescent swellings, a garment in which even the most graceful figure tended to look clumsy. Girls who had achieved a place in the Second XI hockey team wore a pale blue sash, those in the First a green sash with a thin blue line. When I first read Muriel Spark's *The Prime of Miss Jean Brodie* I felt an immediate kinship with her characters leaning across their bicycles wearing their hat brims at different angles. Ours were normally worn turned up at the back and down at the front, but there were a few adventurous spirits who wore the brim turned down at the back. We wore the same uniform for games, and for gym took off our tunics and performed our disciplined contortions in our blouses and dark green knickers. There were no showers and no personal lockers; coats and hats and any belongings were hung on pegs in the cloakroom. Nothing in the whole of my time at the Cambridge High School was ever stolen.

Most of the girls came from the lower-middle or working class; the daughters of university dons and professional men were more likely to go to the Perse School, which was our greatest rival and against whom we played ferocious games of hockey with much clashing of sticks and shouts of encouragement. I wasn't good at games but I was fleet of foot and achieved a precarious place in the Second XI.

There was no member of staff employed to look after our psychological or moral welfare. I think all teachers at that time saw it as part of their job to instil accepted values of personal morality, social responsibility and good behaviour. It requires an immense effort of imagination to picture what the reaction would have been had a girl ever become pregnant. No doubt she would have suddenly disappeared from school, indeed from Cambridge, with soothing explanations of mysterious illness or the need to stay with distant relations. Sex was never discussed, not even in biology lessons, which formed part of General Science in the syllabus. My memory is of producing evil smells from test-tubes with little understanding of the process, experiments with iron filings and magnets, and being told that the atom was the smallest possible element of matter and as such could be neither split nor destroyed. It is ironic to remember that it was even then being split a mile or less away at the Cavendish Laboratory!

Not only was sex a taboo subject but there was an extraordinary reticence about natural functions, including menstruation. I can remember cycling home – I suppose I was about twelve at the time – with a school friend and suggesting that we should hike up the Gog Magog Hills on Saturday afternoon. She replied in a deeply mysterious voice that she couldn't because she wouldn't be well. As she seemed, as usual, in the rudest of health, I was curious as to why she was expecting such a misfortune, but she would only reply: 'Ask your mother.' I didn't ask my mother; parents were the last people to be asked about anything potentially embarrassing. I think my mother did make an attempt when I was younger to prepare me for menstruation, but the explanation must have been incomplete since I somehow got the idea that it occurred once a year; when it did, I complained bitterly that August was a bad month to have started since all future summer holidays would be inconvenienced! I can also remember that my great anxiety was how on earth, if I married, I could conceal this regular event from my husband. I took it for granted that it was a sacred female mystery and that, by disclosing it, I should be a traitor to the whole of my sex.

I suppose that nothing demonstrates the difference in attitudes more clearly than watching television advertisements for sanitary protection where young women wearing tightly fitting white trousers leap in and out of sports cars with happy cries of liberation. There was no internal protection in the 1930s and the commercial sanitary towels were made of cotton wool, cumbersome, not very absorbent and liable to chafe. There were loops at either end for attachment to a belt, giving them the name 'bunnies'. We bought them in Boots the Chemist at a special counter presided over by a grey-haired nurse in full uniform with a great winged cap who handed over the embarrassing package with practised discretion.

But these commercial sanitary towels were expensive and poorer families cut up old sheets into squares, which were hemmed and folded into a kind of bandage, attached to the waist-band with safety pins. Our Victorian forebears had probably coped with just the same unsatisfactory contrivance. Modern sanitary protection is one small victory of modern technology over biological inconvenience, and perhaps not such a small one.

Many of the lessons of Cambridge High School have remained with me although I am not sure whether the classroom in which they were taught still exists. Not long after I left, the school moved to new premises. But fifty years ago we were next door to the Art School, the windows of which overlooked the hard tennis courts and the netball court and from which one of the art students, the young Ronald Searle, could look down on our energetic galumphings. He was even then gaining a reputation as an artist, although I prefer to believe that the allegation that he took us High School girls and, in particular, one dark tousle-haired specimen, as models for the harridans of St Trinian's, is a canard. For one thing, we seldom wore pigtails. They were more typical of our rivals at the Perse School, one of the many subtle social distinctions. Our hair was bobbed, shingled or pudding-basin trimmed under the blue felt hats of winter and our summer panamas.

And how good we were, or rather, how biddable. Admittedly my best friend and I did one afternoon play truant as a gesture to some ill-defined need for self-expression and cycled up the Gog Magog hills where we brewed up tea and fried sausages in our Girl Guide billy cans. I can't recall that it was particularly enjoyable and it must have necessitated some fibbing since this wasn't a school where absences went unnoticed.

We were well behaved by conditioning, not by nature. When children are *en masse* barbarism always lurks beneath the surface. We knew our limitations – this was not the age of child-centred education – but a timid, inexperienced teacher or one still in training could be given a hard time. Not, however, when it came to her examination lesson, at which the examiner would sit at the side of the class, notebook unobtrusively in hand. Here fair play, unstated but instinctively understood, took over. We would sit bolt upright, bright-eyed, hands shooting up like pistons to answer the questions. By the time my younger daughter went to a teacher-training college in the 1960s such a class – attentive, disciplined and obviously learning – would probably have disqualified the student from any chance of becoming a teacher.

History, my second favourite subject and taught by Miss Back, was pure pleasure. I never knew her Christian name. I doubt whether any of the form did. Sixty years ago that was privileged information although those girls given to 'pashes' made it their business to discover the secret and pass it on in giggling triumph to their friends. But I can't remember that anyone had a 'pash' on Miss Back. She exuded common sense, a rational and cheerful dignity which wasn't conducive to such follies. I knew nothing of her life outside the school. I remember seeing her one Saturday evening at a meeting of the Peace Pledge Union to which I had gone out of curiosity; then, as now, I was a non-joiner but an indefatigable taster of ideas. Was she a convinced pacifist? It is impossible to think of her as other than totally rejecting the madness of war, yet I remember that I was surprised to find her at the meeting, perhaps because we could never quite believe that the staff had any life outside the classroom. Did we imagine that they disappeared each evening into some chalky limbo until summoned by the morning assembly bell? Yet if she was a member of the PPU we were never indoctrinated with pacifism or with any other opinion. She saw her job as teaching, not as proselytizing, and yet I am in no doubt of the values – liberal, Christian, scholarly – by which she lived.

We were taught, as much by example as precept, to respect our minds and to use them; to examine the evidence before rushing in with our opinions; to distinguish between fact and theory; to see history through the eyes of the poor and vanquished, not merely those of the powerful and the conquerors; not to believe that something is true simply because it would be pleasant or convenient if it were and, when exposed to propaganda, to ask ourselves, 'In whose interest is it that I should believe this?'

47

Like all the staff except for one widow, Miss Back was a spinster and we took this for granted as we took so much. The post 1914–18 war generation of women, robbed by the holocaust of Flanders of their chance of marriage and motherhood, may have resented their loss, yet in retrospect they seemed to have been neither bitter nor unhappy and the generation they taught, born in the aftermath of that war and destined to reach adulthood at the beginning of the next, benefited from an education which wasn't circumscribed by the demands of the teacher's husband and family. That dedication, too, we took for granted, flourishing unthinking on their deprivation. But even if their chances of finding a husband had been greater, we still wouldn't have been taught by a married woman. In those years – and indeed until the war – marriage meant resignation from the job.

English was marvellously taught, by Miss Scargill and Miss Dalgliesh, after whom I named my detective, Adam Dalgliesh. Years later when she had retired to Edinburgh I visited her after speaking at the book festival and she told me that her father had been called Adam. It never occurred to either teacher that we were incapable of enjoying Shakespeare or reading the great English poets or the major novelists. Miss Dalgliesh would, I suspect, have been incredulous to read today's A-level syllabus. Before the war, even at the level of what was then called the School Certificate, we learned more English literature than many present-day applicants for the English School at university.

And we enjoyed a remarkable continuity of devotion. It was rare indeed for a teacher to leave the High School except by retirement. We were not faced at a critical stage of our pre-examination work by new faces, different methods, unknown personalities. And the school was the right size, large enough to be a lively and diverse community, small enough for each girl to be individually known. We didn't waste time carrying our books from classroom to classroom or building to building at the dictates of a complicated timetable. We all had our own place, our desk, chosen in a noisy scramble at the beginning of a new school year where, surrounded by our cronies, we could create our small island of security. In our lidded desks we could arrange our exercise and text books, fountain pen and pencils and small possessions, knowing that we should find them each morning precisely as we had left them.

In the educational system between the wars there were, of course, wrongs to be remedied and the worst have been remedied. But I sometimes wonder whether we haven't lost almost as much as we have gained. I am not sorry that I was at school at a time when the word 'kid' was reserved for the young of goats.

SATURDAY, 23RD AUGUST

A memorable day. I caught the Oxford Tube – that convenient inter-city coach – at Notting Hill Gate at 8.40 and had a trouble-free and quiet journey. I stopped at Gloucester Green for an iced coffee, and then to St John Street where I chatted to Alixe while watering the garden. The sky was overcast with the promise of rain which never came, but there was a slight breeze and the morning was less oppressive than in London.

My youngest grandchild Beatrice arrived to drive me to her home where her father Peter was cooking the lunch while listening to the ball-by-ball BBC cricket programme. Jane had been feeling under the weather and had vigorously cleaned the house, it being her policy that the less agreeable chores are best kept for unpropitious occasions; feeling really well inclines her to pleasure, not duty. Peter interrupted his cooking to pour me a glass of wine and I gossiped with Jane until lunch was ready, an excellent meal of mixed grilled fish and oven-baked vegetables in olive oil.

In the afternoon we drove to Rousham and walked in the gardens. We saw very few other people and the ordered beauty of lawns and trees was wonderfully refreshing, particularly the view down to the lake with the water-lilies in flower and the golden carp sliding under the dark green surface. We visited the kitchen garden and then sat in the rose garden, Jane and I in silence, listening and inhaling the subtle scents of high summer, while Peter roamed among the rose beds. I thought that I could not have felt happier anywhere else in the world, however beautiful, but then I often think this in England. It is a great disincentive to the ardours, dangers, delays and inevitable disap-pointments of travel. And a perfect day should be recorded. It can't be relived except in memory but it can be celebrated and remembered with gratitude.

MONDAY, 25TH AUGUST

Sunday was a non-productive day. I meant to go to Mass at eleven o'clock but indolence overcame me. I slept for an hour in the afternoon, which was unwise as I had some difficulty getting to sleep last night and was awoken in the early hours by a noisy party in a flat in the Mews which went on until three o'clock. I like to sleep with my window open and one of the drawbacks of summer nights is the increase in noise. Tonight the constant loud thud of a pop group was particularly obnoxious.

The small hours are the worst to lie awake in. I switched on the bedside light and tried to read – P. G. Wodehouse or Nancy Mitford are the best providers of consolation in the treacherous small hours – but couldn't get comfortable and my eyes felt tired and kept watering, smudging my spectacles. I have friends who overcome insomnia, or at least cope with it, by getting up and making tea, but this seems like giving in to sleeplessness. I tried to relax, hoping to slide into unconsciousness.

In theory I could use these uninterrupted hours to think about the next book; after all, I am the first to complain that there isn't enough solitary thinking time. But at three in the morning the mind slips free of conscious control and the thoughts which come are more often depressing than creative.

Last night I found myself back in Cambridge. I can't remember how old I was when my mother was compulsorily admitted to Fulbourne Mental Hospital, nor can I remember how long it was before she came home again. The weeks, perhaps months, before she was finally compulsorily detained, must have been extremely difficult, particularly for my father, but for me they are a complete blank, except for one incident. I was in the double bed asleep with my sister when Father came in and asked me to go quickly and fetch Mrs Mallett, one of our neighbours. I put on shoes and my coat and ran down the street. There was a small pile of gravel deposited there by workmen who were surfacing the road and I ran into this and fell and lay for a moment winded but unhurt. I can remember nothing further of that night except my father coming in after Mrs Mallett had left and ruffling my hair. It was a gesture of tenderness which I don't remember him ever making during my childhood except at that moment. There must have been others, perhaps when I was very young, but this is the only one I remember.

I would go with him every Saturday to visit mother in hospital, my brother and sister being left at home. All I recall of this is the occasional bus ride – a miscellaneous group of passengers making the same journey for the same purpose – the driveway up to the hospital and the smell of the ward. The drug used in those days to sedate the patient permeated clothes, hair, the air we breathed. The visits were always painful. My mother would sit clutching at her hospital dress with restless fingers, looking at us imploringly and constantly reiterating her wish to come home.

While she was away we initially managed. My father had always been extremely capable and, though not demonstrative, he was certainly dutiful. He did his best. Most of the shopping was done on his way home from the office and I cooked the evening meal and the meals at weekends, and tried, with the help of Monica and Edward, to keep the house reasonably clean. The biggest problem was washing; these were the days before washing machines or detergent and it was a problem ensuring that the three of us had clean clothes for Monday school.

And then Dusty arrived. She was a young – but not particularly young – woman living with her sister in Roseford Road, and came by the day to help look after us. I can't imagine why she was living with her sister or why she should have taken the job, since I can't believe that she was paid more than a pittance. I suppose it was convenient as she only had about thirty yards to walk each morning. She was tall, rangy, with bright eager eyes behind large spectacles, a wide mouth and dark springy hair. Her two great pleasures, indeed obsessions, were the National Front, to which she belonged, and the Women's League of Health and Beauty founded by Prunella Stack. She went off to meetings of the former wearing black trousers and a black turtle-neck shirt. Once she took me to a demonstration of the Women's League, and I can recall the rows of women in black satin tight-fitting pants and white blouses, waving and stretching their arms, bending and twisting in unison, an extraordinary if not unimpressive sight.

Dusty made no attempt to indoctrinate us into her Fascist beliefs and as far as I can recall they consisted of admiring the young men who went to the meetings, and of being intensely, if naïvely patriotic. I often wonder what happened to her when the war broke out and disillusionment set in. But she was kind, even-tempered and cheerful, finding no difficulty in coping with my father, and while she was with us life was changed for the better.

One memory is particularly acute. It happened very soon after she arrived. I went up to my bedroom and there, lying folded on the sill beside the open window so that it was aired by the sun, was a clean, ironed nightdress. It is still a powerful image of conscientious caring and it lifted my heart. After trying, not always successfully, to cope with housekeeping and school, I was going to be looked after.

Of we three children I think it was my sister Monica who suffered the most from Mother's illness. Monica was Mother's favourite child. I had the privilege of seniority and was regarded as my father's favourite, and Edward was the youngest and the boy. Monica in between, the least enviable position in any family, always felt herself at a disadvantage. When, a few weeks ago, I talked to her about that time in our lives, she said that no one had ever explained to her what had happened. I had merely told her and Edward one morning that I was taking them for a long walk. When we returned, Mother had disappeared. Monica didn't see her for nearly two years and wasn't even told what had happened to her. I find this astonishing but I believe it to be true. I must have thought that Father was explaining things to her; he must have thought that I would do it. Certainly I can't remember that I ever discussed my visits to the hospital with either of my siblings. If I did indeed leave Monica in ignorance, then I had failed her in a matter more important than cooking breakfast, keeping the house clean and seeing that she had a clean blouse for school on Monday.

WEDNESDAY, 27TH AUGUST

My elder grandson's wedding day. His bride (an Australian, whose family came from Malta) wanted a civil ceremony with no one else present except themselves and their two witnesses. It rained heavily all morning, but I hope it was fine for their ceremony. There is to be a church blessing to which the family will be invited on 4th October in Blythburgh church.

Yesterday I went from Victoria to Horsham, where brother Edward met me and took me to his and his wife Mary's new home in Henfield. I felt rather ashamed not to have visited them earlier, but we had a good day with much family talk. After lunch Edward and I explored the village, which has some very agreeable Regency houses, and then took his usual path along the edge of a field of linseed where we sat together in the strong light of the setting sun and gazed over the golden-brown field towards the Downs. We spoke about childhood and I asked Edward if he had a memory of a single childhood birthday. My own seventy-seventh had reminded me that I couldn't remember any early birthday celebrations. Neither could he.

It seemed to us, talking gently together, that our childhood had been lived on a plateau of apprehension with occasional peaks of acute anxiety or fear. That may have been good for me as a writer, less good, I suspect, for my sister and brother. We were always afraid of my father, as indeed were most of our friends who, when they came to the house, did so with some apprehension. Perfect love may cast out fear, but fear is remarkably potent in casting out love. I think that my father would have liked children who were more affectionate, even while his severity inhibited the open affection of which I think he had received so little in his own childhood.

One of the characteristics which caused us most embarrassment was his almost pathological reluctance to part with money. I remember the misery at the beginning of each term in trying to extract from him my games sub, which I think was either a shilling or one-and-sixpence in old money. I was constantly reprimanded for my carelessness in forgetting it. I could never, of course, have brought myself to say that I had asked for it without success and was too frightened to go on asking.

Father was an indefatigable gardener, but the garden was disciplined rather than tended. The result was always spectacular. Everything flourished in his hands. The garden at Roseford Road was a rough plot when he bought the newly built house, his first over-ambitious house purchase, and he set to work to produce order and plenty in strict geometrical patterns. A square lawn on which we were not permitted to tread was laid front and back. Straight paths were bisected by others at right angles. Vegetables sprouted in precise rows; peas which were never picked until the pods were yellowing, cabbages with hearts as tight as footballs. It was almost intolerable for him to see anything picked. Despite the abundance my mother would creep out surreptitiously to pull up a cabbage where it would be less noticed – always a hopeless task – or to dig up a single root of potatoes, carefully smoothing over the soil. I grew to realize that Father's childhood had been insecure and that, when he began work at fifteen in the Patent Office in London and had to support himself on a meagre wage, he would sometimes go hungry. The garden represented security and abundance. But from time to time, perhaps to impress, perhaps to buy popularity, he would invite colleagues from the office to come and plunder, and they would move among the beanstalks and the peas happily filling their baskets while my mother watched with understandable resentment from the kitchen window.

I can understand my father's insecurity because, for most of my early life, I shared it. When I was a child I couldn't settle to sleep until I had entered into my private world. My imaginings were always the same: I am in a low, large, single-storey building in the Bull Ring in Ludlow. It is composed of innumerable bedrooms, each containing an immense bed. There are hundreds of us sleeping there and in the middle of one of the beds I am anonymously huddled. Outside the building, guards parade, perpetually on watch. No one knows where I am and I couldn't be safer. Thus protected securely, I am able to get to sleep. I can't remember at what age I let go of this nightly ritual.

After we moved from Ludlow to Cambridge, we ate as a family only occasionally on Sunday. We three children and my mother ate in the kitchen and my father had his lunch and dinner brought to him on a tray in the dining-room. I can remember Mother placing it down before him with an expression compounded of resentment and slight apprehension; being brought up in a boys' boarding school was no training for a good cook. Even when she was in hospital and I took over the cooking, Father would still eat on his own. I now realize that, like me, he needed at least one period of absolute solitude during the day and perhaps this was his way of ensuring that he got it.

My father was a great deal more affectionate to his grandchildren than to his children, as often happens, and when he was old and living alone in a small house at Southwold, I grew to admire the qualities he had always possessed: independence, courage and his own brand of sardonic humour. Unfortunately these are not the qualities which are most important to small children. But his own life wasn't easy. He began work at fifteen, fought in the First World War as a sergeant in the Machine-Gun Corps, and spent all his working life in a job which gave him small satisfaction. I like to think that his last years were happy. In his old age I began to realize how much I loved him. But then, I think I always had.

We had dinner at the local restaurant and then went home to bed. Edward gave me a copy of an Australian publication about the history of the 215th Battalion in 1940–45 which made mention of our father's youngest brother, Padre Jimmy James, who served with the Battalion and won the Military Cross for going unaccompanied in a jeep to the German lines to recover the bodies of dead comrades. He was, apparently, the only Australian padre to receive the MC. I met him and his wife on one of my publicity visits to Australia and have an earlier memory of him when he came to London to march in the victory celebrations following the end of the war.

Edward, now seventy-four, is almost blind in one eye and has impaired sight in the second. Apparently the near-blindness is due to deterioration which can't be corrected, so that he has to face the certainty of blindness. He bears it all with his usual stoicism and now listens to audio-tapes instead of reading. He is still able to garden and to see most of his shrubs.

Returning this morning I was met at Victoria by Frances Fyfield, who took me in a taxi to Camden Passage, where we spent an agreeable half-hour trying on jewellery (but not buying) before having an excellent lunch at Frederick's.

SUNDAY, 31ST AUGUST

On Thursday to Southwold for a long weekend with Françoise Manvell. I first met Françoise when I was invited, and went to, Boston University for three months to teach the detective story or, as they say in the United States, the mystery. She is now a widow but was then married to Roger Manvell, who was teaching film at Boston. They were both kind and hospitable to me and I welcomed the companion-ship of compatriots when living abroad for even a few months. Françoise is not strictly speaking a compatriot; she is French and lived in Paris during the occupation and liberation, a time which is fascinating for me to hear about.

We arranged to travel to Southwold separately, as Françoise drove herself from Oxford. I caught my usual train from Liverpool Street and arrived in time to share a lunch of smoked salmon sandwiches in the conservatory with Clare and Lyn who were already there. Clare was peeling apples to make chutney, and the strong smell of apples, vinegar and spices pervaded the kitchen and will undoubtedly remind me of this weekend whenever I smell it again. Françoise arrived shortly after four.

The weekend has been spent resting, walking, talking and, on Friday, driving to Leiston, where Françoise and I enjoyed ourselves hunting in the Trading Post. The owner clears houses and her huge

shed-like shop has the attraction of a childish treasure trove. Apart
from the fun of occasionally finding a treasure or a domestic object
needed but no longer made, there is something poignant and
nostalgic about the accumulated leavings of dead lives: the old
wedding photographs and remnants of tea-services, the sentimental
Victorian prints, the formal photographs from the 1920s of earnest
children posed against obviously spurious backgrounds and gazing
into the lens with concentrated innocence. I remember a similar
photograph taken when I was eleven and had just started at the
Cambridge High School: my mother standing behind a synthetic wall
(she was always sensitive about her size), myself with hair unnaturally tidy, held back with a slide, wearing my pleated gym tunic,
Monica and Edward seated.

Among a pile of objects we both found something to buy: Françoise
a Doulton Victorian toothbrush-holder large enough to make an
attractive flower vase, and a very pretty glass vase, also nineteenth-
century, and myself two turn-of-the-century blue specimen vases,
which I bought as a present for Clare.

I was the first up this morning and heard the news of the death of
the Princess of Wales as soon as I turned on the radio for the seven
o'clock news. My reaction, which must have been shared by millions,
was disbelief, as if the natural order had somehow been reversed.
Death has power over lesser mortals but not this icon. It took a few
seconds of listening to the newscaster's sombre voice to realize that
this wasn't a carefully contrived publicity stunt; this was reality,
horrible, brutal, ugly and final.

The four of us went to St Edmund's Church for the eleven o'clock
service and it seemed appropriate to take part in the order, the dignity
and the well-known prayers of the 1662 mattins. The priest was at
another of his group churches and the service was taken by a layman
wearing doctor's robes. He preached a short but remarkable sermon
which could not have been bettered: Christian, scholarly and sensitive.

After lunch at the Swan, Françoise and I spent most of the afternoon
and evening watching the BBC tribute. It is never easy for public
figures to react appropriately at short notice to such a tragedy. Well-
worn adjectives begin to sound like a mantra and the reiterated
tributes seem fulsome and platitudinous. I thought that the Prime
Minister was impressive, the Archbishop of Canterbury inadequate.
The most moving tributes came from ordinary people whom Princess

Diana had met, sometimes briefly, who spoke of her warmth and her loving concern and who obviously felt that they had had a personal relationship with her. This, I imagine, would have pleased her most.

The process of beatification was well under way by the end of the day and will no doubt continue. There was something so horribly appropriate about the manner of her death and I have the feeling that we were all involved in a Greek tragedy with the whole country as the Chorus. Beautiful, wilful, complicated, destructive and doomed, it is hard to believe that she could have found happiness. Her comfort was always in the love of strangers and, if she most wanted that love to be intense, personal and universal, today, at least, she would be satisfied.

SEPTEMBER

TUESDAY, 2ND SEPTEMBER

Frances Fyfield arrived at eleven o'clock for our last session in connection with a *Times* interview with me. In the course of general discussion about writing we spoke about copy-editing. Frances said that she doubted whether any novel could be absolutely accurate in every detail and that the last person to spot a mistake was usually the author, who was too involved with plot and characters to notice small inconsistencies or typing errors. I know that I am occasionally a careless writer in this respect and, as my books are long and complex, they do need very careful copy-editing; this they certainly receive. Apart from the Faber copy-editor, who is usually excellent, the proofs are read by Peter and Jane. Peter is meticulous about language, deleting, for example, the superfluous adjective in the phrase 'wide panorama', and methodically noting the number of duplicated words.

Ruth Rendell held her publicity party for her new book *Road Rage* at the Groucho, but I was unable to be there as I had undertaken some months ago to speak at the University Women's Club. I managed to reach Ruth at her London house both to explain and to congratulate her on the reviews for *Road Rage*. Ruth, who, with her husband Don, is a long-standing friend, is a remarkable and prolific writer, regularly producing novels which explore with power and high imagination the darker corners of the human psyche. She used to find the conventions of the detective story too restrictive and some critics would agree that her best novels are those written under the pseudonym Barbara Vine. But she is now beginning to use the Wexford saga as an opportunity to deal with social affairs about which she feels concern. Neither Ruth nor I are didactic writers and I never set out to point a moral or to deal specifically with a social problem. But if a novel is set in the modern world, social and political concerns necessarily intrude. In the first book in which my woman detective Kate Miskin appears, *A Taste for Death*, I didn't set out to explore the problems of an intelligent, ambitious and underprivileged young woman fighting her way to seniority and success in the machismo world of the police, but the book would not have been realistic if these problems hadn't been dealt with. Because the detective story is usually set unambiguously in its own time and place, it often gives a clearer idea of contemporary life than does more prestigious literature. If we want to know what it was like to work in a City advertising office in the early 1930s, there is no better book than Dorothy L. Sayers's *Murder Must Advertise*.

The dinner at the University Women's Club was, I think, successful and it is always a pleasure to be in this attractive, comfortable and well-managed club with its ambience of unpretentious feminine tranquillity. But the evening left me exhausted because of the high level of noise at dinner. I realize now that I really cannot tolerate being battered by a cacophony of shouting voices, but it is difficult to know what to do about it. Peter, who is a neuro-scientist, has explained that in youth the human brain has the facility to distinguish between the sounds it wishes to receive and others, thus effectively shutting out loud background noise, but that this ability decreases with age. But then, I am becoming intolerant of almost all loud noises and, in particular, of pop music. It blares out in shops, assaults my ears in taxis, is piped into offices and seeps from the earphones of fellow passengers in trains and on the Underground. And now we have the intrusive nuisance of the ubiquitous mobile phone to disturb the peace of railway journeys. Perhaps the train companies should consider introducing quiet compartments as well as those for non-smokers.

WEDNESDAY, 3RD SEPTEMBER

Derek Parker, who edits the journal of the Society of Authors, came for a brief interview to gather material for an article in the journal following my appointment as President of the Society. Polly-Hodge, as always with male visitors, was outrageously flirtatious and affectionate, laying her head on his knee and effectively covering his trousers with white hairs. Happily he is a cat-lover and didn't mind.

We talked about the Society and whether there would be an advantage in applying for affiliation with the TUC. On the whole I have never been in favour, but certainly wouldn't strongly dissent if a majority of members want affiliation. I don't think there is much evidence that they do. We talked about support for the public library system and he asked my views on whether a small charge should be made for each borrowing. My strong dislike of imposing a charge arises from my early experience when I depended on the Cambridge Public Library for virtually all my reading. The library was education, meeting-place, refuge and treasure trove, although it was poorly equipped and ill-housed compared with the large public libraries of today.

There, too, in the reading room I would read the newspapers. It was there one Saturday morning in 1936 that I first read the news of the uncrowned King Edward VIII's infatuation for a divorced American woman, Mrs Simpson, for whom apparently he was prepared to give up the throne. It seems incredible in these days of media power and intrusiveness that a secret of such importance could be kept from the British public so effectively and for so long. It was achieved because a small group of powerful men, politicians, courtiers and newspaper magnates could exercise a far more effective censorship than almost anything possible today.

The public library was essential to my generation because we couldn't afford books. I pointed out to Derek that it is now possible to buy a classic in paperback for under a pound. The range of paperback fiction is enormous and the huge expenditure on the Lottery doesn't suggest that borrowers would find it an imposition to pay a small charge, perhaps when borrowing new hardback books. But the administrative cost might outweigh the advantage, and I still retain that vestigial dislike of charging for public library borrowing.

Afterwards I shopped in Kensington High Street. The flower stall outside St Mary Abbot's Church had set up a trestle table with a huge pile of tissue paper and there was a continuous sale of flowers to people on their way to Kensington Palace. This extraordinary festival of mourning is like an infection. It is oppressive and poignant, but also alien and disturbing. I have a feeling, uncomfortable and irrational, that something has been released into the atmosphere and it isn't benign. The real woman has become smothered by acres of plastic and decaying flowers. The crowd was extraordinary. The women – and the great majority were women, many with prams or toddlers – walked, eyes fixed with a kind of desperate intensity as if afraid they would be late or were on their way to the first day of a sale. They didn't communicate or even look at each other. One could almost believe that an official edict had gone out that flowers must be laid within three days on pain of condign punishment. There is a growing and disturbing animus against the Royal Family whose reticence is clearly neither understood nor sympathized with. I shall feel relieved when Saturday is over.

FRIDAY, 5TH SEPTEMBER

Yesterday evening Dick Francis held his publication party for his new book, *10lb. Penalty*. Dick is a remarkable writer. He produces a book a year, all of which immediately appear on the bestseller list, usually at number one. He begins writing in January, delivers the manuscript by the end of May, and the book is published in August. Obviously this regularity of output and the disciplined setting aside of five months each year for writing suits him. I don't think I could possibly do it and I admire both his inventiveness and his stamina. For me a novel takes from nine months to a year to plot and plan, and even longer to write. I sometimes envy those writers who produce their best work when under the pressure of time. They make my own leisurely method seem self-indulgent.

Dick's annual novel is always launched at the Ritz and the usual mixture of media people, publishers and crime writers was present. John and Norma Major were guests, both looking extremely well and cheerful. As John has said, 'There is life outside Number 10.' I suspect it is a life Norma prefers. They won't be able to be at my publication party on 6th October as this is the first day of the Conservative Party Conference and John will attend before beginning a lecture tour in the United States.

The Royal Family seem to be giving way to pressure from the people – which of course means pressure from the tabloids – to show their grief more publicly. It seems outrageous that the bereaved should be expected to come down to London publicly to collude in what is increasingly seen as a self-indulgent, almost neurotic display of emotionalism. But it would have been wise if the Queen had spoken briefly on radio and television to say that it was right that she should be with her grandchildren at this time, but that her thoughts and prayers were with all who were grieving, and if the Duke of York and Prince Edward had returned to London at once, perhaps to meet some of those waiting to pay tribute.

Today there was a curious atmosphere in London composed of

unease, expectation and grief. The carpets of flowers are growing before Kensington Palace, St James's and Buckingham Palace, and people are already settling down to spend the night on the funeral route. There was a spell of heavy rain in the afternoon, but a clear night.

In the evening I had supper with Harriet Harvey-Wood, now retired as Director of the Literature Department of the British Council, and her mother. Harriet had shopped in Kensington High Street and said that it was virtually impossible to get out of the tube trains because of the pressure of people on the Underground platform – all carrying flowers. Mrs Harvey-Wood, now over ninety, found the public emotionalism particularly distressing. Her generation, which has survived two world wars, is stoical in grief and mourns in private. And for what exactly are people mourning? I suspect for themselves.

SATURDAY, 6TH SEPTEMBER

I spent most of today until evening watching the funeral on television. It was an extraordinary, indeed unique, event. Apart from a brief preliminary wailing when the gun-carriage first appeared, the crowd was very quiet and the half-feared demonstrations of anger never occurred. For me the most poignant moment was when the young princes, with their father, Prince Philip and Earl Spencer, took their places behind the coffin at St James's Palace. The fact that the boys could manage this walk before thousands of onlookers was a tribute to their fortitude and self-control – qualities which are not much in fashion.

I was glad that it was so sunny. London – the parks, the trees, the buildings – looked very beautiful. It was extraordinary that the whole funeral could be so well organized and so perfectly carried out in just a week. The Abbey service was a successful compromise. I thought that I would find the Elton John song obtrusive but it seemed appropriate; this, after all, was the world in which the Princess was most at home. There was applause both outside and inside the Abbey for Earl Spencer, but I thought his attack on the Royal Family was unnecessary and misguided; the wrong words at the wrong time in the wrong place. I wonder if those sad, mascara-laden eyes will droop in reproach for ever over the House of Windsor, or whether this media-fuelled emotion will burn itself out as quickly as it has arisen.

TUESDAY, 9TH SEPTEMBER

The American Ambassador, Admiral Crowe, and his wife held one of their goodbye parties at the Residence in Regent's Park. There was room in the marquee even for the large number of guests, but as the evening was fine I strolled into the garden. Unusually for a party at Winfield House, I saw few people I knew. The Ambassador gave a short and amusing speech and I particularly liked one story. He said this was his second retirement. The morning after he left the Navy he dashed out of his house and settled himself comfortably with his newspaper in the back of his car. A few minutes later his wife came out to point out gently that, if he wanted the car to go anywhere, he would have to sit in the front and drive! He can't be the only one to tell this story.

The Residency is now to be closed for about two years for necessary repairs, including the removal of asbestos. I shall miss the parties there which, under different ambassadors, I have known always to have a welcoming spontaneity and informality even on more formal occasions.

WEDNESDAY, 10TH SEPTEMBER

To the National Portrait Gallery, one of my favourite London galleries, for the first viewing of a portrait of John Major by John Wonnacott and one of Tony Benn by Humphrey Ocean, both commissioned by the Trustees. The two portraits are very different.

The John Major, considerably larger, shows him sitting in the white room at Number Ten with Norma on a window seat and a view through the open door into the adjoining green room. I like portraits in a domestic setting, particularly with an interesting vista, but I found the perspective somewhat disturbing. The carpet seems to be hung rather than laid, and John's hand and foot look out of proportion. No doubt all this is intended and the picture certainly has a dramatic impact. In front of John is a white glistening object resembling crumpled foil, but which I was told is a piece of modern silver from his collection. I know about his fondness for silver; he showed me with obvious pleasure some pieces from the dinner service when I dined at Number Ten. But I am not sure that the piece included in the portrait is a successful addition. Tony Benn's portrait is much smaller, an amorphous egg-shaped visage but one which did convey something of the sitter's essential character.

Portrait painting seems to be in a state of flux. Perhaps because of the development of photography and its power both to fix and interpret personality with powerful immediacy, artists seem to have lost confidence in representational painting. Few do it well and others, in their desperate search for new ways of looking at life, have sacrificed a recognizable likeness to experimental technique. But a photographic image, however brilliant, can never challenge the best of painting. For me, a painting provides a more intense, more personal and more enduring insight into human personality. A photograph, however brilliant, says all it has to say at once. To return to it is only to reinforce that first immediate response. I can return to a painted portrait again and again, learning more each time about the artist as well as the sitter.

Tony Benn's son came up to me while I was looking at my own portrait by Michael Taylor, and wanted to talk about my use of St Peter-on-the Wall at Bradwell in *Original Sin*. We spoke about setting in the crime novel and I told him that I had wanted to erect a house for one of my characters on a desolate stretch of East Anglian coast and thought Bradwell would suit my purposes admirably. He took a photograph of me in front of my portrait. I read that there is an audio cassette about the portrait giving Michael Taylor's views as artist on me as sitter. I didn't buy it, although I was tempted to hear Michael's views.

When the Trustees of the National Portrait Gallery decided that they wanted to commission a portrait of me, I was invited to meet the Director, Dr Charles Saumarez Smith, and the keeper of the twentieth century collection, to discuss which artist should be chosen. I was asked whether I would prefer a well-known, well-established figure or a brilliant up-and-coming painter, although I don't think the choice was presented in precisely those terms. I was shown postcards of the work of Michael Taylor and I liked the strength and originality of his compositions and the authority with which he used colour.

He came to my house for the sittings, himself chose the room and the pose, and when I showed him the dress I had in mind, liked it, although in the portrait it certainly appears more shapeless than it does when I am wearing it. I enjoyed the thirteen sittings and liked Michael very much. There was no problem in sitting still – there never is for me – but I wanted to use the time and silence to think about my new novel and every time I retreated into that imaginary world, Michael would say, 'You're not looking at me.' He worked with great intensity, seeming to widen and shoot out his eyes as he painted and using copious amounts of toilet paper from a roll to clean his brushes.

We spoke hardly at all during the sittings. There is much I would have liked to have asked him. What did he think of the commercial art world today and of such iconoclastic artists as Damien Hirst? How far did private patrons influence what people feel is important and are prepared to pay for? How difficult was it for a newcomer to find a gallery willing to take him on? Did galleries have too much influence? Did artists feel themselves under pressure to produce quickly or in a certain style? How easy was it to make a living? Were art colleges good or bad for an aspiring artist? But I totally sympathized with Michael's wish not to chat. He was as much in his private world while painting as I am in mine while writing, and at those times interruptions are intolerable.

I did ask him during a break if he was intending to make me look sinister or mysterious, to which he replied, 'I have enough problems putting down what I see without trying to see something else.' He has put down precisely what he saw: an elderly much-lined woman with, I suppose, a certain authority. It is the painting of a seventy-five-year-old by someone still young, and is literally wart and all. It is a powerful painting which I much admire and, like all powerful paintings, provokes controversy. Some of my friends complain that it verges on caricature, but no one says it isn't like me.

THURSDAY, 11TH SEPTEMBER

The children's writer and artist Shirley Hughes is seventy, and four of her publishers joined to give her a party held at the Royal College of Art. Shirley and her husband John are two friends whom I never meet without a lifting of the heart, and see only too rarely. She has had a profound influence on writing for children, particularly young children, through her stories and the vigour of her superb illustrations. Here are real parents, real children, never sentimentalized but drawn with tenderness, humour and humanity. The party was crowded, but not unpleasantly so because of the number of rooms and the fact that the windows could be opened to a generally warm night. There were speeches by Margaret Meek, the educationalist who, like me, occasionally attends All Saints, Margaret Street, by one of Shirley's editors, by Posy Simmons, and by Shirley herself. She blew out seventy candles to general acclamation, after which I left.

There were flowers, teddy bears, other toys, balloons and messages tied to the railings of Kensington Gardens and Hyde Park, although the heaps of dead flowers inside the railings show that the work of clearing has begun.

SUNDAY, 14TH SEPTEMBER

To Southwold on Friday with an Oxford friend, the novelist Ann Pilling. She didn't have the car so came up very early by bus and we took a taxi to Liverpool Street. It was the first time Ann had seen the rebuilt station, which I think architecturally one of the most successful in London. I love the meticulous brickwork and the way in which the great iron arches have been retained and repaired. I can remember the Liverpool Street of my childhood: smoke-filled, mysterious, exciting. To me it represented London and all that word implied of romance, history, pleasure, and a whiff of danger. I came to London very rarely when a schoolgirl, but was once taken by my father to a Promenade Concert at the old Queen's Hall outside the BBC. I remember Sir Henry Wood turning, baton in hand, to scowl at us as if we were a potentially unruly mob. The scowl seemed to be directed personally at me, as if he had detected that, musically, I was unqualified to be there. The music meant little, but I can remember walking down to Oxford Street, by then deserted, and being told by my father that this was the longest street in the world. He was given to confident assertions, most of which I believed.

It has been a good weekend, the beautiful, delicately hued skies and the sea changing from grey-green to pale milky blue. We had much talk, mostly personal on Ann's side, and we also discussed how far the novelist's strong emotions should influence the process of writing. I made the point that a novel can't be just a raw slice of personal experience, however tragic or engulfing. Obviously we must use our own lives as material – what else do we have? – but a novelist must be able to stand aside from this experience, view it with detachment, however painful, and fashion it into a satisfying shape. It is this ability to detach oneself from experience and at the same time portray it with honesty and controlled emotion which makes a novelist. Perhaps it is also this ability to assume the role of privileged spectator, the cold searching gaze, which caused Graham Greene to write that every writer has a splinter of ice in the heart. Even as a child I had a sense that I was two people; the one who experienced the trauma, the pain, the happiness, and the other who stood aside and watched with a disinterested ironic eye. But I know that there are two experiences too overwhelming for such detachment. One would be the death of a child; the second, overwhelming physical agony. Pain, our response to it, our fear of it, makes the whole world kin. Perhaps because no detachment is possible from intense physical agony. I can think of no novel which has described it adequately. The more intense, the higher, more refined and exquisite the physical sensation, whether of agony or ecstasy, the less power have words to describe it.

TUESDAY, 16TH SEPTEMBER

I went this evening to the Royal Society at Carlton Terrace for the AGM of the Society of Authors. It was the last appearance as chairman of Simon Brett, who presented the 112th Annual Report and, as expected, made an entertaining and lively speech. He welcomed his successor, Clare Francis, and also reported that I had been elected by the Council to succeed Sir Victor Pritchett as President of the Society. This has given me immense pleasure. When Mark Le Fanu, Secretary of the Society, wrote to tell me about it I replied that I knew I was following a president of great distinction both as a writer and as a man, and hoped to be worthy of the trust the Society was placing in me. The words were conventional but the emotion was sincere.

After the AGM there was a discussion under the title 'For how much would you sell your soul?' with a panel including Robert McCrum, formerly of Faber and Faber. The discussion concentrated less on money than on the problems raised by indecency and pornography. The general view was that all censorship was wrong, indeed indefensible, but I made the point that there were surely some matters – the depiction on video of the sexual exploitation of young children, for example – which no civilized country ought to tolerate. There are two easy options for any society: total prohibition as in a totalitarian state, or total licence. Both avoid the ardours of decision. Both have the attraction of certainty. The difficult option is to decide where the line should be drawn and this, surely, is the responsibility of any civilized and democratic country.

One of the questioners suggested, although she did not positively state, that I have sold my soul over television since she had seen one of the less successful adaptations. I pointed out that television is a visual medium and that one can't expect ever to be totally satisfied with an adaptation. When people say to me 'Do you like what television has done with your book?', I reply that the director has done nothing to my book, since he has no power to alter a single comma. But it is true that television is increasingly trivial. I have no doubt of the current priorities as far as television is concerned; first in importance is the scheduling, second the star, third the director, fourth – and a long way behind – the drawing power of the writer's name and, last of all, the book. But to turn down the offer of a television series is not a simple decision. The series can dramatically affect paperback sales, which gives the publisher as well as the author a strong interest, and the series provides jobs for actors and adapters.

It is easy for me to say, 'I am rich enough now to do without television and will keep my art undefiled', but I am not sure how far this high-mindedness is justified. I am, however, only too aware what changes may be made to the plot of *A Certain Justice* in order to ensure that the star has an appropriate number of appearances on screen. The story, too, will have to be compressed if a long and complex novel is to be televised in only three episodes. More I fear will be lost than parts of the plot.

SUNDAY, 21ST SEPTEMBER

I arrived home from Heathrow after 9.30 p.m. having spent the weekend in Oslo helping my Norwegian publisher, Aschehoug, celebrate their 125th anniversary. A century and a quarter is apparently a special commemoration in Norway and the event was impressive. It must also have been extremely expensive.

There was a dinner on the Friday night at the Drammensveren Hotel, and on Saturday there was open house at the firm's recently extended offices with a buffet lunch and plenty of drink, and in the evening a concert with 1,500 invited guests. The concert was a celebration in words and music of Aschehoug's 125 years in publishing, and I enjoyed the Norwegian songs and the special mini-opera composed for the occasion, although I could understand none of the rest of the programme, except the words 'Sherlock Holmes' and 'Dr Watson' during the episode celebrating the publication of the Conan Doyle stories.

On the Sunday morning there was a little free time and my escort Ivor (I never registered his surname) took me to see Amundsen's ship, the *Fram*. It is incredible to think that the crew of thirteen were held in the ice together for three years, apparently without anyone going berserk or murdering one of his colleagues. A ship marooned in ice could be a dramatic setting for a detective story, a closed circle of people exposed to the inevitable emotional traumas of enforced intimacy, and a limited number of suspects. This last is important if each suspect is to be given equal space and attention, each motive made credible.

Providing a believable motive for murder is one of the greatest difficulties facing the modern crime writer. In the 1930s readers could apparently believe that A had murdered B because B knew something highly discreditable about A's sex life which he was threatening to reveal. Today, so far from fearing disclosure, people receive good money for writing about the more lurid aspects of their sex lives in the Sunday newspapers. Politicians who are guilty of flagrant infidelities are no longer propelled into the wilderness of ignoble obscurity, but into the lush pastures of media fame and fortune. Blackmail can still provide a credible motive but our priorities for disgust have changed; nowadays it would not be a sexual misdemeanour but racism or child abuse which would invite disaster. Money, the need of it, the lack of it, particularly if the amount is large, is always a credible motive, as is that deep-seated hatred which can render an enemy's very existence insupportable. In one of my early novels an experienced sergeant is reported to have said to the young probationer Adam Dalgliesh that the letter 'L' covers all motives for murder: love, lust, loathing and lucre. He adds, 'They'll tell you, my boy, that the most dangerous emotion in the world is hate. Don't you believe it. The most dangerous emotion is love.' As a writer I find that the most credible motive and, perhaps, the one for which the reader can feel some sympathy, is the murderer's wish to advantage, protect or avenge someone he or she greatly loves. But should the reader feel sympathy for the murderer? Perhaps sympathy is too strong a word; but I think there should be empathy and understanding. In the words of Ivy Compton-Burnett: 'I believe it would go ill with many of us if we were faced with a strong temptation, and I suspect that with some of us it does go ill.'

On board the *Fram* there was a piano and a gramophone for entertainment, and their scientific expeditions by sledge would have added a change of scene and the relief of physical activity. Even so, the whole enterprise was a triumph of courage, will and scientific passion over danger and discomfort. What I wanted to know and didn't discover was how they kept healthy, particularly how they got their vitamins. They obviously shot and ate bears and other wildlife, but they couldn't have had vegetables or fresh fruit.

Ivor was an interesting guide. We talked about his country's educational system, the health service, and social and economic problems which are remarkably similar to ours. We also spoke about language and he said one thing which I found interesting, that much German thoroughness comes from the need to think every sentence through to its concluding verb before speaking it, whereas in English and Norwegian, words can be strung together in an occasionally artless concatenation.

We then went back to the hotel to collect Marilyn French, who wanted to see the Anselm Kiefer pictures at the Astrup Fearnley Museum for Modern Art. I was glad we went. I was impressed and moved by the Kiefers, but the Francis Bacons – violent slabs of meaty flesh – are not pictures I could live with without some risk to mental health. There were three good nudes by Lucian Freud. He paints what he sees with total honesty if little humanity. I should like to own a Freud.

Before coming back on Sunday there was a reading in the Great Hall of the University by two Scandinavian writers, and by Marilyn French, Salman Rushdie and myself. Salman and I had been booked on the same plane at Heathrow and we both went through the VIP channels on arrival, although he was whisked off in a police car with escort and I was found a taxi. I suppose I might have been slightly nervous in flight had I realized that he was a fellow passenger. William Nygaard, my Norwegian publisher, was shot and was lucky to escape being killed when he decided to publish *The Satanic Verses*. He wore a bullet-proof coat during most of the weekend, but I can't say I felt that any of us were particularly at risk. Salman read from *Midnight's Children* exceptionally well, then was hurried away to catch an early plane home. I felt slightly ashamed of my relief that I was booked to travel later.

It was a joy to have Marlene Mitev at the door to welcome me back. She has spent the weekend here looking after Polly-Hodge. When she is here, I realize how much I have missed being greeted at the end of a trip. We shared a room together when we were both working at the Home Office, first in the Whitehall building and then at Queen Anne's Gate. To share an office is to spend more time in one another's company – about eight hours a day – than most people spend with their families. It can also mean sharing more experiences, good and bad. Marlene is intelligent, amusing, kind and, being a Yorkshire-woman, given to speaking plain common sense. We became, and remain, close friends.

It occurs to me that I have mentioned but not described Polly-Hodge. I have shared this house, and to an extent my life, for the past ten years with a white long-haired female cat. Previously I had two Burmese: Cuthbert, plumply indolent and affectionate; Pansy, flirta-tious and over-active. Both were stolen. I never heard anything of Pansy again, but the RSPCA telephoned to say that Cuthbert had been found dead in the Underground but without his collar. I don't know how they traced him to me. I suppose he somehow managed to evade his captors and made a dash for the stairs at Holland Park.

After this I decided not to have another cat. I wasn't entirely uninfluenced by the difficulty of arranging for an animal to be fed while I am away. But then this white cat began to appear in the garden, sleeping on one of the chairs under the glass roof of the loggia. She was excessively nervous and would glide from the chair and disappear at great speed as soon as I opened the kitchen door to feed the birds. But she was frequently in the garden getting – at least to my eyes – thinner and slightly bedraggled. Eventually I could not resist putting out a saucer of Whiskas. When I went down for my early morning tea the next morning she was curled up on the kitchen wicker chair and showed every intention of remaining there.

From that morning she moved in permanently. Knowing this was inevitable I attempted to lay down the conditions under which we would live together. (I dislike anthropomorphizing, but when a cat sits in her Ancient Egyptian pose – head erect, paws together, tail curled, eyes straight ahead – it is difficult to believe that my carefully reasoned arguments are not being understood.) I said that the kitchen would be her territory. An old fur coat would be placed on the chair for her greater comfort. A cat-flap, as she had already discovered, would give access to the garden and the mat by the door was suitably tough for scratching.

Receiving this information, Hodge (as I immediately called her)

71

was mentally laying down the conditions under which she would condescend to live with me. She did not long remain in the kitchen. The corner at the top of the basement stairs is particularly warm since the hot water pipe runs down that wall. There seemed no good reason why she should not be allowed to sleep on the top step. Then it became apparent that she enjoyed watching television with me, provided no war film was being shown when she would immediately leap from my lap and make for the door while keeping close to the wall. So the sitting-room became available to her during the evenings. After that it was only a flight of stairs to my bed where, although she is never allowed to sleep at night, she often finds it convenient to spend the day. Now, of course, there is no corner of the house which is free from white hairs.

It was my then neighbour, the late Lady Moynihan, more knowledgeable than I about people in the neighbourhood, who discovered where Hodge had come from. This coincided with a photograph of me with the cat published in a national newspaper. A letter immediately followed from her previous owners. Apparently Hodge – whose name, I learned, was Polly – had previously lived with the family in Holland Park. When they moved, however, they acquired two more cats and Polly obstinately refused to share her home. It was impossible to keep her in and the vet, when consulted, said that there was nothing they could do to prevent her leaving. Polly-Hodge, cat-like, was prepared to live wild in her old haunts until an acceptable home presented itself, rather than share comfortable accommodation with two interlopers. Her previous owners – although the word *owners* is inappropriate in relation to cats – were happy for me to keep her and Polly-Hodge, now renamed, has remained. Since she never answered to the previous name, the addition of Polly has made no difference. She doesn't have to earn food or houseroom by any service, by tricks of behaviour or by an inordinate display of affection. It is enough that I take daily pleasure in the infinite variety of attitudes, all graceful, in which she composes herself for sleep, the elegant hieratic stillness with which she contemplates life with those inscrutable amber eyes. It is in this attitude that she waits beside her bowl for food. When hungry she never wreathes herself round my legs but sits in a parody of patience unrewarded. Returning to her half-empty bowl she won't deign to eat until I have bent down to scrape the food into the middle. The impression given is that she is awaiting permission to begin eating; more likely she prefers not to touch the edge of the bowl with her whiskers or requires me to perform this small act of servitude.

I have no doubt that she would have found a more desirable home on the Avenue had one presented itself, but nevertheless, irrationally, I feel a sense of pride that she chose me. She is embarrassingly affectionate to all callers, particularly those who dislike cats, loves being photographed – except when she is wanted, when she declines to co-operate – is obstinate, timid and entirely beautiful. I took her to the vet when she first moved in and he thought she was about five years old, so she is now over fifteen and, alas, has that illness common in elderly cats. The symptoms are constant hunger and thirst but, despite huge intake, the cat gets inexorably thinner. But Polly-Hodge still purrs, still grooms herself fastidiously and obviously still enjoys life. When the moment comes when that life is no longer agreeable and it is apparent that she is suffering it will be painlessly ended. We are often more merciful to our animals than we are to each other. Meanwhile we grow old together, she the more gracefully.

WEDNESDAY, 24TH SEPTEMBER

A young photographer, Andy Slack, came to take a portrait photograph for *The Times* to accompany Frances Fyfield's interview. He brought a young woman assistant and I provided tea and cakes before and after the photograph, which was happily stress-free once the young man realized that I strongly dislike talking about my work when being photographed. Photographers, particularly the young ones, seem to feel they should take an interest in an author's craft, and actually imagine that we are gratified to answer the over-familiar questions about working methods, where we get our inspiration, how long it takes to complete a book, etc. At least this one didn't come accompanied by a skull and a dagger and expect me to peer round the edges of doors looking malevolent. Photographers, new to me and setting out to produce images of a dark, sinister and probably emaciated witch-like woman, are disconcerted to find themselves facing a plump, generally benign grandmother. They do their best to fulfil the picture editor's expectations ('You don't happen to have a skull we could use, I suppose?'). Most resign themselves to failure. But I thought the results, judging by the contact prints, were good and Andy was an unfussy photographer. Some of the best photographs I have had taken have been by Jane Bown with no assistant and only a hand-held camera.

I realize that a diary should be written up daily even if the day is without particular events and there seems little of note worth recording. No day is really without interest, being filled with thoughts, memories, plans, moments of particular hope and occasional moments of depression. Every day is lived in the present, but also vicariously in the past and one can write a novel of 100,000 words covering just one hour of a human life. But it seems too egotistical to spend the last hours of every day contemplating the minutiae of unrecoverable moments. I say my prayers and am grateful for the comfort of bed.

THURSDAY, 25TH SEPTEMBER

This evening the Mayor of Kensington, Mr Edward Hess, gave an enjoyable dinner at the Town Hall. At thirty-five he is the youngest mayor the Royal Borough has ever had, and I imagine probably younger than any previous mayor in any borough. He is a lawyer and a number of barristers from his chambers were there, including Gavyn Arthur, who has so generously helped with the research for *A Certain Justice*. Gavyn had his copy with him and passed it to Mr Hess, who obligingly held it aloft at the end of his brief speech and exhorted the company to buy it.

SUNDAY, 28TH SEPTEMBER

This weekend I attended a Conversazione on Culture and Society under the heading 'The Future of the Past' held at Lincoln College, Oxford. The event was interesting and at times enthralling, bringing together more than eighty representatives of Church, finance, the arts, academia and journalism in a three-day discussion of our attitudes towards the past and our cultural perceptions of history and heritage as we have inherited them through literature, art and buildings. My own lecture, on the importance of language and the written word, given this afternoon, was generously received, although I feel that I was boxing somewhat above my weight (always the surest way to ensure a swift knock-out), and most of what I said about literature, language and the importance of encouraging children to read has been said before both by me and by others better qualified to participate. I emphasized that preserving the language doesn't mean resisting change. English has from the beginning been a hybrid; brought to Britain by the Angles, Saxons and Jutes, influenced by Latin and Greek, enriched by the Danes and French-speaking Normans, given strength and beauty by Tyndale's translation of the Bible and Cranmer's Book of Common Prayer. To preserve a language is not to guard it jealously against any alien influence but, in the words of Chambers Dictionary, 'to keep safe from harm or loss; to keep alive; to keep sound; to guard against decay'. A living language responds to the aspirations and needs of each generation but the changes should enrich, not impoverish. We debase our language if, while inventing new words to meet new techniques, we lose that nice precision of definition in vocabulary and construction which makes English an exact as well as a versatile language.

This was the first Conversazione I have attended and it had its own form and procedures, being neither conference nor colloquium. At dinner people at each table conferred and then asked a question of any of the speakers. They were designed, I think, to entertain, challenge or amuse rather than seriously to elicit information. I was asked for Dalgliesh's views on structuralism – or was it post-structuralism? I replied that he had given it careful thought for a number of evenings and had come to the conclusion that it was nonsense. The young chaplain sitting next to me murmured, 'In vain they lay snares at her feet.' I suppose that, if I'd been to university, I might have understood these more complex literary theories. Whether they would have added to my enjoyment of reading or made me a better writer is open to question. The Conversazione was an enjoyable and welcome experience and I was reminded of the conversation between Mr Elliot and his cousin Anne Elliot in *Persuasion*:

'My idea of good company, Mr Elliot, is the company of clever, well-informed people, who have a great deal of conversation; that is what I call good company.'

'You are mistaken,' he said gently. 'That is not good company, that is the best.'

TUESDAY, 30TH SEPTEMBER

Yesterday was one of those catching-up days in which resolutions to tackle the 'pending' file, sort out my summer dresses and put them away, and fit in a hair appointment had all been dissipated in a kind of aimless activity. I did manage to complete, and Joyce faxed to the *Sunday Times*, my review of the *Oxford Dictionary of Literary Quotations* edited by Peter Kemp.

To the making of dictionaries there is no end, particularly under the aegis of the Oxford University Press, and I for one make no complaint. Books of quotations, in particular, afford me one of the most undemanding but satisfying forms of reading pleasure. Oxford University Press have been wise in their choice of editor, Peter bringing to his task a wide knowledge and appreciation of literature both old and contemporary.

I can think of a number of quotations which I should like to have seen included, and no doubt Peter will be inundated with suggestions from friends. All the more reason for a supplement or for an enlarged paperback edition. One quotation I would most like to see in any revised edition are the words of Henry James, writing of Anthony Trollope, 'We trust to novels to maintain us in the practice of great indignations and great generosities.' It is an elevated ideal of fiction but, thinking it over, I am not sure that it is any longer true. Dickens could write a novel which would move his readers to pity or outrage and act as a spur to action, but surely today it is television which, sometimes, powerfully, sometimes superficially, examines for us the dilemmas and concerns of our age, reflects our lives and opens to us the lives of others. Men and women who in Victorian England would have read Dickens are now watching *EastEnders* and *Panorama*.

In particular the so-called literary novel too often seems removed from the day-to-day concerns of ordinary people. The very description 'literary novel' is, for many readers, an indication that the work is not intended for them. With some notable exceptions – David Lodge is one – the worlds of industry and commerce, the very means by which society gains the wealth which supports our art and literature, are alien to the modern novelist, perhaps because they are worlds few of us have experienced. Have we a responsibility to break free from our cabined preoccupations, our fascination with history and our literary exploitation of the evils of the past and address ourselves to more contemporary themes? Is there a novelist today who could write – or would try to write – *War and Peace* or Trollope's *The Way We Live Now* with its brilliant portrayal of the financier Melmotte, the nineteenth-century Robert Maxwell?

Unless the novel, particularly the so-called literary novel, can reach the hearts and minds of ordinary people, reading will increasingly become a minority interest. Novelists, too, surely have a duty to be intelligible if they are to address themselves to a wider audience than the educated middle class and the literary establishment. It would be futile, and indeed silly, to suggest that novelists today can recover the hierarchical and moral certainties of Victorian England. Some writers would argue that we can no longer comfortably write in the tradition of social realism because we no longer know what we mean by reality. I suppose the extremes of literary experimentation are some novelists' way of explaining the arbitrariness and chaos of human existence, an attempt to express the inexpressible. Thomas Hardy wrote that the secret of fiction lies in the adjustment of things uneven to things eternal and universal. But what adjustment can a writer make if, in a world governed for him by chance and chaos, he is no longer able to believe in things eternal and universal?

Publication day for *A Certain Justice* is fast approaching. Faber sent a car to take me to the BBC, where I did an on-line interview from Manchester about the novel, to be used in the afternoon's *Kaleidoscope*. Then to Camden Passage to meet Frances Fyfield and collect a dress for Monday's launch together with a suit and a skirt and jacket. These should see me through most of the publicity.

In the evening Gavyn Arthur gave a dinner at the Carlton Club. I sat between two lawyers, both interesting, and one involved with mental health cases, and we had a long talk about psychopathy. I was glad that he thought my character Garry Ashe a believable portrait of a psychopath. He asked me whether I thought that Ashe would in the end feel any affection or love for Octavia or would begin to respond to her love for him, and I said I was sure not. He agreed. A psychopath who could feel love would not be a psychopath. Some, however, have felt strong affection for a dog. It occurs to me that I can't remember ever reading about a murderer who gave house room to, or was fond of, a cat. The company at dinner was varied, the talk stimulating and interesting, and I met people I should be glad to meet again – which doesn't always happen at the age of seventy-seven. The pity is that life is so busy that I know that I won't.

THURSDAY, 2ND OCTOBER

A journalist from Australia arrived in the afternoon for an interview in connection with the publication of *A Certain Justice*. This is the beginning of the pre-publicity for my Australian tour next year.

In the evening to St Anne's Church in Soho for the launch of Volume 2 of *The Letters of Dorothy L. Sayers*, edited by Dr Barbara Reynolds, for which I have provided a preface. I can detect the influence of Dorothy L. Sayers in my own work together with that of three other writers: Jane Austen, Graham Greene and Evelyn Waugh. I suppose few writers of Sayers's generation have been more controversial. To her admirers she is the novelist who did more than any other of her age to lift the detective story from its status as an inferior puzzle to a respected craft with claims to be taken seriously as popular literature. Her detractors deplore what they see as the snobbery and élitism (she must be the only crime writer to include in her book a letter written in French which she does not deign to translate), focusing their dislike on her aristocratic detective, Lord Peter Wimsey. She wrote her detective novels initially to make money and entertain, and neither is an ignoble aim. And the books do continue to entertain, not least as period popular literature giving us a lively picture of life in the 1920s and 1930s, that period which E. M. Forster described as 'a long weekend between two wars'. The fact that, over forty years after her death, she can still provoke controversy and stimulate argument is a measure of the resilience of her talent and the vitality of her detective.

It is only in recent years, and thanks to her friend Barbara Reynolds, that we have come to respect her as a remarkable letter-writer. This correspondence covers the years 1937–43, the years of the Second World War, of air raids, the threat of invasion, difficult and congested travel, the black-out and inadequate or non-existent domestic help. Nevertheless, they were years of high creativity. She wrote plays, two religious dramas including the notorious radio drama *The Man Born to be King* (the first time an actor had impersonated Christ on the radio), and two theological works as well as articles and hundreds of letters, most in her own hand. The expense of time and effort must have been considerable, deflecting energy from her creative work. But perhaps for Dorothy L. Sayers, as for others, letter-writing was a form of creativity. For someone like myself who has an almost pathological dislike of initiating or replying to correspondence, and does it badly, this is difficult to understand.

And prolific letter-writers, if they achieve fame or notoriety, leave treacherous hostages to fortune. A letter is paradoxically the most revealing and the most deceptive of confessional revelations. We all have our inconsistencies, prejudices, irrationalities which, although strongly felt at the time, may be transitory. A letter captures the mood of the moment. The transitory becomes immutably fixed, part of the evidence for the prosecution or the defence. And we adapt our style to our correspondent. Philip Larkin does not write in the same terms to Kingsley Amis as he does to Charles Monteith, his editor at Faber, or to Barbara Pym. Jane Austen could write with perfect confidence and candour only to Cassandra and the shafts of asperity, cynicism, even of malice, could not have been openly expressed in any other way. In that society, dependent on family and neighbours for entertainment and a social life, discretion and more than a little hypocrisy were necessary if life were to go smoothly, let alone agreeably. Jane Austen may write, 'I was as civil to them as their bad breath would allow me', but she would not have wrinkled her nose when they met. 'Her sweetness of temper never failed', wrote her nephew James Edward Austen-Leigh. On the contrary, it failed frequently, and if it hadn't we would not have had the six great novels.

As a result of editing Dorothy L. Sayers's letters, Barbara Reynolds was able to solve three of the mysteries which have always surrounded her: Who exactly was the William White who was the father of her illegitimate son John Anthony? Why was it not possible for them to marry? Why did she choose Southbourne in Hampshire as the place of birth when, as far as we know, she had no contact with that town?

William White was not the rough, ill-educated motor mechanic he has sometimes been made out to be, but he does appear to have been something of an irresponsible cad. Dorothy and he became lovers on the rebound from her disastrous and unconsummated affair with John Cournos, and in the spring of 1923 she found that she was pregnant. Barbara Reynolds suggests that it may have been only then that she discovered that White was already married and had, in fact, a daughter. He asked his wife to come to London to celebrate the anniversary of their wedding – they seemed to have lived apart for much of the time while remaining on good terms – and he then confided in her about Dorothy's pregnancy and asked her to help. This, with surprising generosity, she agreed to do. Mrs White invited Dorothy to come to Southbourne for the last stages of her pregnancy, took a room for her at a guest house and arranged for her brother, who was a doctor, to attend the birth, which took place in a nursing home. It was not revealed to him that he had been engaged to deliver his brother-in-law's child and Mrs White pledged to keep the baby's existence a secret, and did so until after Dorothy's death in December 1957. It was only then that she wrote to her daughter, revealing to her that she had a half-brother. In 1991 that daughter, now Mrs Napier, decided to write to Anthony. But the letter, which was sent care of the publishers, Victor Gollancz, was returned unopened. John Anthony had then been dead for seven years.

This must have been a traumatic and utterly miserable part of Dorothy's life. She was both egotistical and proud, and now found herself in the humiliating position of any woman who had loved unwisely and been careless or unlucky enough to become pregnant. But I doubt whether, in Sayers's case, it was love; Cournos had cured her of that debilitating waste of spirit.

To have to rely on her lover's wife must have been particularly galling. No wonder, in the novels, Sayers's *alter ego* Harriet Vane makes a number of caustic comments about the humiliating burden of gratitude. It is difficult to know whether Dorothy really got to like Mrs White – in many ways a companion in fortune since they had both been victims of the same feckless, irresponsible man – or whether she accepted her kindness always with a deep if unacknowledged resentment. There is a surprisingly ungracious reference to her benefactress in a letter to Ivy Shrimpton when she had returned to London after leaving Anthony in Ivy's care. 'I was a bit weary yesterday, because I came home to find that the fool I'd let my flat to had locked up the keys inside the flat.' Mrs White had in fact been living there to send on letters to Dorothy and to post her letters from London, notably to her parents. Both of them died without ever knowing that they had a grandson. Mrs White's daughter Valerie was with her mother in London and Barbara Reynolds records that she remembered the flat clearly, in particular a cat called Agag, whose name, Dorothy told her, means 'he who treads lightly', and that there was a large supply of children's books in the flat. If Dorothy provided those it shows a sympathetic understanding of a child's needs.

Some mysteries remain, principally why Dorothy waited until she was returning to work to leave her son in the care of her cousin Ivy Shrimpton. Had she been pressed to have him adopted – then the easiest way out – and later relented? If so, one would like to have thought that the relationship gave her greater pleasure in her later life than in fact proved the case. She received neither disinterested affection nor support from any of the men important to her, including her husband and her son. Small wonder that in Lord Peter Wimsey she created a fantasy figure with whom she could safely fall in love. She moved on from him in later life but she never repudiated him. Unlike the other men in her life, he never let her down.

SATURDAY, 4TH OCTOBER

Today was the blessing of grandson Tom and Mary's marriage, the civil ceremony of which took place last month in a restaurant in Cambridge. I went to Southwold in great hopes that the day would be everything the young people and the family, in particular Clare, needed; for her it was the blessing rather than the civil ceremony which was important.

All went perfectly and there was great happiness. My eldest grandchild Katie had interrupted her solo sponsored walk round the British Isles and had taken a train to be with us. Katie had set out on 2nd April 1997 on a six-month hike over 2,500 miles round Britain in aid of the Calvert Trust Exmoor and the Chernobyl Children's Project. She will just rest for the night and then go back and continue the walk. The weather today was perfect, the sky blue with a few drifting clouds, the light marvellous as it always is in East Anglia, and Blythburgh church, like a great ship moored in the marshes, took one's breath away. Mary and Tom had gone to a great deal of trouble. Mary looked beautiful in a simple sheath dress in bright orange which was good with her skin and large dark eyes. She carried a small posy of marigolds and green foliage and had made similar posies to decorate the ends of the pews.

The ceremony was to have been in a small upper room over the porch, but Mary was afraid that I would find the narrow twisting stairway too claustrophobic to climb. So the blessing was held before the altar with the family sitting opposite each other in the choir stalls. Tom and Mary had devised the ceremony with the help of Father Barry, the parish priest, and it was a mixture of Christian liturgy with a reading by Clare from an Eastern mystic, and translated Gaelic blessings and prayers because Tom and Mary had first met in Ireland. Father Barry seemed to take the innovations in his stride and the service was simple and very moving.

Afterwards we piled out into the sunshine where a patient group of people were waiting for the church to be reopened. They joined in the general laughter and happiness and Clare asked one of them to take a photograph of the group. 'I thought you'd never ask me,' he said. 'I've been waiting here for ages.' Let's hope it comes out.

Afterwards, back at the Southwold house, there was a cake provided by Clare with the Union Jack and Australian flag, and champagne from Peter of a quality seldom met with at weddings large or small. Katie looked bonny and happy. Her journey seems to be a spiritual odyssey as well as a great feat of endurance. Granddaughter Eleanor wasn't well, but had insisted on coming. I think she is finding her teaching job exceptionally arduous. The children, apart from the ill-discipline one expects these days, have had no home training either in manners or social skills, and their attention-span is so short that learning is almost impossible. But Nell said that she was trying hard to establish good relationships with the parents of some of the most difficult children. They might come up to the school to confront her belligerently, but once they understood she was genuinely trying to help their child, they became co-operative and grateful. But it really is an extraordinarily tough job. I'm not surprised that we have a shortage of good teachers. I'm sometimes amazed that we have any.

I'm glad that the day was so successful. It will be a wonderful memory for all of us, and particularly for Clare. Tom is an only son and it will be hard for her to say goodbye to him when he leaves for Australia.

SUNDAY, 5TH OCTOBER

I went to eleven o'clock Mass at All Saints, Margaret Street. One of the post-Communion hymns was 'Jesu, Good Above All Other', a hymn frequently sung at assembly at Cambridge High School. It is odd how hymns can trigger off memories of the past more strongly than visual scenes or smells. At all the schools I attended we had morning assembly consisting of prayers including the Lord's Prayer, a reading from scripture and a hymn. My memory of the British School in Ludlow is that we had no hymn books but sang the same hymns over and over again. Could this really be so? During prayers the older children, those nearing eleven, by some childish unwritten prescription were privileged merely to bow their heads and loosely link their fingers. We, the smaller ones, had to raise our arms, palms pressed.

I can't have been at the National School long before we moved to Cambridge, and I began half-way through the first term of the new school year at the High School. Here too every morning began with assembly. We would file into the hall by form while one of the more musical girls would thump out a march on the piano. The Headmistress, Miss Dovey, commonly called The Dove, would stand there in her gown, the other mistresses ranged against the walls, also gowned. I remember on my first day how impressed I was by this first sight of academic dress, the visible symbol that I was, indeed, a High School pupil.

I was born and bred in the distinctive odour of Anglicanism, which childhood memory identifies as the smell of old prayer books, flowers, brass, stone and polished wood, the whole overlaid by the occasional sweet pungency of incense. I early grew accustomed to its services. Because Father, a middle-grade civil servant, was relatively poor, my parents employed no resident servant to help look after us children, even in those days when wages were low. This meant that, until we moved to Cambridge, when my father gave up going to church, the whole family attended Sunday Evensong together.

I must have been about five years old when we moved from Oxford to Ludlow and I can remember long autumnal Sunday evenings (my memory is always of going to church in the fading light and coming out into darkness): my brother fast asleep against my mother, my sister dozing, and myself reading the Book of Common Prayer to relieve the boredom of sermons which were not only long but invariably well above my understanding. I was fascinated by the

Prayer Book – less by the liturgy than by the accompanying text. I can remember at a very early age being impressed by the rubric in the Communion Service that when in times of plague no one could be found to take communion with the sick then the priest only might do so, and I would sit there in the darkened church with a vivid imagining of crosses on doors, wailing voices and the heroic figure of the cloaked priest moving silently and swiftly through the deserted streets, bearing the sacred vessels.

But my experience of church-going was even earlier. Both my parents had a deep affection for church music, my mother from nostalgia and sentiment, my father because he loved organ music, and they would frequently attend Sung Evensong in the College chapels as well as the services in the Cathedral. I would be wheeled in my pram and left outside the chapel doors (this was an age when mothers had no fear of their children being snatched), or even carried, sleeping, into the chapel. Thus listening to the music and hearing the liturgy of the church were two of my very early and formative experiences and Cranmer's magnificent cadences seeped into my first consciousness.

When we lived in the house called The Woodlands on the fringes of Ludlow our nearest church was over the bridge at Ludford. I have only two memories of Ludford church: the tortoise stove which flared dramatically when the wind changed, reminding me of the tongues of fire at Whitsun, and a remarkable prayer book which had been left in the pew in which we normally sat. It had heavy brass clasps which I would discreetly click open and shut during the service, and one of my earliest temptations was the wish somehow to conceal the prayer book and take it home with me. Surely it wouldn't be stealing. I should be returning with it every Sunday evening. It was the first object I remember wanting to possess with real passion.

I have a memory, too, of Ludford Sunday school. All the children were given a card with blank spaces and each week we were handed a coloured sticker of a biblical scene to fix to the appropriate space. I had no choice about attending Sunday school but, even if I had, it would have been important to complete my card without any humiliating blanks. After a common prayer and hymn we would disperse to sit in little groups according to age. Our group had a teacher who must have been extremely inexperienced; perhaps she was filling in for someone more orthodox. Certainly she spent little time in telling us Bible stories, but did recount the more lurid examples from *Foxe's Book of Martyrs*, which both thrilled and half-terrified us. I don't think these gory details of rackings and burnings kept me awake at night, nor did they affirm me as a natural Protestant.

My mother in particular was naturally ecumenical and had friends who were Roman Catholics and others who were Methodists or belonged to the more esoteric Protestant sects. It was never at any time suggested to me that one form of Christianity was necessarily superior to any other. My mother, indeed, was much in demand as a member of the Talkers Circuit and was frequently asked to address meetings of the Women's Bright Hour. I can remember being taken with her and sitting, legs dangling, among the female audience while my mother gave comforting and lively little homilies on 'Meals in the Bible', 'Journeys in the Bible', or any other similar theme on which she could hang her gentle moralizing. Mother enjoyed amateur theatricals but had no opportunity to participate except at concerts in aid of the church. I remember a performance of *Babes in the Wood* which she wrote or produced (probably both) and in which Edward was a babe, and Monica and I gnomes. Then there was the Sunday school dance troupe. Dressed in such costumes as she could improvise, we would perform deeply inauthentic folk dances, prancing uncertainly across the stage while Mother mouthed encouragement and occasional desperate instructions from the piano.

When we moved from The Woodlands to a tall terraced house in Linney View overlooking the water meadows and close to Ludlow Castle, we began attending St Lawrence's parish church, where my father sang in the choir. Here, too, our usual service was Evensong. There seemed, as I remember, to have been a social distinction between Mattins, sometimes followed by Holy Communion, and the evening service. Those who had servants to cook their Sunday lunch went in the morning; those who, like my mother, had to do all their own housework and cooking, usually found it more convenient to go in the evening. But occasionally on special days we would be taken to a Sung Holy Communion and I can remember the great glory of these occasions and my sense that something mysterious and extremely important was happening at the altar, and that, left in the pew with my brother and sister while my parents went up to receive the wafer and wine, I was temporarily deprived of something which one day would be mine also and which I would enter into as I might an inheritance. It was, too, an important Sunday for us when it was my father's turn to carry the processional cross, the pride of the occasion being somewhat dimmed for me by the terrifying fear that one day he might drop it.

My mother's faith was uncritical, unintellectual, simple and senti-mental. It provided solace, nostalgia, reassurance and such social life as she enjoyed. She liked us to say our evening prayers at her knee, a practice which obviously gave her satisfaction but which I found acutely embarrassing. I accepted that there must be public prayers in church but felt that private prayer should be a matter between me and God. But religion in our home was never made into a source of guilt. We were made to feel guilty enough, but these were sins against an occasionally terrifying earthly father, not against God. God and fear seemed to me two opposing, irreconcilable ideas. And because my mother in particular took a lively part in church affairs, I never from my earliest age assumed that churchgoers were necessarily morally superior to other people, since experience showed me that they were not. There were the seemingly inevitable disputes at Easter-time and Harvest Festival about who should and should not decorate the altar and pulpit, and my mother voiced her dissatisfaction at always being given one of the darkest windows. There were the usual arguments between the organist and the vicar about the hymns and the music, and the annual church fête and sale of work provoked mutterings about members of the congregation notable for their bossiness. But the church was always there, immutable, unchanging, comforting and secure, and the year given a recognizable shape by its festivals and seasons.

When we moved to Cambridge we no longer worshipped as a family. My brother gained a place in the choir at Clare College, which kept him busy singing the services on Sunday and attending rehearsals on some weekdays, and my mother attended St Mary's parish church. Occasionally I went with her but my school friend and I preferred the smaller St Edward's Church, where within two years we were both prepared for confirmation by Father Colin Marr. Looking back, it seems that I took confirmation as very much a rite of passage unaccompanied by any particular spiritual enthusiasm. In those days candidates were not confirmed in their own parish church but together in a large group either in the cathedral or in a church sufficiently large for the purpose. My best friend Joan and I were confirmed together at St Luke's Church in Cambridge by the Bishop of Ely and I remember the massed pews of white-clad veiled girls and, opposite, the boys in their blue Sunday-best suits.

St Edward's Church, in defiance of its traditions, was going through a brief period of High Anglicanism, and we both went to confession before confirmation. Father Colin had suggested that it would be helpful if we listed our sins so that none were forgotten, and I can remember to my chagrin that Joan's list was twice the length of mine, and my relief at discovering that, whereas I had put down 'unkindness to members of the family' as one sin, she had listed her family members separately to produce a far more impressive total. Even so, I felt that my offering was hardly worthy of Father Colin's attention, a thought which, alas, would not occur to me today. Occasionally our current boyfriends from the Perse or the boys' grammar school (the word 'followers' would be a more appropriate description since we never encouraged them) would attend the morning service in an attempt to ingratiate themselves with us and we would spend much time during the sermon throwing them discouraging and disapproving looks.

But it was King's College Chapel which, during these years of early adolescence, provided for me my most meaningful religious experience. Evensong was sung at half-past three on Sundays and in the evening on weekdays, and I would often drop in when cycling home from school. I can recall the solemnity, the grandeur and the beauty of the building, the high, soaring magnificence of the roof, the candle-lit gloom, the decorous procession of the boys of the choir, the order and the beauty of the traditional service. This, I believed then and still do believe, was what worship should be. I think I probably realized even then that I was in danger of confusing worship of God with a strong emotional and aesthetic response to architecture, music and literature, but it seemed to me that religion could be an aesthetic experience and that God should be worshipped in the beauty of holiness.

From an early age I have taken little pleasure in sermons; it is the more reprehensible that I have occasionally succumbed to the temptation to accept invitations to deliver them. Special children's services have always been anathema to me and I greatly deplore the present fashion for rewriting the Eucharistic prayer to make it suitable for children. I must have listened to thousands of sermons during a lifetime of churchgoing, but few have remained permanently in memory. The fault no doubt lies in my arrogance. From childhood I wanted to question the preacher and to engage in discussion, particularly when the points he was putting forward differed greatly from those propounded in the previous Sunday sermon. After all, even in school we could put up our hands, ask a question, seek elucidation of half-understood points. There seemed something unnatural in a whole congregation listening in silence to one person's voice without the chance to intervene.

But if as a child I disliked the sermon, I loved the hymns, and this affection has remained with me. The soaring triumph of the processional Easter hymns, the celebration of All Saints' Day, with the hymn 'For All the Saints', which was my mother's favourite, and the plangent melancholy of the evening hymns, particularly 'The Day Thou Gavest, Lord, Has Ended', sung while the church windows darkened and the mind moved forward to the walk through the churchyard between the gleaming tombstones in the evening dusk. Some of my early religious memories are of the hymns and my mother's rich and over-loud contralto and my own piping treble. Some of them still have the power to move me to tears.

The Church of England in my childhood was the national church in a very special sense, the visible symbol of the country's moral and religious aspirations, a country which, despite great differences of class, wealth and privilege, was unified by generally accepted values and by a common tradition, history and culture, just as the church was unified by Cranmer's magnificent liturgy. There were, of course, varieties of practice and little superficial resemblance between the multi-candled ceremonial, the incense and Stations of the Cross found in the extreme High Church and the simplicities of an evangelical church which could have been mistaken for a non-conformist chapel. But it was possible to attend different churches – on holiday, for example – and feel immediately at home, finding in the pew, not a service sheet with a series number, but the familiar and unifying Book of Common Prayer.

The importance of the Church of England as the national church was perhaps most clearly shown on Armistice Day, when whole communities gathered in their parish church, united in sorrowful remembrance. To be born in 1920, two years after the end of the slaughter of a generation, was to be aware from one's earliest years of a universal grieving which was part of the air one breathed. Today I frequently hear people and families referred to as being Christian as if they were members of a minority and slightly eccentric sect. In my childhood the great majority of the population, whether or not they regularly attended a place of worship, thought of themselves as Christians, and most described themselves as C of E. The English have always respected and felt a devotion to their national church, provided they are not expected regularly to attend its services.

My early religious experience, like all the experiences of childhood, has both formed and influenced my subsequent years. I have inherited a love of and devotion to the Church of England which is still strong, although I sometimes find it difficult today to recognize the Church into which I was baptized. Much of its former dignity, scholarly tolerance, beauty and order, have been not so much lost as wantonly thrown away, together with its incomparable liturgy. The King James Bible and the Book of Common Prayer have both been central to my life and to my craft as a novelist. In particular, the words of the Prayer Book are so much part of my consciousness that I do not need to remember them, search for them or concentrate on them, but can release my mind to enter into that communion with the unseen, unknowable God which I call prayer. I still see myself as a searcher after truth rather than as one confident she has found answers to the great and eternal questions of human existence, not least the problem of the suffering of the innocent, and at seventy-seven I do not think I shall find all the answers now.

MONDAY, 6TH OCTOBER

Publication day of *A Certain Justice*, which was launched at a party given by Faber this evening in Middle Temple Hall. For me publication day is never an unalloyed pleasure. Like several writers I know, I would sometimes like to go abroad incognito and lie low until the fuss is over, returning only when the best and worst are known. But it helps to have a few preliminary good reviews, or the assurance of them, and in this I have been fortunate.

A Certain Justice is one of the novels I have most enjoyed writing, largely because of my fascination with criminal law and the fun and interest I had in researching the book. It began, as do nearly all my novels, with the setting. I had been to the 11.15 service in the Temple Church, to which I occasionally go when I feel the need to hear Mattins beautifully said in accordance with the Book of Common

Prayer and with superb accompanying music. Strolling after the service through the Temple and into Middle Temple Lane, I was struck by the contrast between the peace, the traditions, the history and the ordered beauty of this unique part of London and the appalling events with which criminal barristers daily deal in courts like the Old Bailey. I thought that it would be exciting to bring murder, the ultimate crime, into the heart of this bastion of law and order, striking down a female barrister of the criminal Bar in her own chambers. At once, as has happened with all my detective novels, this initial inspiration was followed by the heart-lifting certainty that I would write another book.

I was extremely lucky with the research. By chance at a public dinner I sat next to Gavyn Arthur, who inquired what I was working on. When I said I was researching a new novel to be set in the Middle Temple, he told me that he was in Chambers there and would be happy to help. This help, generously given, proved invaluable. Within minutes he had saved me from what could have been a serious error if I had myself failed to detect it. He asked which detective I was employing on the case. When I said Adam Dalgliesh, he reminded me that the Temple is within the jurisdiction of the City of London Police, not of New Scotland Yard. This was something I knew but had completely forgotten and might not have remembered in time. I have got over the difficulty by placing my imaginary court and chambers on the boundary between the two jurisdictions so that at least part of the unfortunate victim's body lies within the territory of the Metropolitan Police. Gavyn Arthur provided me with maps of the Temple showing the entrances and exits, arranged for me to speak to lawyers and clerks in Chambers, to have lunch with the judges at the Old Bailey and to watch a trial in Court Number One. He also kindly vetted the details of legal procedure in the court scene with which the book opens. It was with genuine gratitude that I acknowledged his help in my foreword.

I suppose that one of the small deprivations of age is that nothing, and certainly not great success or triumph, is ever as exciting as it was in youth. This is probably a mercy, since pain and distress are also less acute. But I woke with a thankful heart for having been given the book. This is always how my writing has seemed to me; nothing to do with my own cleverness but born of a talent which I have done nothing personally to deserve.

Faber sent my usual driver to collect Joyce and myself and we arrived in very good time. Middle Temple Hall was ideal for the launch. As always it looked magnificent and the publicity department at Faber had been clever over the embellishments.

The party was a great success and I think everyone there enjoyed it. I was a little afraid that we might break up into groups; lawyers, writers, journalists, family and so on, but that didn't happen, and everyone seemed to find a kindred spirit to talk to. There was great advantage in having plenty of room for the one hundred or so present. I can no longer tolerate crowded launch parties where the level of din is so high that ears and brain are continually assaulted, I can't speak without inducing a sore throat, and am totally unable to hear anyone. This really was a civilized occasion.

Matthew Evans, Chairman of Faber, made a short, funny and informal speech and I replied equally briefly. It was a huge relief to be holding the party with some excellent reviews behind me. I am always desperately sorry for writers who have to go ahead with these jollities in the knowledge that the book has been poorly received, but it must be even worse for actors who spend long weeks in rehearsal and then are dependent on one or two really influential reviewers.

I'm frequently asked how much I care about reviews. I'm tempted to say not at all, but this is hardly honest. Most of us do very much welcome good reviews, not only for our own satisfaction, but because of the pleasure they give to publishers and friends. The majority of mine have been so good that I can have no possible complaint. One reviewer was maliciously scathing but he is not someone I would worry about. There are, of course, some reviewers who use reviewing to compensate for professional, creative or sexual failure and others who criticize the author not for the book written, but for the one they think he should have written. There are also those who are reviewing not the book but the writer, and who strongly dislike what they think he stands for, his class, his sex or, most frequently of all, his politics. But these are relatively few, and it is stupid for any writer to take the slightest notice of them.

When the party ended I got the family together – Lyn and Clare, Peter and Jane – and we were driven to the Savoy for a very late dinner. I had booked in the River Restaurant, hoping for a quiet meal and a river view, but there was a somewhat noisy small orchestra. Jane, knowing how this would affect me, beckoned to the head waiter and asked if we could go to another part of the hotel. They disappeared together and returned five minutes later to say that Jane had approved a table for five in the Grill Room. There we ate in comfort a traditional but uninspiring meal, and then dropped Clare and Lyn by taxi at Oxford Circus and came home here so that Jane and Peter could pick up their car and drive back to Oxford. By then all of us were tired, myself particularly, too tired to write this before bed. But it was a good day, for which I am very grateful.

Thinking of reviews has encouraged me mentally to draw up a list of somewhat presumptuous advice for reviewers, among whom I list myself.

1. Always read the whole of the book before you write your review.
2. Don't undertake to review a book if it is written in a genre you particularly dislike.
3. Review the book the author has written, not the one you think he/ she should have written.
4. If you have prejudices – and you're entitled to them – face them frankly and, if appropriate, acknowledge them.
5. Be scathingly witty if you must and can, but never be deliberately cruel, except to those writers who themselves deal in cruelty, and therefore presumably expect it.
6. If you absolutely hate the book and have nothing either interesting or positive to say, why review it? Any review gives a book much-wanted publicity and it is a pity to waste space on a book which is meretricious or dishonest when you could be saying something of value about one worth reading. An exception to this rule is an eagerly awaited major work by a well-known writer when the verdict of leading critics is expected.
7. If you are given a book to review by a close friend and you strongly dislike it, don't review it. We none of us like hurting our friends and the temptation to be over-kind is too strong.
8. Resist the temptation to use a review to pay back old scores or to vent your dislike of the author's sex, class, politics, religion or lifestyle. Try to believe that it is possible for people of whom you disapprove to write a good book.

TUESDAY, 7TH OCTOBER

Publicity began in earnest today. Andy arrived to take me to Hatchard's, calling in at Faber to pick up Nicola Winter from

Publicity. There I spent an hour signing with a non-stop line, many of them Americans. It is always a pleasure to meet readers and mine are so generous and grateful that it makes me feel humble. Then upstairs to sign books which had been ordered, many of them with specific dedications. These can occasionally be a problem, some readers requesting protestations of passionate devotion while others want a message to Mum, Dad or a husband which should, I feel, more appropriately be written by the purchaser than by me.

Roger Katz and his team helped. He must be one of the most enthusiastic booksellers in London and one of the best read. We worked away, meanwhile discussing the Booker list, the general view being that it was inexplicable. I paused briefly for some excellent sandwiches and a bottle of red wine over which Roger had taken considerable trouble. Altogether I signed over 700 books.

Then on to Lincoln's Inn, where the BBC filmed me for a small interlude to be inserted in *The Late Show*. I had two passages to read and a short interview, then some outdoor shots in the cloisters.

I arrived home in time to see Joyce and talk over yesterday's party, always a pleasure, and then watched the news before an early bed. I went to one of my bookcases to find a novel for my bedtime reading, something familiar but not too familiar, nothing new or too exciting since I need tonight to promote sleep, not discourage it. Inevitably I found myself still taking down books half an hour later.

I have always wanted to have a library, a room in which I can shelve all my books, and there is really no reason why this shouldn't have been possible. It just happens that the houses I have owned over the years have never seemed suitable and today, as always, I have books in every room, arranged in no particular order. Recently I have at least made an effort to sort them into categories so that I know where to look for fiction, for poetry or for biography, but it is a slow business because the crowded shelves disgorge an extraordinary variety of books acquired over sixty years, some of which I had forgotten I owned.

When, I wondered, did I acquire this copy of Michael Arlen's *The Green Hat*? It was apparently a bestseller in its day but now, opening it, I find it impossible to continue after even one page. Then there are the two novels by Ernest Raymond, also bestsellers between the wars. My copy of *Tell England* is probably the one I first read as a fourteen-year-old, ending in floods of tears after the final chapter, which makes it plain that the young soldier–narrator has died with his two friends in the First World War. This book was lent to all my friends who shared my passionate interest in this boys' story of public school life which could have had no possible relevance to our own school experience. With increasing years and sophistication I probably wondered how the idealistic schoolmaster, Radley, escaped the suspicions of the police; nowadays he would certainly be invited to a session with the local social worker. But the book was published in a more innocent age and I suppose he was an example of the dedicated bachelor schoolmaster whose devotion to boys was emotional rather than physical.

The other Ernest Raymond novel, shelved next to it, *We the Accused*, had a more lasting influence on me. It dealt with a murder case obviously based on the Crippen/Ethel le Neve tragedy and was the first book I read which described the reality of a judicial hanging. After reading it I became a lifelong opponent of capital punishment.

Another volume, which literally fell at my feet since it had been pushed behind the Ernest Raymonds, was a chubby red-covered book, which proclaims itself on the frontispiece as 'An Authentic History of Maria Marten, or the Red Barn' and which, although it carries no date, must have been published soon after the execution of William Corder for the murder of his pregnant fiancée in the Red Barn in Polstead, Suffolk. I recall that it was given to me by a fellow traveller on the train from Ipswich to Liverpool Street and feel some guilt that I can't now remember his name. The murder is remarkable because Mrs Ann Marten, stepmother of Maria, had frequent dreams that Maria had been murdered and her body buried in the Red Barn. For a time her husband paid no attention, but in the end he took a spade and went with a friend called Bowtell to begin his search. After removing a foot-and-a-half of soil they discovered Maria's body.

After Corder left Polstead, confident that his secret was safe, he went to London and advertised for a wife. The interest in the little red book is that it contains both his advertisement and the many letters he received from women obviously desperate to escape their lives of deprivation, demeaning dependence or hopeless poverty. Some of the women are obviously well educated, but in 1827 would have had no profession open to them except that of governess. The advertisement which seduced them into replying appeared in the *Morning Herald* on 13th November and was as follows:

MATRIMONY – A Private Gentleman, aged 24, entirely independent, whose disposition is not to be exceeded, has lately lost the
chief of his family by the hand of Providence, which has
occasioned discord among the remainder, under circumstances
most disagreeable to relate. To any female of respectability who
would study for domestic comfort, and willing to confide her
future happiness in one every way qualified to render the
marriage state desirable, as the advertiser is in affluence, the lady
must have the power of some property, which may remain in her
own possession. Many very happy marriages have taken place
through means similar to this now resorted to, and it is hoped no
one will answer this through impertinent curiosity, but should
this meet the eye of any agreeable lady who feels desirous of
meeting with a sociable, tender, kind, and sympathizing companion, they will find this advertisement worthy of notice. Honour
and secrecy may be relied on. As some little security against idle
applications, it is requested that letters may be addressed (post-
paid) to A.Z., care of Mr Foster, stationer, No. 68, Leadenhall
Street, which will meet with the most respectful attention.

What is extraordinary is that William Corder did indeed find a
suitable and affectionate wife by this means. They married and set up
a private school and when eventually, after the discovery of Maria
Marten's body, he was apprehended, she remained a support to her
husband to the day of his execution.

WEDNESDAY, 8TH OCTOBER

John Mortimer gave a luncheon today at the Royal Society of
Literature to say goodbye as our Chairman. There were about twenty
people present, most of whom I knew, and some of them friends I
hadn't seen for too long. I sat between John and A. N. Wilson – a
guarantee of good conversation spiced with gossip.

John is leaving the Society because he needs to devote his time and
energy to the Royal Court Theatre, which has received a Lottery
grant. Like many Lottery grants, this alleviates some problems but
produces others. There is little point in giving a capital grant of
millions if a theatre can't meet its running costs, or of expecting it to
contribute an equal sum when it's already overdrawn. John is to be
succeeded as Chairman by Michael Holroyd, so we'll be in good and

experienced hands. John has done well by the Society. When he arrived we were one of those long-established and peculiarly English organizations which people respect and regard as important but know virtually nothing about. There are considerable advantages in being an organization which manages to be highly respected without having to do anything in particular, but John thought that we should be more active in promoting literature, and now indeed we are. This has been achieved without any loss of the spirit and ethos of the Society, a tribute to John's influence and wisdom.

At 5.45 Andy called to take me to the bookshop Books Etc. in Charing Cross Road, where I was to give a short talk, answer questions and then sign copies of the novel. There was a full house and the questions following the talk were lively, continuous and intelligent. These mixtures of talk and signing at bookshops are usually referred to as 'events', which puts me in mind of horse trials although, thankfully, they don't in my case last for three days, and the only high jumps come in question time.

One of the questions I was asked is how I arrive at the title of a novel. I find the question of titles intriguing. I suppose the romantically minded see the process of choosing a title as the equivalent of naming a child. The title remains while the creation is in being and evokes different reactions from those who hear or read it. What one hopes to achieve is a title which is memorable, euphonious, original and appropriate to the work. Many English novels have what I think of as utilitarian titles – short, highly relevant but hardly imaginative, often the name of the chief character: *David Copperfield, Jane Eyre, Tristram Shandy, Daniel Deronda*. Then there are the place names, often used when the setting is so fundamental to the story that it assumes the importance of a character: *Mansfield Park, Wuthering Heights, Howard's End*. The utilitarian title may also describe the central theme of the work: *Pride and Prejudice, Sense and Sensibility*. Titles I find particularly memorable are: *All Passion Spent* by Vita Sackville-West, *A Handful of Dust* by Evelyn Waugh, and *Appointment in Samarra* by John O'Hara. Both the latter would make wonderful titles for crime novels and I wish I'd thought of them first.

O'Hara's title for his novel set in America during the Depression is brilliant but would, of course, be meaningless if he hadn't prefaced it with the short fable about Death encountering a servant in the market place. The servant returns to his master, terrified because Death has met him and made a threatening gesture towards him. He must escape immediately and hide himself in Samarra. Later that day his master goes to the market and, encountering Death, asks why he made a threatening gesture, to which Death replies: 'It was not a threatening gesture, merely one of surprise. I did not expect to see your servant in the market as I have an appointment with him this evening in Samarra.'

My own titles come to me either very early, usually before I begin writing, or are difficult to find. I find it unsettling to have to work with a provisional title, almost as unsettling as changing the name of a character, and it is always a relief to have the title settled before I begin writing. I had no trouble, for example, with *Death of an Expert Witness* or *An Unsuitable Job for a Woman*, or with titles taken from the Book of Common Prayer or the Bible, which always provide an intriguing resonance: *Original Sin*, *Devices and Desires*. Two, however, caused me particular trouble.

My novel *Innocent Blood*, which deals with an adopted eighteen-year-old discovering her true parents, was originally called *The Blood Tie*. The book had reached the stage of page proofs when Faber discovered that the title had been used very recently. There is, of course, no copyright in titles, but no novelist wants to duplicate a recent title, or one already associated in readers' minds with an existing book. It proved extremely difficult to find an alternative. *The Blood Relation*, an uninspiring choice, had also been used recently. The book was ready to be printed and still no satisfactory title had been found despite frequent searches through *The Oxford Book of Quotations* – always a useful source when in trouble. Remembering how a Roman Catholic friend of mine prays to St Anthony for the recovery of things lost, it occurred to me that the saint might be prepared to help a Protestant find something which, although not lost in the strict sense, had certainly eluded discovery. So I said the appropriate words that night in bed, and awoke next morning with the title *Innocent Blood* in my mind, and on my lips. It was an infinitely better choice than the one originally proposed and I immediately telephoned Faber in London and Scribner's in New York with the happy news. My friend, apparently unsurprised at my success, merely enquired what the saint had 'charged' – or rather, what I had subsequently paid. I made a mental note to fulfil my dues when next passing a Roman Catholic church.

The other title which caused problems was *A Taste for Death*. This was taken from four lines of verse which I had read, I think in a *Spectator* article, some years previously:

> Some can gaze and not be sick,
> But I could never learn the trick.
> There's this to say for blood and breath
> They give a man a taste for death.

At the time I scribbled down the four lines, telling myself that 'A Taste for Death' would be an admirable title for my next novel and would, indeed, probably prove suitable no matter what the plot. When the novel was finished, I tried to find the source of the verse, expecting little difficulty. In fact the lines were totally elusive. My editor and I, helped by Faber staff, culled Auden, Kipling and any other poet who seemed likely to be the author. Again the weeks passed and the novel was due to be printed. It seemed to me that the title was meaningless without the verse, but it could hardly be printed from memory and without acknowledgement. At the last minute the source was discovered simultaneously by an elderly lady living in the Cathedral Close at Norwich and a young woman working on the book pages of the *New York Times*. The lines are by A. E. Housman, published among his later work, untitled and not part of a longer poem. So perhaps it isn't surprising that the quotation eluded us for so long.

FRIDAY, 10TH OCTOBER

To Cheltenham by car with Nicola to give a talk at the Cheltenham Literary Festival. All the publicists with whom I have worked both here, in America and in Australia have been women and I don't find this surprising. The job requires a combination of qualities which I think are more often found in women than men: an eye for detail, particularly time (missing a train can upset the whole schedule), an ability both to get on with a wide variety of people while protecting the writer from overenthusiastic demands, and to be supportive, encouraging, soothing or bracing in response to the individual author's personality and needs. Writers are not the easiest of people, especially soon after publication day, always a time of trauma. This morning both of us set out in good heart.

It has been a glorious day with great snub-nosed clouds like ethereal dirigibles against a sky of astonishing blue. The feel of the air was spring, the colours the beginning of a late autumn. I like Cheltenham and the city looked its best in the sunlight, the long red banners advertising the Festival giving it the air of an elderly respectable dowager a little surprised at her unaccustomed gaiety. The Festival is one of the most successful and best organized of the English literary events and attracts large and knowledgeable audiences. There were 350 for my talk. I enjoyed myself and so, I think, did they.

It is difficult to assess how a talk will go, but much seems to depend on whether I am tired, on the ambience and on the initial response of the audience. I find it surprising that writers today are expected to be public performers. Addressing an audience of 350 for forty to forty-five minutes and then taking questions is a public performance and writers, often the most solitary of people, are seldom actors. I wonder how Virginia Woolf would have coped with today's demand that successful writers be seen and heard.

I returned to find a call on the answerphone from granddaughter Beatrice. She is due here with her bridge partner, Rachel, and Rachel's boyfriend to play bridge in the English squad. Bea said that there were two more friends, whom she ironically described as clean-living boys, who had no bed for the night, so she has told them that they could turn up with their sleeping bags and sleep at my house. Last year there was only one clean-living lad. Next year, no doubt, there will be three or four clean-living boys trooping in with their sleeping bags. However, there is plenty of room and I like civilized, lively and intelligent young people, although I find this passion for bridge incomprehensible in anyone under forty.

This evening there was a call from Paul Bogaards of Alfred Knopf about my prospective American tour in January. I had queried whether I could really manage it. I am due to begin at Boston, then on to New York, Washington, Chicago, Dayton, Pittsburgh, Dallas, Houston, Seattle, San Francisco, Los Angeles and then down to Miami in just over a fortnight. Paul went through the itinerary with me and pointed out that, with one exception, the flights were not as long as he had expected. He thought it was manageable and I knew that it was important, so I gave in as I usually do. Time will show whether this was wise. But I can be sure of two things: the tour will be organized with efficiency and carried out in comfort.

SATURDAY, 11TH OCTOBER

I was driven to Cambridge by Will Atkinson of Faber through continuously slanting rain to sign books at Heffer's. We were fortunate to find a parking space in the garage close to the shop, and then dashed through the downpour into Waterstone's to sign stock. The queue at Heffer's was long by half-past twelve, and progress slow, mainly because of greeting old friends. Afterwards, as usual, Heffer's provided luncheon in the boardroom and I gave an interview for the local radio. Grandson Tom and his new wife Mary appeared and Will and I called in at their house for tea before driving back to London in the early evening.

TUESDAY, 14TH OCTOBER

To the Booker dinner with Rosemary Goad, who has edited all my books. It was one of the most enjoyable Booker dinners for us, largely because we shared a table with Anne Elletson, late of Faber and now a BBC producer, who is always a delight to meet. Others at our table were Clare Short with her newly discovered son; Martyn Goff, administrator of the Prize, and Geordie Greig of the *Sunday Times*. There was some muttering about the choice of winner, but not, of course, from Martyn, who is always a model of discretion. All members of the Booker Management Committee are sent copies of the shortlist and I have made a start with the winner, Arundhati Roy's *The God of Small Things*, but haven't got very far. It seems to me somewhat lush and overwritten, a beginner's attempt at a Naipaul or a Rushdie. But I admit to prejudice: I seldom enjoy books seen through the eyes of children, *The Go-Between* being a notable exception.

In announcing the prize, the Chairman, Professor Gillian Beer, suggested there was merit in finding a first novelist as prize-winner; I think this is a mistaken view. The Booker jury are there to reward the best novel of the year. Was this the best? Hardly, I felt. But then, if we set up ten different juries of five, it is unlikely – except in a rare year – that they would award the prize to the same book.

Next year will mark the thirtieth anniversary of the Booker Prize. On the whole I think it has succeeded in its aim of celebrating the best of contemporary fiction, although there have been years in which it was difficult to see the winning novel as even worthy of the shortlist, let alone the accolade of best novel of the year. But the Prize has always been controversial and this isn't surprising and is, perhaps, part of its appeal. When I chaired the panel of judges in 1987 with Selina Hastings, Allan Massie, Trevor McDonald and John B. Thompson as my colleagues, we recognized at our first meeting that literary judgement is inevitably subjective and that one person's masterpiece is another's pretentious and incomprehensible absurdity. For this reason we agreed never to impugn each other's taste.

The problem for the judges, which existed when I was Chairman and still exists, is the number of entries. By the time I had got to the hundredth novel I was beginning to doubt my own judgement. The Management Committee has made efforts to cut down the number of entries, but too many novels are entered which hardly merit publication, let alone gaining the shortlist. Then there is the problem that publishing houses with a distinguished list can enter only the same number as smaller houses which may only have published a couple of novels. The entry is further complicated by self-publication, and now by publication on the Internet. Somehow the numbers will have to be reduced, but how?

If I were in sole charge of a literary prize I would arrange things differently. I would appoint a panel of a dozen or so people consisting of literary editors, well-regarded reviewers, booksellers and members of the general public who are lovers of fiction. Each member would submit a list of up to fifty novels which he or she thought worthy of consideration, although there would be no obligation to read all of them. From the total it would be possible to compile one list of fifty novels from those which appeared most frequently. The judging panel would select the winner from this fifty, but they would also have the option of calling in an additional ten. In this way the reading task would be far more manageable, it is unlikely that any novel of merit would be overlooked, and the panel would still have the power to call in a book by a previously unknown author which didn't appear on the shortlist.

It is for the chairman of the Booker panel of judges to decide how the judging panel shall carry out its job, although it is expected that all members will read all the novels. The worst way of arriving at the ultimate shortlist of some five or six is for each panel member to nominate his or her favourite. I believe this was done one year, but it is difficult to see how it could result in a generally accepted first choice. I wanted to achieve a shortlist of novels which all the judges thought worthy of the Prize even though we each had a particular favourite. The shortlist is inevitably a compromise. I would certainly have included at least one novel, Ian McEwan's *A Child in Time*, which another judge heartily disliked and spoke against very strongly, so the five of us would probably, if judging alone, have produced five different shortlists. One has to remember that the Booker novel can't reasonably be regarded as the best novel of the year – only time will determine that – but is simply the book which five very different people, brought together at one moment in time and after being sated with months of fiction reading, feel is worthy of the Prize. Our final choice of Penelope Lively's *Moon Tiger* was only arrived at after a long argument which nearly made us late for the Guildhall dinner, and the choice was not unanimous.

The Booker, like most literary prizes, has probably given more pleasure than pain, has certainly stimulated interest in fiction and has provided its share of entertainment, controversy, malice and general ill will. But if I were trying to encourage a young person to read and enjoy modern fiction I am not sure I would begin by presenting him or her with the Booker shortlist.

MONDAY, 20TH OCTOBER

On Thursday afternoon I flew to the Isle of Man to give a lecture in St German's Cathedral, organized by the Friends of the Cathedral, on Friday, and an afternoon talk on Saturday to the island's Prayer Book Society. I stayed with Mrs Salisbury-Jones in her stone house in the centre of Castletown. From my top-floor window I could glimpse the sea which, under the red and gold sky of early morning, looked like a sheet of gleaming metal. Even the sand was golden-yellow. Mrs Salisbury-Jones was welcoming and hospitable and took great trouble to show me the island on Saturday morning and on Sunday.

The architecture is generally undistinguished but the island itself much more interesting and attractive than I remembered from one previous visit. It seems that all the variety of scenery found in the rest of the United Kingdom is present in this small island. The charming little ports reminded me of Dorset and the West Country. The central hills with the valleys and streams were like parts of Scotland, while the plain in the west leading down to a pebbled shore with dunes and marram grass and great round stones reminded me strongly of East Anglia. The weather was wonderful and I shall retain a very clear memory of Sunday afternoon when we drove to Peel. We found a seat against the castle walls and sat in the strength of the mellow sunshine looking across Peel harbour and eating particularly good crab rolls.

I liked the inscription on Bishop Sam's tomb in the ruins of the Cathedral: 'In this house which I share with my brothers the worms in hope of the resurrection to life lie I, Sam, by divine grace Bishop of this Island. Stay reader, look and laugh at the Bishop's palace. Died 30th May, Anno 1662, Samuel Rutter, Lord Bishop of Sodor and Man.'

THURSDAY, 23RD OCTOBER

This evening I spoke at a joint *Times*-Dillons literary event at the Institute of Education. I was apprehensive that there wouldn't be much of an audience, since the charge of £10 seemed to me high. However, there were about 350 people present; an interested and very warm audience. There was no shortage of questions and a long line at the signing afterwards.

Afterwards, Peter Stothard, the editor, took about twelve of us out to dinner at the Etoile, where I sat next to the Deputy Chief Constable of Thames Valley Constabulary. He offered to show me a murder incident room when I am next in Oxford, and this will be helpful. Apparently some of my details in *Original Sin* were not totally accurate.

Not all the questions after a talk are about my work. Some people expect me to be an expert on crime fiction (which I am not), and I'm frequently asked about my response to real-life crimes and to the death penalty. I reply that I have always been an abolitionist, but that this stance is hardly rational since I do believe that the death penalty deters. I am, therefore, prepared to see people put at additional risk of being murdered rather than live in a country which enacts the death penalty. I expect my hatred of the death penalty is influenced by my horror of hanging, surely a barbaric if effective way of putting people to death.

It seems to me that when I was a child there was far more public and newspaper interest in murder trials than there is today. Perhaps those detailed accounts, often with photographs, satisfied the public's fascination with murder which, today, is catered for by television series on crime and the police. I can remember the pages of broadsheet which covered the trial in 1931 of Alfred Arthur Rouse, who murdered a hitchhiker whose identity is still unknown, and can recall the newspaper pictures of the burnt-out car. But the murder which evoked a personal response was that of Vera Page, also in 1931, perhaps because, like me, she was an eleven-year-old. Her body – she had been raped and strangled – was found on the morning of 16th December in the tradesmen's entrance of a house in Addison Road, Kensington. She had gone after school to show her swimming certificates to her grandmother and never returned home. I can clearly recall her face from the newspaper photographs: dark haired, and with the eager bright-eyed look of a child for whom life is an enchantment. A neighbour, Percy Orlando Rust, was an obvious suspect. He had worn a finger-stall similar to one found on the body, he had no alibi, and there were other physical clues linking him to the crime. During questioning by the coroner a woman stood up in court and shouted, 'That man is telling lies, sir.' But the coroner's jury found the evidence against Rust insufficient and no one was ever brought to trial. It still seems inexplicable to me that the police, provided with so much physical evidence, couldn't solve the case. Today, with DNA, there would be no difficulty. It is extraordinary how that child's face is imprinted on my imagination. Perhaps there persists in the human psyche an atavistic belief that a murder must be solved if the dead are to rest in peace.

TUESDAY, 28TH OCTOBER

Gill Frost arrived to give me a massage at 8 a.m. and at 9.30 a journalist rang from New Zealand for a telephone interview, followed by a call at 10 o'clock from an Australian journalist.

In the afternoon Andy arrived with Rosemary in the car to drive us to Chipping Norton for a talk in the small theatre there, followed by a signing. Rosemary has her left arm in a sling as she fell on the rocks at Purbeck during the weekend and broke her wrist. We went first to have supper with Penelope and Jack Lively at their medieval farmhouse at Great Rollright. They then drove us to Chipping Norton, where Andy had taken his car to find himself a pub meal, and be ready later to drive us back to London.

The theatre was full, the audience lively and encouraging with particularly good questions, although I was very tired at the end of the session, trying to sign for stock while being interviewed simultaneously by a local journalist. But this was a very worthwhile signing, arranged by Elizabeth Sleight, who is the proprietor of a small independent bookshop in Chipping Norton and is dedicated, enthusiastic and successful in attracting writers to talk and sign.

I was asked, as I often am, about one of the novels which isn't a detective story and doesn't feature Adam Dalgliesh: *Innocent Blood*. This is the only one of my novels influenced by a real-life murder case. It had, in fact, a twofold genesis: a murder and an act of Parliament.

The inspiration first came when I was working at the Home Office and was concerned with some of the provisions relating to care orders in the Children's Act 1975. This was a DHSS not a Home Office Bill, but my division had an interest in the provisions relating to juvenile courts. But the Bill was primarily concerned with adoption. Adoption proceedings were confidential. A mother placing her child for adoption would not be told the name of the adopters and they would not know the identity of the birth mother. An adopted child would grow up with no way of finding out its natural parentage. Parliament took the view that young people had a right to this knowledge, even though it meant breaking faith with both those who had adopted a child under the previous arrangement and those who had parted with a child in the assurance of secrecy. The Bill provided that a young person of eighteen, after counselling with a social worker, should be able to see his or her birth certificate and have the possibility of beginning a search for the natural parents.

The murder, which took place some years before the abolition of capital punishment, was the case of Daniel Raven. Raven's wife had recently given birth to their first child, a son, in a Muswell Hill nursing-home. The young father called to visit his wife and, on the way home, went to the house of his parents-in-law, a Mr and Mrs Goodman, and battered them to death with a television aerial. He was an obvious suspect and the police were not short of damning evidence, including his bloodstained clothing which he had attempted to burn. He was tried, convicted and hanged. When I heard on the radio that Daniel Raven had been executed that morning for the murder of the Goodmans, I thought primarily not of him, nor of his victims, but of the young mother and her baby. How, if ever, could she break the news? What would she answer when her son asked why he had no father or what had happened to his maternal grandparents? Imagining myself in her place, I wondered whether I would even consider placing the child for adoption.

When the Children's Bill was going through Parliament, the memory of this case surfaced and the idea for the novel was born. I would write about an eighteen-year-old, a highly intelligent but unloving girl adopted by a psychologist and his wife, who began to search for her parents. She would have fantasized about her earlier life; that her father was an aristocrat, her mother perhaps a servant girl in the ancestral home. She would discover that her father had murdered a young girl, her mother had colluded, and that both had been sentenced to life imprisonment. Her father had died in prison, but her mother was soon to be released on licence. The book would have a double theme: a crime story relating how the father of the dead child, patiently waiting for the release of the convicted woman, begins to track her down in London; secondly the growth of love between the daughter and the mother after the daughter's decision that they should set up house together.

Although the novel didn't begin with a place, setting is as important to *Innocent Blood* as it is to my detective stories. The father of the murdered child, Norman Scase, tracks his daughter's murderess through London. The city's underground system, its raucous street markets, lanes and streets, and the darkly numinous roof of Westminster Cathedral are all integral parts of the story. *Innocent Blood* was one of three novels – the other two being *Death of an Expert Witness* and *A Taste for Death* – which could not have been written, or at least written with such authority, without my Home Office experience.

Perhaps this is why I carried on working years after it would have been possible to live by my writing – if occasionally precariously. I found that to be part of the working world was a powerful inspiration as well as providing useful background information. And it was *Innocent Blood* which made me prosperous. Before it was published, I had decided to leave the Home Office six months before my retirement date and had carefully calculated that I would be able to live in reasonable comfort until I received my lump sum and pension in August 1980. The book was modestly successful in Britain. It came at a difficult time for my publishers and was meanly produced, but in the States it rapidly became number one on the New York bestseller list and received rave reviews. The film and paperback rights were sold in the same week. *Innocent Blood* meant the end of anxiety about money, and for that I was grateful.

The film was, in fact, never made, but to sell a lucrative option without having to watch the result on the screen is considered by many writers to be an advantage. Producers still occasionally want to make it, but the company with the rights is holding on to them.

NOVEMBER

I have just had a highly enjoyable if exhausting weekend. Eliza Oxley had asked me some months ago if I would talk at a dinner in aid of the Charminster Conservative Party, the dinner to be held at Wolfeton, one of the oldest and most historic country houses in Dorset. I would have driven down with Rosemary, but because of her broken left wrist she can't drive. So Andy again took charge and we drove down, using minor roads where possible, under a sunny sky and through autumn foliage to Stockbridge. There we first had a walk round the craft shop, where Rosemary bought me a necklace as an early Christmas present, and then went to the Vine pub for lunch.

At Charminster House, where I was to stay overnight, I rested while the others went to finish preparations at Wolfeton. The evening was hugely enjoyable. There were torches flaming to show us the way to the massive gatehouse flanked with two solid towers. Wolfeton must be grim and probably cold when uninhabited, but with great log fires and banks of candles it looked wonderful. It was a typical and perfect Agatha Christie evening. The oak-panelled rooms, the pictures, the flickering candles and the mysterious shadows made Wolfeton the ideal setting for a 1930s mystery. Even the names on the table-plan were entirely in keeping – and I found myself allocating my fellow diners to their appropriate roles – Captain Gueterbock, Brigadier Proudman, Mrs Mould-Graham, Miss Archdale and Captain Thimbleby all have the authentic Christie ring. The guests arrived in a mood to enjoy themselves and my after-dinner talk received more praise and applause than it deserved.

Andy arrived to collect us in time to hear the talk. As a townsman he couldn't get used to the total blackness of a country night, or indeed to the silence and emptiness of Charminster House. Eliza had left a cold dinner for him but I think he would much have preferred to seek the conviviality of a local pub if he had dared to venture out. He said he closed the curtains, shut the doors firmly and wouldn't even leave the sanctuary of the kitchen to walk the ten yards down the passage to the television room. Instead he was fearfully aware of the row of bells, each labelled with its room, and sat there expecting one of them to begin ringing in the empty house. I suppose country people can be equally ill at ease in town, and wonder how we survive behind our grilles while the wicked and violent city rages outside.

I sympathize with Andy. Although I spent my early years in Ludlow amid beautiful country, I am happiest in towns and cities. When I visit Tom and Mary Norman in rural Dorset I always feel I am venturing on dangerous and alien territory. The two cats chase mice around the kitchen table unremarked on by anyone but me, and small bodies of rodents are left outside the pantry door as morning offerings. One is never surprised to find the heads of chickens murdered by a fox and laid out in a circle like some pagan rite, while dinner guests complain that the otters, a protected species, are attacking their dogs. At night the darkness presses against the windows like a black carpet while the silence is occasionally broken by the shrieks and screams of tormented animals. A night in deep country is a demonstration of nature red in tooth and claw.

I would certainly feel nervous if required to spend the night alone at Wolfeton, which I am sure has its ghosts. The house is charged with a sense of the past and if it is not haunted in the usual sense, it is certainly inhabited by more presences than those of the present owners, Nigel and Katharine Thimbleby. During the sixteenth century a priest called Cornelius was imprisoned in the gatehouse. He was so attractive that his gaolers, the Trenchards, and their circle (including Walter Ralegh) would dispute with him amiably and they became friends. But they couldn't save him from being tried in Dorchester, condemned, hanged, drawn and quartered. It is said that his footsteps can still be heard climbing to his room in the gatehouse.

In 1506 the Archduke of Austria and his Spanish bride were forced by storms to put in at Weymouth and were taken to Wolfeton to await better weather. Neither the visitors nor the Trenchards could speak each other's language, but luckily John Trenchard had a cousin, John Russell, who knew Spanish and came over to interpret, making himself so useful that, when the Archduke and princess went to visit Henry VII at Windsor, he went with them. From this royal meeting was founded the House of Russell and the Dukedom of Bedford. It makes a change from the more usual founding of great dynasties by illicit encounters between the sheets.

MONDAY, 3RD NOVEMBER

This is the month, in 1949, when I began my working career in the Health Service, having answered an advertisement, I think in the *Evening Standard*, for clerical assistants in the newly formed service. I applied to Paddington Hospital Management Committee in the Harrow Road, a choice which now seems to me highly eccentric, was duly short-listed and presented myself for interview at the group's headquarters next door to what was then Paddington General Hospital. I was one of a large group of aspirants. It was apparent that the administrators of the highly diverse hospitals and outpatient clinics, which had been somewhat illogically grouped together, had been asked to submit requests for additional staff and that what was being held was a kind of labour market. I found favour with Mrs – or it may have been Miss – McBain who ran the London Skin Hospital in Fitzroy Square. She was an intimidating woman, grey-haired, stocky and with the face of an angry Pekinese, and I think she rather relished the effect her gruff, no-nonsense manner had on the male members of the Hospital Management Committee.

The London Skin Hospital was one of the many small specialist hospitals which abounded at that time, supported by payments from the patients and by voluntary help and subscriptions, treating a faithful band of patients who seemed neither to expect to get better, nor to much resent the fact that they appeared weekly for some years. My duties were simple. Patients attending for the first time were issued with appointment cards and numbers. A numerical filing system had to be instituted, and reports of the number of patients attending submitted, I think monthly, to Group Headquarters. I would make appointments when the patients rang up, get out the records and have them ready for the dermatologist when he or she arrived. Making the appointments merely meant adding the patient's name to the clinic. The Skin Hospital believed firmly in a policy of first-come, first-served, and indeed this was generally acceptable to the patients.

The staff, other than the medical staff, consisted of Mrs McBain, Sister Ewell, a devout High Anglican, Mrs Clayton, a highly efficient pharmacist, and the porter, referred to as Reid, who had, I gathered, more or less run the hospital singlehandedly during the war years, having been fortunate enough to be at school at a time when literacy and numeracy were assiduously taught. I would arrive promptly at nine, don my white coat and Mrs McBain would arrive some hours later on a convenient train from Hove where she lived. I had a feeling that my job was not strictly necessary or, at least, could have been done by existing staff, but there was a general feeling of optimism, of public money liberally available, and a sense that people, no longer working for a charity, need not over-exert themselves. But the staff at the London Skin Hospital were fiercely anti-National Health Service, seeing it as the triumph of state bureaucracy over personal charitable service. Mrs McBain would pretend not to recognize patients: 'It's no good saying you've been coming here for years, Mrs Collins. You're just a number to us now.' I liked Mrs McBain, who had, like many women of forbidding appearance, a charitable heart and who, I suspect, liked me, since otherwise I should have been returned to Paddington Group Headquarters with scant ceremony.

Although the small staff of the London Skin Hospital were unenthusiastic about the Health Service, most of us welcomed it unreservedly. The assurance that medical treatment, including hospital care, would be free at the time of need lifted a huge weight of anxiety from many shoulders. It did from mine. I could remember when my mother suffered from renal colic due to stones in the kidney. I must have been nine or ten at the time. Because it cost money to visit or call in the doctor, she went on enduring spasms of atrocious agony until she finally collapsed in the butcher's shop and was taken by ambulance to Shrewsbury Hospital. It was good to know that this need not happen to anyone ever again.

But we were all surprisingly over-optimistic. Members of Parliament admitted that the initial cost of the service might be high, but said that the annual expenditure would decrease as people were treated for long-standing conditions, and received their free wigs, dentures and appliances. After that the free service would ensure that the nation became healthier year by year. No one then could have believed that medical science and technology would make it possible to transplant kidneys and hearts, or to overcome infertility by fertilizing the ovum outside the woman's body. No one could foresee the onset of new diseases such as AIDS. On looking back it seems strange that we took no account of an ageing population and the demands that an increasing population of the over-seventies would make on a free service.

In addition to filing and getting out records, I was responsible for the stamp book. All letters sent were entered in the ledger by name and I was supposed to reconcile on a daily basis the total of stamps left with letters sent, a task which I found tedious and accordingly neglected. As the weeks passed it seemed even more difficult to tackle it, and when the auditors unexpectedly arrived, as is the wont of auditors, they seized on the book in triumph and bore it down to their basement office with evident satisfaction. Some hours later, they arrived to admit with reluctance that the stamp book was correct to the last stamp, while pointing out that it was deplorable that it hadn't been reconciled daily. I said smugly that I had seen no reason for that chore since I knew the book was accurate. Accuracy to the last penny can only have been a matter of the purest luck. I did tot up the book daily thereafter but never again succeeded in getting it right.

My record unsullied by financial misdemeanour, I applied for promotion to Grade C at Group Headquarters. The job was that of Committee Clerk, which meant sitting in at the meetings, taking a record of what was said, writing the minutes and later collating all the papers and sending them out to members of the House Committees, who oversaw the individual hospitals, to the sub-committees of the Hospital Management Committee and to the Management Committee itself. I never managed to learn shorthand but devised my own quick way of writing and luckily found I had a good memory for speech so that the job wasn't overdemanding.

It was about this time that I began to realize that Connor, who had returned mentally ill from overseas service, might never be well again and that I might have to support the family indefinitely. I was then living with my parents-in-law at Ilford, Essex, who provided unfailing support and, until they retired to Suffolk, a loving and stable home for Clare and Jane. I was going to need, not a job, but a career. I began going to evening classes at the City of London College in Moorgate to study for a diploma in hospital administration. Without it any further progress would be impossible. A small group of us would go to the College together after work, eating a light supper in the canteen, usually of soft roes on toast, before the classes began. The syllabus covered hospital supplies, building and planning, personnel management, bookkeeping and law, the latter for me being by far the most interesting. We were taught by a vivacious, rotund and obviously excellent lawyer called Schmitov, I imagine originally a refugee, with a penchant for the dramatic. This meant that he acted out all the cases: pretending to travel in a cab round Regent's Park for immoral purposes, thus vitiating the contract between him and the driver, or purchasing a desirable ball gown from a West End store and lying to the assistant about his age, illustrating the interesting legal point whereby a ball gown could not in law be regarded as a necessity.

I found the bookkeeping the most difficult – indeed, at first totally incomprehensible. It seemed to me that all transactions were being entered on the wrong side of the ledger. We were taught by an Irishman with a heavy accent who, early ignoring me as a hopeless case, would repeatedly say, 'Yer have to learn the teery, boys.' Alas, 'the teery' perpetually eluded me. But I did eventually pass the final examination with honours, gaining the regional prize. Without this I doubt whether I would have gained my next promotion, which was to replace the head of the committee section when he, too, was transferred to higher things. I was now beginning to earn the kind of salary which might mean I could support the family without help from my parents-in-law. The next move at one grade higher was to the North West Metropolitan Regional Hospital Board and its offices opposite Paddington Station, where I remained until 1968.

Now that there is so much concern with waiting lists, treatment priorities and the rationing of limited resources, it is easy to forget that not all demands could be met in those heady early years of the service. One of the greatest problems facing the country after the war was tuberculosis. Paddington Hospital actually had huts in the hospital grounds where the TB patients were nursed, inhaling the not very salubrious air of the Harrow Road. There was the TB waiting list for admission to sanatoria, and another for the young chronic sick, with illnesses such as disseminated sclerosis, who only too often had to be nursed in long-stay geriatric wards. My section was responsible for the latter waiting list and I was interested in how human beings differ in their response to chronic illness. There were families in which a wife or a husband was coping with an almost intolerable burden of care and yet could barely contemplate the thought that the partner might have to leave home and be institutionalized. I remember another case in which a wife was battering on the doors of the Regional Board almost as soon as the diagnosis was made, complaining bitterly that her husband could no longer get to the lavatory and had to use a bottle in the presence of the children. It was deeply depressing to contemplate a family in which a disabled father was made to feel ashamed because he couldn't get unaided to the lavatory. The section of which I was head was responsible for a variety of duties in addition to the young chronic sick waiting list: the compilation of the regional statistics based on returns made by each hospital, the mental health service and legal actions against the Regional Hospital Board, which were handled by an outside firm of solicitors.

By the time I went to the North West Metropolitan Regional Hospital Board, my father-in-law had retired from general practice in Ilford, and he and my mother-in-law moved to a village outside Halesworth in Suffolk. The house we shared in Ilford was sold and I had to find a new home for the four of us. I thought it would be pleasant to live in Richmond, but taking a day off to reconnoitre I was told by all the house agents I visited that even a small house or flat in this desirable borough couldn't be purchased under £4,000. So on their advice I took a bus to Kingston-on-Thames and there found a small semi-detached Victorian cottage in Richmond Park Road for just over half that sum. It is almost unbelievable now to think that a house could be bought so cheaply. The journey from Kingston-on-Thames to London was slow, but it was a delight to be so close to the park.

It was while we lived at Kingston-on-Thames that my elder daughter, Clare, married and moved with her husband, Lyn, to America, where Lyn had been offered a job in Huntsville, Alabama, on the space programme. She did not see her father again. Connor died at home on 5th August 1964, aged forty-four years. While he was alive I hadn't felt it possible to change my job. He would periodically discharge himself from hospital, sometimes at very short notice, and I never knew quite what I would have to face when I returned home from the office. It was not a propitious time to look for promotion or for a new job, which would only impose additional strain. But now I felt the strong need to look for a change of direction. I saw an advertisement, I think in *The Times*, inviting applications for the grade of Principal in the Home Civil Service. I sent for particulars, only to receive a reply saying that my educational qualifications were nowhere near the standard required. The following year the advertisement appeared again, but was differently worded. Now, those applicants who hadn't a good honours degree could take a written examination followed by a series of interviews. I applied again and was successful, coming third in the country on the final list. This wasn't quite as impressive as it appears. Many of the questions covered the kind of work I had been doing in the Health Service, writing reports, sitting in committees, replying to letters of complaint. I was lucky, too, in finding that the intelligence test was one based on a sequence of geometric shapes, the only kind with which I have never had difficulty. My place on the list of successful candidates gave me, if not a choice of departments, at least a say in where I should be posted and I asked for either the Home Office or the Department of Education. On 1st March 1968 I entered the Home Office as a Principal and began what was probably the most interesting and happiest part of my working life.

TUESDAY, 4TH NOVEMBER

To Edinburgh yesterday afternoon by air with Joanna Mackle, a director of Faber, for a talk in the Assembly Rooms followed by a signing. Afterwards we went to dinner with my grandson James – reading politics at Edinburgh University – in his flat in Henderson Row. James and his girlfriend have made the flat strongly individual with bold primary colours on the walls throughout, the paint applied with more enthusiasm than finesse. Like his father he is an excellent cook and we had rabbit in a curry sauce with salad and a lemon cake to follow. His aunt Mona and her husband were also in the party and we argued amiably, if forcefully, about education, about which she knows a great deal and I considerably less.

After the Assembly Rooms talk I was asked the question which comes up frequently during question-and-answer sessions: Do I draw my characters from real life? I am not surprised that this is a popular question. Characterization is at the heart of a novel and people are always intrigued about the novelist's method of creating fictional men and women who live as vividly in the imagination as real people. The creation of characters is, I suspect, as mysterious to many novelists as it is to their readers. I usually reply that I don't draw characters directly from real life and then explain that, by this, I mean I don't take someone I know and, after making a few judicious alterations to height, age, appearance or occupation, put the essentials of that person into a novel. But I go on to admit that to state that characters are not drawn from life is to be disingenuous. All characterization comes from life; where else can it have its origin?

Some writers make no apology for drawing directly from people they know. A name can be put to almost every C. P. Snow character, as it can to the most successful characters of Nancy Mitford. But for most of us the creation of character is rather more complicated.

Dickens drew directly from life. Indeed, in a letter to a Mr Haines in 1837 he stated that he needed a magistrate for his next number of *Oliver Twist* and, having cast about for 'a magistrate whose harshness and insolence would render him a fit subject to be shown up', stumbled upon Mr Laing of Hatton Garden. He knew the man's character perfectly well but wanted to describe his personal appearance and therefore wondered whether he might be smuggled into the Hatton Garden office for a few minutes under Mr Haines's auspices. I suspect that, in today's world, Dickens would be at constant risk of an action for libel. Similarly, he responded to a complaint from Leigh Hunt that he had been portrayed as Harold Skimpole in *Bleak House* by apologizing for Leigh Hunt's pain, but excused himself by saying that when he felt he was getting too close to reality, he stopped himself. Besides, he did not fancy that Leigh Hunt would ever recognize himself. He ended: 'Under similar disguises my own mother and father are in my books, and you might as well see your likeness in Micawber.'

Some novelists have taken pains to emphasize that they don't draw directly from life, almost as if they find the accusation demeaning. Charlotte Brontë, writing to Ellen Nussey in 1849, protested that she was not to suppose any of the characters in *Shirley* was intended as a literal portrait. 'It would not suit the rules of art, nor of my own feelings, to write in that style. We only suffer reality to *suggest*, never to *dictate*.' This is a subtle but, I think, a valid distinction. George Eliot, in a letter ten years later, claimed that there was 'not a single portrait in *Adam Bede* ... The whole course of the story, the descriptions of scenery and houses, the characters and dialogue, everything is a combination from widely sundered elements of experience.' Gustave Flaubert wrote that there was nothing true in *Madame Bovary*. 'It is a story of pure invention: I have put none of my own feelings into it, nor anything of my own life. The illusion, on the contrary (if there is any), comes from the very objectivity of the work.' But it is difficult to believe that Flaubert had not at some time encountered a Madame Bovary or someone very like her.

Certainly I find it difficult to believe that any successful fictional character has been created which did not catch the first flicker of life from the burning coal of a living person. That person may very well, of course, be the author himself, and frequently is. We may not always have access to the pain, joy, disgust, embarrassment, remorse of other people – how can we have? – but our own emotions, our own pains and joys, are always available to us. These, remembered, and relived, sometimes with discomfort, and filtered through the imagination become the raw stuff of fiction.

Once the main emotive thrust is established – the essentials of character, the formative experiences of childhood and the vicissitudes of adult life – then, for me, a character takes root in my mind and is able to grow and develop. But the character never really comes alive until I begin writing. Then it feels to me as if the character and his whole story already exist in some limbo of my imagination and that what I am doing is getting in touch with a living person and putting his story down in black and white, a process less of creation than of revelation. And during the writing the character will reveal himself or herself more clearly, will display unexpected quirks of personality and will sometimes act in a way I neither planned nor expected. For in my kind of fiction, of course, no character can completely escape his author. I can't have a murderer deciding that he would prefer to be an innocent suspect. When I am asked if my characters do occasionally take control, I have to reply that their freedom is necessarily limited, but because they change and develop as the manuscript lengthens, I never get exactly the novel I was so carefully planning.

Real people reveal themselves and are revealed by what they do, what they say, what they think and by what other people say and think about them. So it is with characters in fiction. I was interested when I read – I can't remember where – how Evelyn Waugh responded to a reader who pointed out that he never describes what his characters are thinking. He said, 'I don't know what they're thinking, I only know what they do.' This is the opposite of the stream-of-consciousness revelation of character, the Molly Bloom soliloquy in *Ulysses* being one of the best examples. Character can also be revealed through setting, through the personal choice of what to wear, the outward appearance we present to the world, the objects with which we choose to surround ourselves. It is possible in a novel to describe a room, books, pictures, ornaments, or a bare uncluttered, functional space and immediately bring the owner to life, an example of the interdependence of all the elements in a novel. We are always two people: the essential self, perhaps never fully known, and the carefully constructed carapace which protects that self and becomes the person we present to the world.

For me, one of the fascinations of detective fiction is the exploration of character under the revealing trauma of a murder enquiry. Murder is the unique crime, the only one for which we can never make reparation to the victim. Murder destroys privacy, both of the living and of the dead. It forces us to confront what we are and what we are capable of being. No wonder it has fascinated writers and readers since Cain murdered Abel.

WEDNESDAY, 5TH NOVEMBER

To lunch at Penguin's offices off Kensington High Street, where we discussed plans for the promotion of the mass-market edition of *A Certain Justice*. Then at 4.30 Michele Buck and Tim Vaughan from Anglia (now United Film and Television Productions) called to talk about the television version of the book.

It was on this day, 5th November, in 1989, when I first went to Czechoslovakia for a nine-day visit on behalf of the British Council, of which I was a member from 1988 to 1993. It was my first excursion behind the Iron Curtain except for a day's visit to East Berlin when I was in Berlin in 1986, again for the British Council. The hotel in Prague was comfortable and modernized, but the service surly. I had a translator constantly with me and on the first morning was due to meet a journalist in the foyer of the hotel. Before she arrived, my translator suggested we should have coffee at the bar. So we perched on two high stools where my interviewer eventually joined us. I offered her coffee and suggested that we should now take our cups to the comfortable chairs around one of the low tables, since it was hardly practicable to conduct an interview while seated in a line at the bar.

My translator at once demurred. 'It is not allowed,' she said. 'Coffee is at the bar only.' I said that I, as a guest of the hotel, had paid for the coffee and could see no reason why we should not drink it at one of the tables. I was perfectly prepared to carry the cups back to the bar afterwards. So we went to the table but my translator was obviously not at ease. A few minutes later she broke off her translation to say,

'You are right. You are a guest in this hotel. Why can't we have coffee at this table?' I replied that she should stay close to my side, as she intended, and by the end of my visit would no doubt be as bloody-minded as a Briton.

Everywhere I sensed this sensitivity to what was or was not allowed. A small television crew with one camera came to make a film about me, part of which was shot outside the Cathedral. It was bitterly cold and afterwards I suggested that they should come back with me to the hotel for coffee or a drink. Only the director spoke English and he said that this would not be possible. The hotel was for rich foreigners and those who had foreign exchange. I persuaded them to come back and I think they enjoyed the coffee, but they were not at ease.

Everywhere there was a sense of impending change. The roads were lined with the tinny-looking cars of East Germans who had come over the border. The dominoes were tumbling and although I saw on every wall, particularly in the schools where I spoke, a large framed photograph of the President, Gustáv Husák, I felt I was not the only person present who was wondering how long it would hang there.

The school visits were disappointing. The young people sat in attentive silence and all, as far as I could judge, seemed interested in what I told them about the craft of the detective story and what was happening in English literature. But at question time they were absolutely silent. This was in such marked contrast from my experience of lively, questioning young audiences in Germany, Italy or Spain, let alone English-speaking countries, that I asked the reason. The staff said pupils were not encouraged ever to question what they had been told and a period of questions and discussion would be alien to their culture.

I spent one evening speaking to an officially recognized organiza-tion of writers. They told me that the state was generous to writers and that there was a beautiful residential centre in which they could stay without payment when writing their books. I asked whether a Czech whose books were critical of the government would also be able to enjoy this privilege. There was a silence and then one of the writers replied no. The evening was curious, the air heavy with questions unasked and the knowledge that life was about to change fundamentally and perhaps in directions no one could foresee.

I was driven to Slovakia by a British Council driver through a landscape of fir trees which reminded me of the novels of John le Carré and of an early scene from the BBC production of *Tinker, Tailor, Soldier, Spy* where the British agent is betrayed and shot. I almost expected to hear the crackle of gunfire and see the solitary figure dodging among the trees.

We stopped on the way for coffee and the driver spoke about communism and the acknowledgement of and apology for past mistakes recently made in Russia. Looking across the table I saw that he was close to tears. He broke out vehemently: 'Thousands were killed, thousands have no jobs, no hope, thousands are in prison. And now they say, "Was a mistake"!'

When I lived in Cambridge in the early days of the war I met a Czechoslovak airman and we would go dancing together on Saturday nights at the pretentiously named McGrath Ballroom, one of the regular Cambridge haunts of air crews based on airfields near the city. He was tall and exceptionally good-looking, but the relationship, which never really grew beyond a romantic friendship, was hampered because we could only communicate in rather poor French. He gave me a very beautiful cameo ring which, to my lasting regret, I lost sometime during the war. He had a passionate hatred of Germans. When I enquired whether he was a bomber or a fighter pilot, he growled, *'Je suis chasseur!'*, as if it were a battle cry. This vehemence was in contrast to the British fighter pilots I knew who took a matter-of-fact attitude to the task in hand, showing little hatred of the enemy with whom they shared the same dangerous skies. We were due to meet at the ballroom in January 1941 but my Czech didn't arrive, and I knew none of his fellow Czech pilots from whom I could enquire.

When I was in Prague my publishers told me that the Czechs who had fought for the allies and survived were subsequently ostracized. Professional men lost their jobs and most were denied civil liberties. But he said that the climate was now changing and that his firm had produced a book with pictures and records of those who had flown in the Free Czech Air Force. He gave me a copy, and I recognized my Czechoslovak pilot. There was a cross and a date in January 1941 beside his name, confirming what I already knew.

THURSDAY, 6TH NOVEMBER
This is the time of year when all the main literary editors of the broadsheets telephone and ask what books I have most enjoyed

during the year. It is a curious exercise affording some readers the chance to give a plug to their friends while others choose extraordinarily erudite volumes which it is hard to believe they have actually read for pleasure.

It has been a particularly good year for biographies, which I now read and enjoy far more than fiction. I still have much reading pleasure in store, but, of those I have finished, I greatly enjoyed and have named Claire Tomalin's sensitive and elegantly written *Jane Austen: a Life*, and Jenny Uglow's *Hogarth: a Life and a World*, an absorbing study of a great artist and his age. Iain Pears's unmemorably named *An Instance of the Fingerpost* is a fictional *tour de force* set in Oxford in the 1660s which combines erudition with mystery. But the novel I most admired this year is *Enduring Love* by Ian McEwan; the brilliant first chapter alone should have assured it a place on the Booker shortlist. It doesn't altogether fulfil this promise and it isn't a comfortable novel, but it would be interesting to know why the judges rejected it.

THURSDAY, 13TH NOVEMBER

I am writing this in my room at the Waldorf Astoria at the end of the *QE2* cruise which began on Friday, 7th November. This was my third trip as a guest lecturer and by far the most enjoyable. The *QE2* is a ship which needs getting used to; at first too much like a floating hotel to provide what I love, a sense of being at sea. But now I know my way around and have begun to understand the affection which regular travellers obviously feel. Some of them cross the Atlantic by no other way, taking the same cabin, meeting the same people, and speaking knowledgeably about their favourite captains.

This time I persuaded Rosemary to come with me, the perfect travelling companion since she is invariably good-humoured, relishes the variety, challenge and drollery of new experience and can be relied upon to be stalwart in an emergency. Her broken wrist is still in plaster, and the official photograph taken of us coming aboard has caught her, arm in sling, with a momentary look of submissive depression, with me at her side, twice as large, ruddy-faced and beaming. The only appropriate caption would be 'Murderess and her victim come aboard'!

The trip was memorable for the storm which began on Saturday. We were warned that the weather would worsen, and it did so spectacularly. Rosemary and I took our sea-sickness pills, which were effective, but a row of cabins had their 'Do not disturb' signs on the doors all day, and the Queen's Grill, where we had our table, had more empty places than passengers. One of the waiters told me that a member of the crew in their quarters had become extremely unpopular by showing *The Poseidon Adventure* on video. It was difficult at times to keep upright and the captain broadcast to us that the open deck was prohibited. Before this announcement Rosemary and I, desperate for sea air, had tried to force open one of the doors on the boat deck, but immediately had to clutch each other to avoid being hurled across the deck.

But it was worth putting up with inconvenience to see the Atlantic in a storm. As far as we could see the ocean had solidified and become a heaving mountain range of granite and rock, violently restless and yet intimidatingly dense and impervious. As far as the horizon the great grey ridges reared themselves up, valleys widened and became chasms, and volcano after volcano rose with majestic slowness to erupt, not with bursts of fire, but with explosions of spume. Outside our cabin window we watched the ocean rising in shining curves of grey mottled with white which disintegrated with a sound like gunfire and flung spray against the glass. On Saturday night a particularly large wave must have shaken the ship, the sound something between a crack and an explosion. Our clothes were wrenched from the hangers and flung across the floor while bottles and glasses skidded and broke, and the chairs spun and crashed against the cabin wall. It was extraordinary to think that a ship the size of the *QE2*, 70,000 tons in weight, thirteen storeys high and a half-mile walk round the decks, could be so shaken.

But by Sunday night the storm had eased and on Monday midday a fitful sun was shining on a calm purple-blue ocean and we were able to sit and read on deck. When the *QE2* finally goes out of service, I wonder how many regular sea crossings of the Atlantic there will be and how many passengers will be able to experience the tumultuous power of the Atlantic in a gale.

We found we were to share our table, always at first a depressing prospect. But the two passengers – Donald and Renée Bain – were delightful, entertaining and companionable Americans. Donald, among his varied literary achievements – he is the author of the *Murder, She Wrote* series – writes books for celebrities who want to be published authors without the actual bother of having to write themselves. He was extremely discreet about his clients, but I can see the attraction. The book sells on the celebrity's name and the writer collects 50 per cent of the royalties. But it is not without its disadvantages, particularly when the celebrity draws a languid hand across his or her brow and complains that the emotional stress of creative writing, not to mention the publicity, is becoming too much. Under Don's guidance I threw craps in the casino, the first time I have ever gambled. I limited myself to $100 and left the table with $198. Rosemary played the one-armed bandits until I confiscated all her quarters.

The arrival in New York down the Hudson was as spectacular as ever. One should always arrive in great cities by sea or river. As we managed our own luggage we were able to disembark early and, despite pouring rain, set off to check in at the Waldorf Astoria and then to the Frick and the Metropolitan Museum. Rosemary will have a day in New York before flying back to London tomorrow, while I go on to a Canadian tour.

FRIDAY, 21ST NOVEMBER

It is 9.30 p.m. and I am seated on Air Canada flight 96 for London Heathrow after a successful, if tiring, Canadian tour.

On Friday 14th I arrived very late in Toronto and was met by Pat Cairns, one of the publicity directors, and taken to the Four Seasons Hotel. Next day, Saturday, my Canadian publisher, Louise Dennys, gave a celebration party at her Toronto apartment. Louise is a remarkable woman, beautiful, intelligent and kind, and I value her both as my Canadian publisher and as a friend. The party was due to last for two hours, but went on considerably longer and I was introduced in swift succession to one Toronto celebrity after another. Although I was comfortably seated while this went on, the noise level and the effort of responding to each new personality were inevitably tiring.

At the dinner afterwards, one of the guests, an eminent woman lawyer, inveighed passionately against the dominance of the legal profession in England by male barristers and the prejudice and hostility shown to women at the Bar. She instanced Helena Kennedy and the unfairness with which, she alleged, this particular lawyer had had to contend. I was tempted to point out that the brilliant Helena Kennedy had, in the end, done rather well for herself. I am always irritated by criticism of England when I am abroad and I tried to point out that women were entering the law in greater numbers and that, although I obviously had no personal knowledge, I believed that things were improving. However, as the diatribe continued, I found myself saying tartly that I was becoming tired of women presenting themselves as victims.

I have been out of the regular working world now for so long that I have to resist the temptation to take lightly difficulties which other women may be experiencing in their professional lives. During my career in the Health Service and Civil Service I certainly worked with a few men who disliked women, which was disagreeable enough, and occasionally with some who disliked me, which was even less agreeable. But I cannot in honesty say that, once in post, I ever experienced real discrimination. Admittedly when I went before appointing committees in the National Health Service to gain promotion, I accepted that I would have to be not only better qualified than the male candidates, but considerably better qualified. This can hardly be regarded as equality of opportunity. The discrimination was partly because hospital administration was seen primarily as a male career if only to balance the considerable power that matrons then exercised in the hospital world. In the Home Office I experienced no trace of discrimination, but I accept from what is told to me that in some professions it does exist and that sexual discrimination and harassment can't be dismissed as the obsessive preoccupation of extreme feminists. But it is remarkable how much has been achieved for women during my lifetime. When I was a child I can't remember ever coming into contact with any professional women who were not either nurses or schoolteachers. Obviously there were women doctors, dentists, solicitors, but I never met them.

The career opportunities available to us grammar school girls in the 1930s were limited, particularly those of us who had no chance of going on to university. I can recall a sentence from the Cambridge High School prospectus which, after pointing out that girls could enter the sixth form and be prepared for teacher training college or could take a secretarial course, added: 'The school thus prepares pupils either for a career or for the ordinary pursuits of womanhood.' The ordinary pursuits of womanhood consisted of finding a husband, bearing his children, looking after the home and, if money and leisure afforded, undertaking voluntary work in the community. No girl I knew at school went on to a university although a number became teachers.

When I entered the Health Service in 1949 I was paid less than a man on the same grade doing comparable work simply because I was a woman. Then, after my father-in-law retired and I had to find a home for myself, my husband and the children, I was told that a mortgage would not be granted without my husband's signature. Eventually I was able to persuade the mortgage company of the impracticability of this since Connor was unable to earn and spent most of his time in hospitals, but it was a long struggle.

But all the benefits and advantages we women have won during my lifetime have their compensating disadvantages. Professional women with small children certainly work harder and under greater stress today than ever I experienced. I was, of course, fortunate in living with my parents-in-law so that, although I had to work, my daughters were assured of devoted and reliable daily care. The relationship between the sexes is more fraught with uncertainty and anxiety than when I was a girl. Girls growing up today have privileges and opportunities which would have seemed unbelievable to that fourteen-year-old schoolgirl before the war, but I do not think that their lives are necessarily easier and I do not envy them.

Despite the arguments at dinner, Friday was a happy day. It is always a delight to see Louise and her husband Ric Young, who has more energy than any other man I know. It is impossible to dine in a restaurant with him without at least half the staff and three-quarters of the other diners coming over to greet him and Louise, and to chat.

Monday 17th November was the real beginning of the tour, with a continuous programme of radio and television in the morning and afternoon, and a reading at Trinity Church followed by a book-signing. After this, a Canadian friend, Vern Heinrich, collected me and took me for a quiet dinner to his and his wife's Toronto home. It was good to sit and eat in quiet comfort away from the questioning voices.

The next morning I flew Air Canada to Montreal for the usual schedule of television, radio and newsprint events, followed by dinner and a talk with two other writers at the Ritz Carlton Hotel. I went to bed early to be up in good time for the 8.40 a.m. flight to Ottawa, where Louise joined me at the Château Laurier Hotel. I was in Ottawa for one event only, at the National Arts Centre for a talk followed by a signing.

Kathy Reichs, author of *Déjà Dead*, had read with me in Montreal and was again part of the event. She is a highly intelligent, lively and likeable forensic anthropologist and is being strongly promoted as the new Patricia Cornwell. The strength of her novel is the insight it gives into the scientific procedures of a murder investigation, and with its gruesomely authentic background, its contemporary heroine, Dr Temperance Brennan, an ex-alcoholic, and the interesting setting in bilingual Montreal, I predict that it will be a bestseller. The event was sold out well before the night and Kathy Reichs's talk to the crowded audience was as fascinating as it was unexpected. She decided to talk about her work, not her novel, and image after gaudy image of mutilated and decomposed bodies was thrown upon the screen; one of particular horror to the squeamish showed a dead male with his hands hacked off seeming to hold out the bloodstained stumps in piteous entreaty. The audience, composed predominantly of middle-aged women, seemed totally unflustered by this realism, but the audience for a concert in another part of the Arts Centre, enjoying an opportune interval, pressed their faces to the glass partition in some wonder at the strong stomachs of the mystery book-buying public.

Listening to Kathy Reichs giving her presentation I pondered on the difference between the books written by women crime writers in the Golden Age and women writing today. Dorothy L. Sayers, Ngaio Marsh, Margery Allingham, all created gentlemanly detectives operating predominantly in a middle-class or upper-class world: Lord Peter Wimsey, son of a duke; Roderick Alleyn, son of a baronet; Albert Campion of unspecified but aristocratic lineage. This emphasis on gentility wasn't entirely snobbish. The detective story is popular entertainment and readers in the 1930s preferred their heroes to be at least their social equal and to demonstrate qualities which were then regarded as essential for the hero: courage, reticence, intelligence and good manners. There was small regard for credibility, particularly in the method of murder. The relations between the police and omni-talented private eye were unrealistic. Forensic and police details were usually inaccurate or omitted. There was an avoidance of violence, sometimes indeed an absence of blood, and the villain invariably received his or her just deserts without too much regard for psychological subtleties.

The 1930s were years of remarkable freedom from domestic crime and although there were areas of the inner cities which must have been as violent as they are today, pictures of social disruption were not being brought daily into our drawing-rooms by television. It was therefore possible to live in a small country town or village and feel almost entirely secure. Reading the detective stories of the 1930s brings the decades between the wars vividly to life. What we find in these essentially gentle mysteries is an ordered society in which virtue is regarded as normal, crime an aberration, and in which there is small sympathy for the criminal. It is accepted, although seldom stated, that murderers, when convicted, will hang. Agatha Christie, arch-purveyor of cosy reassurance, is careful not to emphasize this fact, but Dorothy L. Sayers in *Busman's Honeymoon* actually has the temerity to confront Lord Peter Wimsey with the logical end to his detective activities, when he crouches weeping in his wife's arms on the morning when Frank Crutchley is executed. I couldn't help feeling when I first read the novel that Lord Peter was somewhat over-sensitive; no one after all had forced him to become a detective.

One of the criticisms made today of the 1930s detective story is that it pandered to the snobbery of the middle class. Certainly I can't think of a single crime novel of the 1930s in which a servant or member of the working class is either the murderer or plays a major part in the story. It is almost as if the working class were there to feed the detective with useful scraps of information, provide comic relief, and occasionally be sacrificed as an additional, but seldom the main, victim. This uncritical acceptance of the division of class runs through virtually all the detective stories of the 1930s, although it is perhaps strongest in Dorothy L. Sayers and Ngaio Marsh. But if the detective story was snobbish by present-day standards, so was virtually all popular entertainment including commercial drama, as I know from the series of Plays of the Year on my bookshelf. Here the name of a cook or house parlour-maid in the cast list is a guarantee that the playwright is aiming to inject a leaven of domestic humour.

Dorothy L. Sayers, among much in her novels that is incredible, or over-romanticized, does deal realistically with the 1930s problem of the superfluous women, not only the pathetic spinsters in their boarding houses and cheap hotels, but women with intelligence, initiative, and often with education, for whom society offered no real intellectual outlet. I can't think of a single detective story written by a woman in the 1930s which features a woman lawyer, a woman doctor, a woman politician, or indeed a woman in any real position of political or commercial power.

In her biography of Margery Allingham, Julie Thorogood states that the fashion historian James Laver, a correspondent of the novelist, described the era between the wars as 'hectic, frivolous, frustrated, puzzled, frantic', and Margery Allingham herself said, 'Whatever happens, never go pretending that things were going well before the war. Never deceive yourself that you could not foresee a dead end.' They were not, of course, going well, but in general the detective story was concerned to provide diversion from the ills of society, not to dwell on them or propose a solution. In Christie, for example, there is no real horror, no real blood or grief; indeed, even the murders are sanitized. And we know at the end that the corpse will pick itself up, shake itself down, and normality will be restored to Mayhem Parva, the fly-in-amber village, which, despite its above-average homicide rate, never really loses its peace or innocence.

The heroes created by women writing today could hardly be more different. Forensic and medical details are invariably accurate and women make use of their own expertise. Patricia Cornwell, whose detective, Dr Kay Scarpetta, is a forensic medical examiner, herself worked in this field; Kathy Reichs is of course a forensic anthropologist, whilst Sarah Dunant with Hannah Woolf, Sue Grafton with Kinsey Millhone, Sara Paretsky with V. I. Warshawski, and Joan Smith with her academic Loretta Lawson have created tough private eyes all over thirty, independent, highly professional and operating successfully in a predominantly male world. None of these fictional women is a single working mother or a married woman with children, trying to cope with her job whilst negotiating with a series of *au pairs* and torn with guilt about leaving her children. This is not the kind of realism which most readers of crime novels want. Adam Dalgliesh is similarly unencumbered. I ruthlessly killed off his wife in childbirth even before beginning my first novel. Neither his poetry nor his professional life are inconvenienced by the pram in the hall. To that extent, I suppose, we still deal in fantasy, and it is only the fashion in fantasy which changes.

DECEMBER

MONDAY, 1ST DECEMBER

It was on this date seven years ago that I learned I was to receive a life peerage. I remember that the post was particularly heavy that morning and I gathered up the letters to open at the kitchen table while I drank coffee. The stiff white envelope came from 10 Downing Street and I opened it with no particular expectations. When I read the first line, 'I have it in mind on the occasion of the forthcoming list of New Year Honours to submit your name to the Queen' – I immediately assumed that my OBE was to be upgraded to CBE. There was scarcely time for this thought to take hold before I read the rest of the letter and learnt that I was to be recommended for a life peerage.

Looking back now over the past seven years I feel some guilt that I have taken so little part in the affairs of the House. I wasn't appointed as what is commonly known as a working peer, but I did expect to show my face more regularly than I have. The problem has been with my writing life, particularly the public and charitable appearances and overseas tours, which are arranged months in advance, whereas the business of the House comes up at very short notice. Another problem has been my reluctance to speak without having become a more regular attender and better conversant with the traditions and procedures of the House. But I should be doing more and doing it better.

I made my maiden speech on the subject of literature and the preservation of the English language. Nearly all new peers confess that, whatever experience they may have of public speaking, their maiden speech in the House of Lords is an ordeal. There is no reason why this should be so as the tradition of the House is to be unfailingly courteous and supportive to the new member, and maiden speeches, however inadequate, are by custom received with tributes of praise and congratulations from following speakers. And so it was with me.

And now, if the Government's intention in its manifesto is to be carried out, the House will change fundamentally and will, indeed, cease to be the House of Lords. Although few people would wish to defend the right of hereditary peers to have a part in the government of the country merely because of their birthright, to seek to reform the House by first abolishing the hereditary peers without deciding the final constitution and form of the second chamber seems to me dangerous and irresponsible folly. The first step to reform would surely be to prohibit any elder son from taking his father's place when the peer dies, and to exclude from the chamber all those who don't have a record of regular attendance. This would enable the work of the House to be carried on while the long-term future was discussed at leisure. There should be no hurry about changing an institution which has served for 700 years.

The proper way is to appoint a Royal Commission and to give them adequate time in which to take evidence from a wide variety of people and interests. The reform of the House is more complex than a government anxious for quick results is prepared to admit. Reform of the second chamber involves considering the relationship between the two Houses, and between the Westminster Parliament and the legislative bodies in Scotland, Wales and Northern Ireland. It is also for consideration whether the second chamber should have powers in relation to European legislation. The Royal Commission would need to consider whether the Lords should be appointed or elected and, if elected, by what means and for how long; whether the present system of appointment, if continued, is sufficiently democratic and open to scrutiny; and whether it is desirable that the power of a second and revising chamber should be increased. If the second chamber is elected or partly elected, it will, of course, have a democratic legitimacy which it now lacks, and it could well flex its muscles to be a far more effective check on the executive. At present the Lords, only too aware that all members are there by privilege not by election, are afraid to exercise those powers which are already theirs. A more democratically constituted Upper House would be more powerful and more troublesome to the Government; is this likely to be acceptable to the Commons?

I am not sure, either, whether we really need a second chamber composed mainly of professional full-time politicians. There is something to be said for the present system whereby men and women with particular expertise will try to attend and make their contribution when their subject comes up. A danger, too, in an elected chamber is that the House will lose that sturdy independence which has characterized not only those on the cross-benches, but peers who have declared a political allegiance. And when the hereditary peers go, will there be any point in retaining life peers? The ermine, the title, the coat of arms for those who decide to have one, the induction ceremony, all will become meaningless flummery if the House has in fact become the equivalent of a senate.

The House as at present constituted may be an anomaly and one difficult to justify democratically, but it does work effectively and if it is to be changed, it must be changed for the better and not merely to gratify the more ignoble impulses of class resentment or envy. Our present system of government makes a strong revising chamber essential to the cause of democracy. Because of the first-past-the-post voting system, which does have the advantage of producing strong government, nearly every government is elected on a minority vote; there are always more people who didn't want the party in power than those who did. The second chamber should have a keen ear to hear their grievances and the courage and independence to voice their concerns. No one doubts that the final authority rests with the elected chamber but it is carrying hypocrisy too far to pretend that the elected chamber always represents in every respect the will of the majority of the people.

Whatever happens, the House will be far duller without the hereditary peers, and I must try to attend more often while it retains some of the vigour, independence, excitement and breadth of knowledge which characterizes it at present. And is it too much to hope that the reforms will be made in a spirit of dignity, courtesy and generosity? The hereditary peers have served the country well, some of them with distinction. They deserve our thanks before they go. But then, ours is not a dignified, courteous or generous-minded age.

WEDNESDAY, 3RD DECEMBER

I arrived last Friday at Grand Cayman, flying from Gatwick to spend a week with Dick and Mary Francis. The journey is much easier now that there are direct flights. Previously I had to transfer at Miami, a tedious time-consuming business, since the airport has apparently no transfer lounge and I had to go through Immigration merely in order to change

1a On my father's knee, aged two and a half, with my mother and sister Monica.

1b *Babes in the Wood* at Ludlow. My brother as a babe and my sister and I as gnomes. I think this was a pantomime in aid of Ludford church.

2a My mother with her Sunday-School dancers. Wearing improvised costumes we pranced uncertainly across the stage in highly inauthentic country dances with mother at the piano.

2b As Leontes in *The Winter's Tale*. Cambridge High School for Girls, 1934.

3 With my mother, Monica and Edward. Cambridge, 1931. This was probably taken to be sent to relations and friends at Christmas. I don't know why my father wasn't included.

4 With my first-born, Clare, in 1942.

5a With Connor, on leave from the RAMC, and Jane at Chigwell Row, Essex.

5b With Connor at Clare's wedding, 27th April 1963.

6a Clare and Jane in the garden at White Hall, Chigwell Row, *c.* 1962.

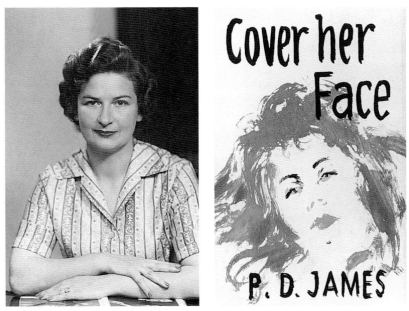

6b Publicity photograph for *Cover Her Face*, with the dust jacket by Charles Mozley, 1962.

7 In New York, 1980, for the American publication of *Innocent Blood*, which reached Number One on the *New York Times* bestseller list.

8 The first Anglia television series, *Death of an Expert Witness*, in 1983. With John Rosenberg (Producer), Herbie Wise (Director) and Roy Marsden as Adam Dalgliesh.

9 In Berlin with Ruth Rendell before the wall came down.

10 Speaking at Chatsworth after presenting the Heywood Hill literary prizes, 19th June 1998. The Duke's dog showed a flattering interest throughout.

11 At home with Polly-Hodge, 1998.

12a St Paul's Cathedral 28th June 1995. My largest and most attentive audience. Reading the Bidding Prayer I was asked to write for the thanksgiving service to celebrate the centenary of the National Trust.

12b With the Board of Governors and the Board of Management of the BBC at Lucknam Park.

13 With my sponsors, Baroness Blatch and Lord Butterfield, before taking my seat in the House of Lords, 19th February 1991.

14 Photographed by Jane Bown at Blythburgh.

15 With my fellow honorary graduands Pat Barker and Richard Griffiths, and the Chancellor Sir Peter Ustinov, Durham, 30th June 1988.

16a A young painter and an elderly subject. My portrait by Michael Taylor in the National Portrait Gallery, painted in 1996.

16b On the beach at Southwold, planning murder.

planes. This is my second visit and, as before, I stepped out of the aircraft into warm, sweet-smelling air and saw Mary and Dick waiting for me under the leafy canopy which leads to the airport building.

Our daily routine is well established. Dick and Mary's apartment is on Seven Mile Beach within yards of the warm translucent sea. In the morning, before breakfast, Dick and I walk along the firm sand, splashing through the surf for half a mile in either direction, returning to take our morning swim with Mary, who gets up later. Early in her marriage she had polio very badly, was in an iron lung and nearly died. She can't tolerate the English winter, which is the reason why she and Dick live in Grand Cayman. After our swim I laze under the palm trees until it is time for lunch. The afternoon is similarly sybaritic and I don't put on shoes or change from shorts and T-shirt until it is time to go out for a meal. The restaurants are varied and good, and I particularly like the Wharf Restaurant, where we sit under the lights on the pier in warm scented darkness, and wait for the tarpons to be fed, swirling and leaping as the bucket empties in a silver stream.

Grand Cayman is one of the few remaining British colonies and the people are obviously well content with a system which produces security and prosperity. I learned something of the history. Columbus discovered Grand Cayman on his fourth journey in 1503, apparently by accident when blown off course on his way to take on water at Dominica. He named it Tortuga after the turtles for which it was, and remains, famous. Francis Drake arrived in 1586. Because the island is unwatered there seems to have been no indigenous population and the earliest inhabitants were pirates, remittance men and escaping slaves.

It is a colony without taxes and since people keep all the money they earn, there is no need for the equivalent of a welfare state. It is a socio-economic system which could only work in a small and self-contained community. Income is derived from a tax on imports and on every legal document signed in the colony; since Grand Cayman, for obvious reasons, is one of the world's most flourishing financial centres, this imposition is lucrative. I went to a meeting of the Legislative Assembly. There are fifteen members elected by districts and an Executive Council of five elected by the Assembly with the Governor General and Attorney General as *ex-officio* members. The Assembly is modelled on the House of Commons with a Speaker but no Prime Minister. The debate I listened to was lively, with the multi-racial members questioning the Customs Officer on the problem of controlling the traffic in drugs. Grand Cayman is a convenient staging post for drugs entering or leaving the United States. I was intrigued to see that the Minister of Health was called Anthony Eden.

Grand Cayman is an island with remarkably little crime, which is hardly surprising since almost everyone is personally known and the only way of leaving is by boat or air.

I have stayed at a number of British embassies abroad when on my travels and always there has been high security, often with armed guards. Walking along the beach with Dick I saw that the Governor's garden stretches down to the beach with no fence and a simple notice on a post stuck into the sand: 'Please respect the Governor's privacy.' That notice seemed to sum up the spirit of the island.

SATURDAY, 6TH DECEMBER

I arrived home in the early afternoon. Andy was waiting for me at Gatwick and drove me to Marks & Spencer on my way home to stock up with food. Polly-Hodge gave me her usual cool greeting to demonstrate displeasure at my absence, and then followed me around the house for the rest of the day. Everything was in good order. Joyce, with her usual efficiency, had sorted the post into matters requiring attention, those that were urgent and papers for information only. What on earth would I do without her?

Next week is going to be exceptionally busy, but I shall think about that tomorrow.

SUNDAY, 7TH DECEMBER

I awoke after a very good night's sleep with the firm intention of going to 11 o'clock Mass. I set out with a quarter of an hour to get to Margaret Street, but neither bus nor taxi appeared and I was obstinately disinclined to go down into the Underground. Eventually a 94 appeared, but the journey was slow and it was obvious by the time we reached Marble Arch that I would be at least twenty minutes late for the service. So I went into Marks & Spencer instead and bought myself a skirt. I was rewarded for this triumph of Mammon over God by leaving my umbrella in the bus.

Waiting for the 94, I was reminded somewhat irrationally of Billy Brown of London Town, that squat round little man of the war years with his bowler hat and rolled umbrella invented by some Mandelson of the Ministry of Information to demonstrate the perfect citizen. Billy

Brown never lost his ration card, never travelled unnecessarily and his blackout was always impeccable, showing no chink of light. The poster showed him standing at a bus stop with his left hand raised and read: 'Face the driver, raise your hand / You'll find that he will understand.' Underneath some wit had written: 'Of course he will, the silly cuss / But will he stop the bloody bus?'

FRIDAY, 12TH DECEMBER

The last few days, all filled with activity, seem to have merged together.

On Monday at 9 o'clock Faber sent Andy to take me to Queen Square, where I signed 1,000 copies of the novel between half-past nine and a quarter past twelve, a feat achieved by setting up a production line of someone to open the book at the title page and slide it before me and someone else to close it and pack it.

On Tuesday morning I attended a lunch for the Regent's Park and Kensington North Conservative Association Women's Group at the Henry VIII Hotel in Paddington, and spoke afterwards. I had arranged for Andy to collect me at 3.15 and take me direct to Buckingham Palace, where there was a meeting of the Patrons of the Royal Society Project Science. The Duke of Edinburgh as usual got through the business sharply and we then retired to a room overlooking The Mall for tea. This is served in surprisingly large cups and accompanied by delicately sized and delicious sandwiches.

We then went to the Royal Society for the President's reception. Despite my ignorance of science, I love going to the Royal Society, particularly to look at the documents, the books and the pictures, and there are always interesting people to meet. On Tuesday I had a lively discussion with a young scientist about religious belief. He said that, as a Roman Catholic, he had never been troubled by any conflict between science and religion; they represented two entirely different modes of thought. I said that surely some of the more esoteric doctrines, such as the physical Assumption of the Virgin Mary, were hard to accept. I don't think he did accept it. He said that religion should be reduced to its essentials and the extraneous paraphernalia ignored, although perhaps the word 'reduced' isn't really appropriate. 'At heart,' he said, 'it's really very simple.'

On Wednesday morning I was at the British Council to give a short talk at a lunchtime meeting in aid of the Council's Benevolent Fund. They had held a poetry competition and I was asked to read the winning poem. It is always good to return to the Council to meet old friends and to hear what is happening in the Literature Department. One of the most encouraging things I have learned recently is the success of an application to the Lottery to co-operate with a publisher in sending a complete set of Everyman books, not only to every secondary school in the United Kingdom, but also to all overseas British Council libraries. We have in English a language of incomparable beauty, versatility and richness and a literature, particularly poetry, surely unsurpassed, and it is extraordinary to me how little we understand of its importance to this country's reputation overseas.

Yesterday, 11th December, I was one of the speakers with Roy Hattersley and my American editor, Charles Elliott, at *The Oldie* lunch at Simpsons. It was, as usual, crowded, cheerful, and the food was excellent, if hardly suitable for oldies counting calories. Roy Hattersley spoke entertainingly about what he saw as a deterioration in public life since the days of Attlee, and Charles was interesting on the difference between gardening in the United States and in England – or, in his case, in the Welsh Marches. We were to speak for ten minutes only so I was fairly lighthearted, but I misjudged the event. For some reason I hadn't realized that I was expected to discuss my latest novel. Instead I attempted not very successfully to be amusing.

This morning Joanna Mackle called for me at 9 a.m. and I drove with her to Faber to sign another 750 copies of *A Certain Justice*. The 1,000 I signed last Monday have already been sold.

Back in the afternoon to attempt to catch up with the post, and then in the evening to talk to the Association of Women Solicitors and Lawyers at St John's Gate in Clerkenwell. They had procured copies of the novel, which I signed, and which were sold after the dinner. The meal was supposed to start at 7.30 but it was closer to 8.10 before we sat down and 9.50 before I rose to speak, which is much too late to do justice to any subject.

Another late night, which is making me realize even more that winter evening engagements will have to be cut down.

SATURDAY, 13TH DECEMBER
This morning to Westminster Abbey to lay a wreath on behalf of the Johnson Society of London. As usual, and through anxiety not to be late, I arrived too early so walked up as far as the Army and Navy Stores and then back to fill in time. I had it in mind to sit quietly in St

Faith's Chapel in the Abbey, but access to this was blocked; indeed it seemed impossible for anyone to go further than the main nave without passing the desk and paying a charge to see the Royal Chapels. The Abbey was very crowded and I wondered how long this ancient monument could withstand the tramping feet and press of so many millions. The middle part of the nave was roped off for private prayer, or for those wishing to sit quietly, but the background noise was like the subdued roar of the sea.

The party from the Johnson Society was due to congregate near the tomb of the Unknown Soldier at twelve o'clock, at which hour the Sub-Dean announced that there would be a short prayer, and invited people to stand still or sit for this. Most stood, but others continued their somewhat aimless perambulations, whilst a family with two small boys made an exit, half-hurried, half-furtive, as if afraid of spiritual contamination.

The short ceremony at Johnson's grave was impressive and rather moving. We processed with the Beadle in front, followed by the Sub-Dean and then myself, carrying the wreath of laurels and white carnations, then members of the Society. After the Dean had spoken a short welcome, I laid the wreath. I had been asked to say a few words and I decided on the following:

I lay this wreath on behalf of the Johnson Society of London to honour a great Englishman and this country's greatest man of letters: Samuel Johnson, moralist, essayist, lexicographer, critic, poet, genius of both the written and the spoken word. We honour him both as a writer and as a man, remembering his generosity and humanity and the courage with which his great heart endured poverty, frustration, neglect and private pain. With all lovers of the English language, which he celebrated and glorified, we rejoice in the legacy of literature which is his lasting memorial. It is fitting that he should be buried here in the London he loved and among the greatest of our land; fitting too that, on the anniversary of his death, I should end these few words by speaking in his memory the prayer which he himself wrote and offered up before writing: 'Almighty God, the giver of all good things, without whose help all labour is ineffectual, and without whose grace all wisdom is folly: grant, I beseech thee, that in this undertaking thy Holy Spirit may not be withheld from me, but that I may promote thy glory, and the salvation of myself and others: grant this, O Lord, for the sake of thy son, Jesus Christ. Amen.'

I wondered whether it was entirely accurate to describe Johnson as our nation's greatest man of letters, but decided that it was. Shakespeare is thought of primarily as a poet, Dickens as a novelist. The term 'man of letters' suggests a polymath of literature as well as one whose whole working life has been devoted to its cause. Laying the wreath, I thought how much Connor would have liked to have been with us. Samuel Johnson was his great hero.

After the wreath-laying we went to the Vitello d'Oro near Church House for an Italian meal, and then to a small conference room where I gave my talk. The Society had suggested that 'The Moral Responsibility of the Novelist' would be an appropriate title, and I found this more challenging than my usual talk about the craft of writing detective fiction. Inevitably an overriding question asserts itself: if the novelist has a moral responsibility, what is the morality from which that responsibility derives? The answer would have been obvious to a devout Christian like Samuel Johnson, as it was to George Eliot or any of the Brontës, but we no longer live in a predominantly Christian society. Thus to speak of a novelist's moral responsibility seems to imply that there is an immutable value system, an accepted view of the universe and man's place in it, with a set of ethical rules of conduct to which all right-minded people conform. Even if this were true – and I do not think we can claim that it is in our increasingly secular and fragmented society – one could question whether it is the business of any creative artist to express or promote it. Dr Johnson, of course, had his own view of the matter:

It is justly considered as the greatest excellency of art, to imitate nature; but it is necessary to distinguish those parts of nature, which are most proper for imitation; greater care is still required in representing life, which is so often coloured by passion or deformed by wickedness. If the world be promiscuously described, I cannot see of what use it can be to read the account; or why it may not be as safe to turn the eye immediately upon mankind as upon a mirror which shows all that presents itself without discrimination.

Many of the Victorian novelists, and particularly Anthony Trollope, laid claims to moral purpose in the novel and were probably prudent to do so. After all, there still hung about novel-reading the sulphurous whiff of indolent and almost decadent self-indulgence. I don't think that even the most didactic novelist today would claim that his or her words should reform either institutions or people, although we may all have an urge to nudge society's inclinations in a direction more agreeable to our own beliefs and prejudices. I imagine most writers today would probably agree with that eighteenth-century, less well-known writer, Richard Cumberland:

> All that I am bound to do as a story-maker is to make a story. I am not bound to reform the constitution of my country in the same breath, nor even, (Heaven be thanked!) to overturn it, although that may be the easier task of the two. Nature is my guide; man's nature, not his natural rights. The one ushers me by the straight avenue to the human heart, the other bewilders me in a maze of metaphysics.

Certainly, for me, the intention of any novelist must surely be to make that straight avenue to the human heart.

In the talk I went on to discuss the novelist's responsibility under the headings of subject matter, characterization and style. It can, I think, be argued that it is absurd to claim that the question of moral responsibility can enter into the novelist's choice of subject simply because the idea of choice, of a conscious selection or rejection, is illusory. Every novelist writes what he or she needs to write, a subconscious compulsion to express and explain his unique view of reality. If creativity is the successful resolution of internal conflict, the creative writer seeks out of this conflict to make sense of his experience of the world, to impose order on disorder and to construct a controlled pattern from his own internal chaos. In support of this theory, that a writer's choice of subject is more apparent than real, we can see how genre writers tend to stay with that genre, and how easily we recognize the mind's topography in such very different novelists as Thomas Hardy, Graham Greene, Virginia Woolf, Barbara Pym, John le Carré, Jane Austen, P. G. Wodehouse, all of whom create a distinctive and immediately recognizable world.

The crime novelist does not reject romantic fiction or science fiction in favour of murder through conscious choice. He or she needs to deal with the atavistic fear of death, to exorcize the terror of violence and to restore at least fictional peace and tranquillity after the disruptive terror of murder, and to affirm the sanctity of human life and the possibility of justice, even if it is only the fallible justice of men. A distinguished writer of novels of espionage like John le Carré is as much fascinated by personal treachery and betrayal as he is by the shoddy international bureaucracy of spying and the dangers and excitement of the chase. Espionage is his internal as well as his external world.

Even so, there must be an element of choice both in subject and treatment; no artist is so at the mercy of his subconscious that he is totally without control of his imagination. But if the novelist has a duty to consider the effect of what he writes on the sensitivities of his readers, it is surely also justifiable to ask whether those sensitivities are reasonable or whether criticism and complaints are a subtle attempt at censorship. There are fashionable views on gender, race and political correctness which a writer would be ill-advised to ignore if he wishes to avoid controversy, and which take some courage to confront.

When it comes to style, it seems to me that the only moral responsibility is for the writer to do his conscientious best with such talent as he has been given to eschew plagiarism, avoid slovenly or meretricious writing, abjure jargon and platitudes and to strive always for that distinctive individual voice which we call style.

I ended the talk by considering the morality of the fiction I have chosen to write. I do, in fact, get asked from time to time whether it is justifiable to use murder, sometimes appalling murder, to produce books which are primarily for entertainment and relaxation. In short, does the detective story trivialize death and suffering? And isn't it true that the detective story too often subjugates all the elements of a good novel – psychological truth, setting and atmosphere, characterization – to the dominant needs of the plot, so that the writer, handcuffed to the need to provide a puzzle and shackled to the conventions of the genre, can never write with total honesty or truth? Some of these criticisms are as perverse and irrelevant as complaining that Jane Austen fails to deal adequately with the Napoleonic Wars or with the barbarism of the early-nineteenth-century criminal justice system, or that Bertie Wooster has an imperfect understanding of the socio-economic consequences of twentieth-century capitalism.

Sometimes I am asked whether I am afraid that readers will get murderous ideas from my books. This is not a risk I take seriously: detective novelists are hardly in the business of promoting successful and undetected crime. But I do impose a censorship, sometimes subconscious, on what I write. I can't read descriptions of torture or watch these scenes on film or television, and I would never describe the explosion of a terrorist bomb in the Underground. This isn't because terrorists need my imagination to provide them with murderous ideas; it is a superstitious dread that the event might actually happen and I would never afterwards be absolutely sure that I hadn't contributed to the horror.

I very seldom describe the act of murder, but make no apology for describing the dead victim realistically, and indeed vividly. The moment in a detective story when the body is discovered is one of horror and high drama, and the reader should experience both. I always describe the scene through the eyes of the character in the novel who discovers the body, and the scene is often most effective when that character is herself or himself innocent. The scene in *A Taste for Death* where the bodies of the ex-Minister of the Crown and the tramp are incongruously yoked in death in the vestry of a church in Paddington provides that contrast which, I think, is so effective in detective fiction, between horror and normality, evil and goodness. The fact that the bodies are discovered by Miss Wharton and Darren adds to the horror. In the description I repeat the word 'blood' again and again because it was this all-pervasive redness which suffused Miss Wharton's mind as it did her retina. In *Devices and Desires*, however, the body of Hilary Robarts is discovered by Adam Dalgliesh walking along the shore at nightfall. The description is analytical, cool, and Dalgliesh's response after the initial shock is always that of a professional detective.

All this is rather removed from the subject of today's talk. I have given myself quite a lot to think about; I am not sure whether the audience found it equally interesting.

MONDAY, 15TH DECEMBER

To Westminster for a meeting in Church House of the Liturgical Commission. I don't think I am particularly useful on the Commission, to which I was appointed by Archbishop Robert Runcie shortly before he retired. I enjoy the meetings I am able to get to, but the detailed work of revision is largely done in small groups. I like my fellow members, who tolerate my theological ignorance with Christian charity, but they are, of course, concerned to write or rewrite liturgy and my interest as a Vice-President of the Prayer Book Society is in attempting to preserve the treasure we have.

The Commission generates more paper than almost any other committee on which I have sat. The highly experienced Secretary, David Hebblethwaite, copes manfully, but my filing-cabinet drawer, which Joyce has labelled 'God', contains more bulging files than there are on any other subject. The bureaucracy of the Church of England would be terrifying if it were efficient.

The Church of England hasn't shown much interest in or respect for its rich heritage of literature during the last decades and some parish priests, many of whom can't cope with Cranmerian prose, would point out that their concerns lie elsewhere than in preserving what they see as an archaic and irrelevant liturgy. What surprises me is the neglect of the King James Bible and the Book of Common Prayer by academics and its absence from the A-level English syllabus. Even for people uninterested in or unconvinced by Cranmer's reformation theology, his Prayer Book is one of the great glories of English literature. It is difficult, too, to understand how students can read Shakespeare or view with understanding some of the greatest paintings in our galleries without some knowledge of the Authorized Version of the Bible or Tyndale's translation on which it is based. I have been told by friends who teach English at universities that they have to give a short course in basic Christianity to some of their English students before some books of the canon are comprehensible.

In his magisterial biography of Thomas Cranmer, published in 1996, Diarmid MacCulloch said that Cranmer is among 'a select band of Tudor writers, from Tyndale to Shakespeare, who set English on its future course' and that 'millions who have never heard of Cranmer or of the muddled heroism of his death have echoes of his words in their minds'. I wonder how long those words and cadences will, in fact, echo. I must resist paranoia, but it is sometimes difficult not to believe that there are people with a more sinister purpose than the neglect of two of the nation's most seminal books. If you want to destroy a country's traditions and soften it up for a culture you personally find more to your liking, there is no better way to begin than by an attack on its language and literature.

WEDNESDAY, 24TH DECEMBER

It was on this day in 1979 that I retired from the Home Office. The second part of my service was less satisfying than the first. I was transferred to the Children's Department, whose responsibilities were then being reallocated to the Department of Health and Social Security, and then to the Criminal Policy Department, where I was concerned with juvenile courts and the law relating to juvenile offenders. The Department's chief concern was the Children and Young Person's Act 1969 which revised the law relating to juveniles and set up, among other provisions, the care order. The job of the Civil Service is to help implement Government policy, not to criticize it – and certainly not at my level, of Principal – but it seemed to me that the Act, based, as far as I know, on no research evidence, was mistaken from the beginning. The underlying premise was that any delinquency or serious criminal behaviour in a child or young person is the result of the juvenile's circumstances and environment. Put this right and all will be well. In serious cases, therefore, the Juvenile Court would have power to place the offender in local authority care where he would receive the loving and responsible guidance and protection which he could expect from a good parent. Children at risk of abuse or ill-treatment could be similarly placed in care if the necessary conditions were satisfied.

The Maria Colwell tragedy, when Maria, under supervision by her local authority, was murdered by her stepfather, had an immediate impact on legislative proposals for strengthening the child protection provisions of the 1969 Act. Ministers announced that it would never be allowed to happen again. It has, of course, happened again, and not infrequently. I feel some sympathy with social workers, who are faced with an appalling dilemma. They are criticized if they leave a child in her home and she is subsequently abused or even murdered; they are criticized if they too readily take her into care. It doesn't surprise me that they have so often got it wrong; what does surprise me is the extraordinary and irrational optimism with which Parliament and the profession assumed they could get it right.

The years have shown how misguided the Act was. The official view put forward by the DHSS at the time and endorsed by ministers generally, was that any defects in its working were due to lack of resources. Of course there were not adequate resources; there never are. All governments are fond of legislating for what they see as social reforms well in advance of providing the necessary funds for implementing the changes. But the main problem was not lack of money, it was the lack of skill and experience. The new local authority Social Services were formed in the wake of the Seebohm and Redcliffe-Maud reorganizations. There was to be one integrated training for social workers, who were presumed to be able to undertake any aspect of the work. Inexperienced young people imbued with the latest socio-economic theories were faced with some of the most intractable problems of child delinquency or child abuse. It is small wonder that both the supervision orders and the care orders were largely ineffective. We have now had some years of experience of what local authority residential care has meant for thousands of deprived, unhappy young people.

I decided that I should leave on Christmas Eve at the age of fifty-nine years and six months. I was not due to receive my lump sum and to start my pension until my sixtieth birthday on 3rd August, but the success of *Innocent Blood* made early retirement possible. I had given the usual goodbye party earlier in the week and the office was very quiet and almost empty when I cleared the last drawer, washed my tea mug, packed it away in my tote-bag and closed the door for the last time. They had been twelve good years. I had gained experience which had been invaluable in writing *Death of an Expert Witness* and *Innocent Blood*, and was to prove equally valuable in future. I left with considerable respect for this much-misunderstood department and I had made more than one lasting friend. My life as a bureaucrat was now at an end and it was time to go.

DIARY 1998

JANUARY

I spent today completing my packing for the American tour which begins tomorrow, and tackling the bulging 'Pending' file with Joyce. I had a telephone interview with the *Dayton Daily News*, advance publicity for my arrival there on 16th January. Dayton, Ohio, has not been included before in any of my American tours, but I have what is in effect a fan club there, largely due to the friendship and the vigorous support of a local journalist, Rosamond Young. Rosamond has persuaded my publishers, Alfred A. Knopf, that a visit to her town would be well worth the detour; knowing her, I've no doubt that it will be.

Perhaps the greatest change in publishing since my girlhood has been the death – sometimes dramatic, sometimes after a protracted period of ailing – of small individual publishing houses and the emergence of conglomerates, many of them international firms with wide and varying interests of which publishing is only a part. Publishing is, indeed, in danger of becoming an international monopoly with serious consequences not only for writers, but for the future of literature. A second great change, which has been strongly influenced by the first, is in the marketing of books. Before the war if you produced a new work of fiction, it would, if accepted, be published and, if the writer were well-known or lucky, reviewed and discreetly advertised. There might be journalistic features in newspapers and magazines and if the book were considered scandalous, as was *The Well of Loneliness*, the consequent furore would keep journalists and readers in a state of profitable indignation for weeks. A new novel was like a boat: the frail craft would be launched and left to breast the waves of public taste and the winds of critical acclaim or disdain either to sink or swim, without much help from the publisher. Some publishers, indeed, seemed to consider their imprint so prestigious that writers were fortunate to be published by them; it would be unreasonable for the author to expect his publisher actively to sell the book or to concern himself overmuch with such sordid commercial concerns as sales figures or promotion.

Nowadays a new novel, particularly one which looks as if it has a chance of getting on to a national or international bestseller list, is promoted, packaged and sold like a new perfume. In this process the author is expected to take an active part, notably through author tours. To some this is a pleasure, to others an ordeal, while some few resolutely decline to participate. How far this hinders their sales is, I think, open to question. I can never find any reliable research on the profitability of author tours but, as publishers are still prepared to spend thousands of pounds arranging them, they must consider the time and effort worthwhile.

Sometimes my family and friends say to me before a major tour, 'Why do you do it? Surely you don't need to?' Part of the answer, I think, is my always feeble wish to be accommodating, particularly as I have a personal affection for my publishers both at home and in the USA. There is also the assurance that I shall travel in extreme comfort, be looked after all the way, shall meet friends from previous tours and probably enjoy new experiences. But I think the chief reason is the pleasure of meeting my readers face-to-face. Readers of crime fiction are remarkably loyal, knowledgeable and enthusiastic. I have never faced an audience before a signing without a sense of being among personal friends.

I have learned now to pace myself; I know, too, what is and what is not possible. A few years ago I made it plain that I wanted the minimum of socializing on tour; indeed, that what I liked best was to go back to my hotel at the end of the day, have room service and relax. This was difficult for the hospitable Americans to understand. They hated the thought that their author was spending the evening alone. But it really was impossible to cope with a day of publicity and follow it with a party in which the same questions – 'Where do you get your ideas? When did you know you wanted to be a writer? Do you use a word-processor?' – are reiterated over the wine or the dinner table.

I also early laid it down that I only wanted two press interviews at a time. Ten or so years ago I was on my USA tour in San Francisco when I had one press interview from 9 to 10, another from 10 to 11, and the third from 11 to 12. Each journalist had brought a tape recorder to place between us and what I endured was three hours of continuous interrogation. Until that experience I had always in my naïvety found it difficult to understand why suspects questioned by the police confessed when they were innocent. I now know how psychologically distressing, indeed traumatic, interrogation can be. But at least, had I been a police suspect it is doubtful whether the questioning would have lasted for three virtually uninterrupted hours. So now press interviews are interspersed with television or radio. I find the last two much easier, indeed often enjoyable. The other person is actively participating in the discussion and we share a joint wish to make the broadcast or programme interesting to the viewer or listener and satisfying for ourselves.

I have seen great cities which I would not otherwise have visited, have received much generosity and kindness and have shared much laughter. I imagine that I shall continue to undertake major writer tours as long as I continue to write and have the strength. But this method of selling books, promoting the writer rather as if he or she were a pop star, seems a curious, even a farcical, concomitance. I note that today a new writer who is young and physically attractive starts with a considerable initial advantage. He or she will be a hit on the publicity trail; the image is promotable and acceptable. There is, too, a curious development of which *Swan*, a novel supposedly written by the model Naomi Campbell, is an example. We live in an age which, despite its apparent sophistication and its technological advancement, is remarkable for silliness and gullibility. What can be the possible interest of reading a book reputedly written by Naomi Campbell unless she has in fact written it?

Soon we shall get to the stage where a bestseller will be written by a computer with all the necessary ingredients of sex and violence fed into the machine. The publisher will then find a young man or woman with a fashionable face, appropriate body measurements, and a sensational emotional and sexual life, and place his or her name on the title page. I suppose the book could then be sold on the Internet and would no doubt cause a literary sensation.

In the meantime there still seems to be considerable interest in an elderly grandmother who writes traditional English detective fiction. And so I embark tomorrow on the major American tour, which will take me to twelve cities in nineteen days.

MONDAY, 19TH JANUARY

I arrived in Dallas yesterday from Pittsburgh, am here for two nights, and shall leave on Tuesday for Houston. I am still in good health and spirits after ten hectic days. I arrived in Boston on 9th January and then continued to New York, Washington, Chicago, Dayton and Pittsburgh. I have seen little of any of these cities, except for the interiors of television and radio studios, bookshops, and the venues for talks and lectures. But all the experiences have been good so far, with large and enthusiastic audiences, sometimes numbering as many as 400. This is less a tribute to my drawing power or popularity than an indication of cultural differences between our two nations. Even if it were rumoured that Graham Greene had risen from the dead, I doubt whether we would get audiences of this size in England to listen to a writer.

I was glad Knopf included Dayton in the tour. Roz Young more than fulfilled her promise; my signing and talk at Books and Company was more like being welcomed home after a long absence than a first visit, and it was interesting to spend the night at a hotel which wasn't five-star and where I could meet and eat with a cross-section of Americans.

It is a truism to say that Texas is large, but it is this immensity, the sense of space stretching out, flat, featureless, limitless, sky and land indistinguishable, which strikes me every time I travel in the state, inducing a faint agoraphobia. I feel the absence of water, of sea or lake or river, like a parched throat. The Dallas skyline could be almost any American city. Approaching from the airport, the roads curve on their high T-shaped struts of concrete. The exit signs point to different communities, sometimes disconcertingly called cities. Most of these seem to have grown up, or rather been spontaneously brought into being, since my last visit. The city itself, indeed, seems the creation of real estate; nothing here is huddled together, space is there for the taking. But how could one live in any of these communities without a car? Unable to drive, for me it would be too like living in an open prison with fellow inmates of the same class, background and income; every physical need catered for admirably and often with imagination but in an intimacy more circumscribed than solitary confinement.

The hotel had a notice to say that it was illegal to bring in concealed weapons. Does this mean that loaded guns held at the ready are acceptable? An interview in the morning with a journalist from the

Dallas Morning News was loosely based on a former *Vanity Fair* interview which has surfaced often during this tour. The interviewer, like many others, asked about Princess Diana. Why wouldn't the Queen grieve? I was tempted to point out that, had I been the Queen, my grieving, though sincere, would not have been excessive. Instead I said that not everyone showed grief by pinning teddy-bears and flowers to the railings of public parks. We then went on for some reason to talk about Myra Hindley. Had I visited her in prison? No. Why not? I replied that, since there was nothing I needed to say to her, or presumably she to me, and nothing I could usefully do for her, a visit would be too much like morbid voyeurism.

I had my hair washed and set at a salon opposite the hotel in a high complex of shops with a centre courtyard with water and trees, balconies and seats set out where shoppers could rest in comfort. I found it cool and pleasant. In the salon a young stylist was trimming the beard of an older customer, kneeling in front of him like a supplicant and delicately parting, combing and snipping the silken hairs of the long beard with a concentrated, almost loving dedication. I hadn't seen this done before.

WEDNESDAY, 28TH JANUARY

I am writing this on the BA flight on my way home from Miami. The captain promised a relatively smooth flight, but this was optimistic and my wine slopped over the pristine tablecloth as soon as it was served. I like the redesigned first-class cabin of British Airways. I am sitting, as I did on my way out, in my own capsule, my window seat isolated from the rest of the cabin by a curved partition with a panel of buttons to my left to operate the various seat positions. This I find more convenient than the previous system of having them in the armrests where I could never comfortably reach them when wearing a seat-belt, nor easily identify which button was which. The main advantage of the redesigned seat is that one can lie flat and attempt to sleep. One button when pressed elongates the seat into a bed and each passenger is provided with a duvet and pillow. At least one male passenger changed early into his pyjamas and settled down dinnerless for the night. This morning the cabin, with passengers neatly folding their duvets, had the appearance of a small and exceptionally luxurious school or army dormitory. I had no appetite for breakfast, but early morning tea arrived on a small tray with elegant teapot and jug. First-class travel, provided one hasn't to pay for it oneself, is the most insidiously addictive of life's luxuries.

My hotel in Miami, the Biltmore, was the largest and most impressive at which I had stayed. I love five-star American hotels, not because of the luxury, but because they are so wonderfully efficient and anonymous. One is a transient among other transients. Nothing is here of previous visitors and I shall leave behind nothing of myself. To return to the room after an absence is to find everything immaculate as if the absolving hands of the chambermaid have smoothed away more than the detritus of the past day. I think I could write in such a place. On tour, however, there is hardly time even to appreciate the comfort. But I shall remember breakfast at the Biltmore. I ate it in warm sunshine in the courtyard under a palm tree and beside the largest hotel swimming pool in the United States; each breakfast was separately cooked in an open-air kitchen, the smell of bacon over-laying the warm scent of flowers and water.

The last day of the tour in Miami was the only one on which there was spare time. My minder took me to see Miami Beach. A thin rain was falling and a sluggish tide crept wearily over the deserted and pitted sand. Versace's house, the gates locked, looked elegant and incongruous among the sugar-candy colours of the innumerable hotels. For someone whose ideal of a day at the sea is a secluded and empty cove, Miami in high season must be Hell-on-Sea. From there we were driven to the botanical gardens. The weather had by then improved and we enjoyed a quiet walk under the trees and by the lakes.

There was still some time to spare before leaving for the airport, so my last event in the States was a visit to a cinema to see *Titanic*, something I could just as well have done back home. It is over-long but the special effects are certainly memorable and will no doubt achieve an Oscar. I didn't believe in the young lovers and was irritated by the usual Hollywood anti-British bias. The Englishmen all wore evening dress to demonstrate their upper-class unfeeling arrogance, even on the last night of the voyage, when they would not have changed for dinner, while the Irish were happy innocents dancing their jigs below deck. One of the crew, who in real-life had behaved impeccably, was shown as a murdering coward, which I thought unforgivable. The young hero, Leonardo di Caprio, clung to the wreckage on which Kate Winslett was elegantly lying to deliver a poignant valedictory speech before sinking slowly out of sight. I felt the energy required for this could have been better spent in swimming to a similar piece of wreckage and keeping himself alive. But I have no doubt the film will be an immense success with adolescent girls all over the world. It was an odd way of spending my last evening.

Soon we shall prepare for landing and the tour will finally be over. It has been far less exhausting than I feared, except for the days in New York and Washington. I enjoyed the company of the three publicists from Knopf who accompanied me – Sophie, Jill and Gabriella – all enthusiastic, intelligent and highly capable. I could not have been better looked after.

THURSDAY, 29TH JANUARY

Joanna from Faber telephoned yesterday to discuss the cover for the trade paperback of *A Certain Justice* and we talked about the new Ted Hughes collection of poems, *Birthday Letters*. She promised to send a copy and it arrived this morning. It was impossible not to begin reading at once and just as impossible to stop once I'd begun. Inevitably one's response to the poems is influenced by the joint tragedies; how could it be otherwise? I have always felt great sympathy for Ted Hughes and huge respect for the dignified silence with which he has endured years of calumny. No woman who is the mother of young children and kills herself can be sane, and this degree of mental pain has its roots far deeper than the imperfections of a marriage. Equally no one who has never had to live with a partner who is mentally ill can possibly understand what this means. Two people are in separate hells, but each intensifies the other. Those who have not experienced this contaminating misery should keep silent.

But now Ted Hughes's thirty-five years of silence are broken. I have never found him an easy poet, but then why should he be? Poetry is like religion: sometimes the vision is immediate and almost frightening in its intensity; sometimes it is reached with difficulty, giving intimations only, and those confused and partial. Here the verse, unimpeded by a jumble of feral imagery, flows like a clear strong stream bearing the weight of pity, terror and regret. The poems are too honest to read as an attempt at justification. They may be a means of exorcism. Certainly they are a tribute of love.

FEBRUARY

I looked forward to today as I do to any day on which I am to see a daughter or a grandchild. I was invited to deliver a lecture to the Cambridge Union on 'Fiction: Has it a Future?' and arranged in the morning to have lunch with Beatrice, to see her room at college and then, after the lecture, to spend the night with Clare.

It has been a bright day but exceedingly cold. There is something about the coldness of Cambridge that is peculiarly raw and I wished I'd been warmer clad. However, I bought a second scarf on my walk from the centre of the city to Trinity, and this helped. Beatrice took me to lunch at a restaurant specializing in pasta, and then I saw and admired her room and rested on her bed while she did some quiet reading before going to a lecture. When she returned she and a fellow student walked me to the Union, where the officers of the Union took me to dinner before the talk.

Both my young escorts are reading history and they asked me what it was like living in Cambridge during the war, and why was it, did I think, that my generation had been so dilatory and so reluctant to stand up to Hitler? I explained that this was very largely the result of the First World War. When my parents talked about the past, they seemed always to be dwelling on the war and on the destruction of a whole generation of young men. My generation was born under a pall of inarticulate grieving. One of my earliest Ludlow memories is of a terraced house with a photograph of a fresh-faced private, himself hardly more than a child, in the window between small Union Jacks. It was one of many such humble and poignant shrines. Then later we read the poets of the Great War, Wilfred Owen, Siegfried Sassoon, Isaac Rosenberg, saw the films, particularly *All Quiet on the Western Front*, and read the war novels. We grew up with the conviction that war in its horror, its brutality and its degradation was the greatest calamity possible and must at all costs be avoided. The words 'never again', spoken or unspoken, were ever-present.

My father, who fought in the 1914–18 war, could never really believe that Europe could allow it to happen again, not even when, on 3rd September 1939, war was declared. And even if we were to 'stand up to Hitler' – a euphemism for going to war – when and how would that be possible? We had disarmed. Even if the mothers of England had been happy to see their sons slaughtered in the defence of the Rhineland or Czechoslovakia, the men and the money weren't there. In the end we realized, as did Europe, that the confrontation was inevitable and began to re-arm. We went to war with none of the patriotic fervour or enthusiasm of 1914, but with the grim realization that this war was both inevitable and just, and would have to be seen through.

The young men thought it wrong to judge the past by the standards of the present and they are of course right. No doubt in a hundred years' time our descendants will marvel that we were able to watch the death by starvation or the massacre of thousands on our television screens and yet did nothing to stop it. Yet what could we have done about Rwanda? Admittedly, given sufficient will, an army could have been sent to stop the killings; but what would follow? Could we permanently occupy a country and rule it? Stopping fighting is one thing; effecting reconciliation between tribes which have been hating each other for generations is less easy. I doubt whether it can ever be achieved by the intervention of a foreign power.

We talked about what it was like to live in Cambridge in the early days of the war. I can recall a series of sounds and images: the disciplined tramp of young feet as companies of airmen in training marched through the streets with flashes in their caps; the city crowded with unfamiliar people – evacuated civil servants, academics from other universities, refugees; dancing at the McGrath Ballroom with young airmen from the East Anglian fighter and bomber stations in the knowledge that the boy I danced with one Saturday might not be there the following week. His friends would just say 'he couldn't come'. I wouldn't ask why, partly because I knew and partly because they were not there to remember death.

A particular memory is of going to work one morning at the Ministry of Food to find the lawn of Christ's College completely covered with sleeping and exhausted soldiers, gaunt-faced and mudstained and still in their battledress. They were part of the remnant of the Dunkirk evacuation. I'll never know how and by what means they found themselves apparently dumped at this incongruous staging post.

Our entertainment came from the wireless and from films. The war years produced some memorable films: *Stagecoach*, *Gone with the Wind*, *The Wizard of Oz* and *Of Mice and Men* all appeared in 1939. Queues would lengthen outside the cinemas while we waited for what we called 'the big picture' to end. The performance was continuous and as the couples came out, the doorman would call 'four one-and-six-pennies', and the queue would shuffle forward. The British film industry geared itself for the propaganda war. Some early films I saw, in their banality, probably provided more comfort to the enemy than encouragement for us, but Carol Reed's *The Way Ahead* and *This Happy Breed*, and Laurence Olivier's *Henry V* remain in the memory. I began for the first time to watch French films with Connor: *Les Enfants du Paradis*, *Le Jour se Lève*. During the war cinema was at its most creative, its most influential and its most entertaining. I have seldom gone to the cinema since with the same anticipatory pleasure.

We were comparatively safe in Cambridge. A few inadvertent bombs were dropped and there were casualties but the main thrust of the war was elsewhere. I remember climbing the Gog Magog Hills and seeing the distant red glare of the sky where London was burning, remember, too, hearing our heavy bombers leaving on their raids, seeming to lift themselves grunting into the air. There is one persistent and vivid memory. I had spent an afternoon with an elderly friend of my mother's, visiting a relation of hers who lived in a distant village. We were returning to Cambridge by bus in the darkness when the Germans raided the East Anglian airfields. We rumbled slowly on between the low hedges and the flat landscape, hearing the crash of distant bombs and ringed by fire. It reminded me of the burning of stubble after the harvest. The blacked-out bus didn't stop – what would have been the point? – but I remember that we all sat in absolute silence. It wasn't the silence of fear, more the weariness of the journey and a resigned acceptance. My elderly companion slept, slumped against me. The raids weren't close enough for there to be real danger, but I had a sensation of grinding onward inexorably through a deserted landscape that had become alien and surreal. The sights and sounds of Cambridge at war come back clearly, but the emotion is more elusive. I have no recollection of fear – not then – or, I think, of any apprehension that the war would be lost. I suppose I felt healthy, alive, optimistic, eager for life; in other words, I felt young.

SUNDAY, 8TH FEBRUARY

This was a golden day with weather to match: sunny, even warm, and with a clear blue sky. Jane and Peter arrived shortly after ten and we took a hurried glance at the papers before setting out for our walk. We went to Holland Park, wended our way down the most agreeable streets north of Kensington Library, then through to Hyde Park and as far as Watt's statue of energy. I had taken some bread with me and on our return we threw pellets to the seagulls which swooped and shrieked, snatching the bread on the wing. Some of the people strolling in the sunshine round the pond must have been carrying their weight of unhappiness, but the air seemed to sing with pleasure. The old men were racing their model boats, the children chasing the pigeons, others sitting in the sunshine reading their books, the lovers strolling hand-in-hand.

We walked round the sunken garden at the Palace, now in its winter decrepitude but bringing back memories of tulips and the scents of high summer. Peter hadn't visited it before. Walking out over the grass I hoped again that the proposed Princess Diana Memorial Garden would not be built here. There is already the sunken garden, and the great stretch of green is so important – and not only to the residents of Kensington walking their dogs. Surely some more appropriate place can be found.

Afterwards we went back to Holland Park and had an early lunch at the Belvedere; a good meal eaten in pleasant surroundings and in peace before the usual Sunday lunchtime rush. The plan was then to go on by car to the Tate. Jane demurred at first, feeling tired, but we persuaded her, after which she admitted to the prospect of pleasure.

The Tate was busy, as it always is on a Sunday afternoon, but not disagreeably so. We visited one of my favourite pictures, William Dyce's *Pegwell Bay*. I like Victorian painting, including genre painting, and this has always appealed to me largely, I suppose, because it's a seascape and I love the contrast of the gaunt, dark, almost ageless cliffs and the Victorian figures in the foreground. But for so peaceful and innocent a view I find it a disturbing picture, one which always induces in me the same gentle melancholy. The painter stands underneath the cliffs looking up at the faintly discernible comet streaking across the sky, but the women are preoccupied in collecting shells, almost as if they were totally detached from the beauty around them and oblivious to the wonder in the sky. One knows that the shells would later be used to decorate boxes or photograph frames, one of the ways in which the underemployed middle-class Victorian woman managed to pass her time. The picture seems to speak of the transience and pointlessness of human life, of the brief span of our days measured against the intensity of space and time. But I love it and wish I had it on my walls.

Jane wanted to see the Bacons, so Peter and I walked through the Turner galleries. I know that Turner is a great painter – but I don't respond to him as I do to lesser geniuses. Peter and Jane drove straight home from the gallery after dropping me in Holland Park Avenue. It has been one of those days which will remain in memory, one more to be carefully shored up against ruin.

THURSDAY, 12TH FEBRUARY

I went at 2 o'clock to Bush House to discuss on the BBC World Service *Thrones, Dominations*, Jill Paton Walsh's completion of an unfinished novel by Dorothy L. Sayers. Our interviewer was Harriett Gilbert. I had been sent the six chapters some time ago and asked whether I would like to complete the novel, but I didn't think it could satisfactorily be done. The fragment, obviously very much a first draft, was about 40,000 words long and DLS was clearly less concerned with plotting a detective story than with the preoccupation previously dealt with in *Gaudy Night*: how does a woman with both heart and brain reconcile the emotional and sexual side of her nature with her intellect?

She certainly never managed to do this satisfactorily herself. It is interesting how often unintelligent, even stupid, women manage their emotional lives more satisfactorily than do their cleverer sisters. When Harriet Vane says in *Gaudy Night* that the reason she values the life of the mind is because this is the only part of her life she hasn't made a mess of, she is obviously speaking for her author. DLS was made deeply unhappy, even distraught, by her unconsummated love affair with John Cournos, subsequently found sexual satisfaction but no commitment in the arms of a married philanderer, and finally married a divorced man who resented her fame and sank into alcoholic bad temper. No wonder she distrusted the emotions. For Dorothy L. Sayers, even her religion was a matter of intellectual assent to dogma, not an emotional response to a personal God.

Jill Paton Walsh, an admirer both of Sayers and of Lord Peter, has managed to reflect the Sayers style, remain true to the proposed theme and provide a detective story very much in the mode of the 1930s. She has not incorporated the whole of the Sayers draft, wisely excluding the more embarrassing passages. I easily detected the vital clue and had little doubt about the identity of the murderer but this, too, made the book typical of its age. I doubt whether anyone could have done it better.

Afterwards I went to the House to listen to the second reading of the Crime and Punishment Bill and two speeches on the abolition of *doli incapax*, the requirement of courts to be satisfied that children accused of criminal acts know that the acts are seriously wrong, not merely childish bad behaviour. I made a brief and not particularly relevant intervention in which I recounted an incident I saw in a juvenile court. An agreeable small delinquent with the face of a roguish angel and attired in a multi-striped hand-knitted pullover had been accused of letting off an airgun in a supermarket. His response to the question whether he knew it was wrong – 'I knew it was against the law, but I didn't know it was wrong' – provided a nice problem of law for the juvenile justices.

SATURDAY, 14TH FEBRUARY

Yesterday I had dinner at the Dorchester with Rosemary Herbert, the journalist from Boston whom I first met when she interviewed me about twenty years ago and who has become something of an expert on crime writing. Rosemary is at present Editor-in-Chief of a compendium of crime writing to be published by Oxford University Press. She is anxious for me to co-operate with an anthology of the best crime short stories in the last hundred years, to be published at the Millennium. The suggestion is that I write the foreword and introductions to the selected stories. I said I would not wish to be published by a publisher other than Faber and suggested that she provide a written proposal which I could consider, and if necessary discuss.

I am not a natural collaborator and I suspect that few novelists are. A novel is essentially the product of an individual voice and a single concentrated mind. Drama can be collaborative and textbooks frequently are, but I can think of no major work of fiction written by more than one author. Canaletto might ask an apprentice to paint in an inch or two of waves, but I can't imagine Dickens, however hard pressed, handing over a synopsis to a pupil and asking him to help out with some of the duller chapters.

A car called this morning to drive me to Birmingham to take part in the BBC quiz programme *Call my Bluff*. Our captain was Alan Coren and my fellow panellist the actor Michael Maloney. On the other side were Kate Adie, Sandi Toksvig and Robert Daws. I can remember when Frank Muir sat on one side against Patrick Campbell, now alas both dead. I am told that they took the game with deadly seriousness and both hated to lose. Luckily our captain was less fanatical, but I was surprised how glad I was not to have made a fool of myself. The final score for both games was a draw of three points each.

The game was recorded at the International Convention Centre and I was astounded how much the centre of Birmingham has changed for the better. I remember going to my father-in-law's funeral some fifteen years ago and walking out of Birmingham station to take a look at the city while waiting for my connection. The Bull Ring appalled me: a concrete monstrosity in which only motorists, criminals and psychopaths could feel at home. It is still in place, but I believe the city fathers plan to demolish it. In contrast, the development by the canal is impressive and obviously designed for human beings. Old brick buildings have been restored and there are outdoor cafés and walkways by the canal. Gradually some cities are putting right the follies of the 1960s.

SUNDAY, 22ND FEBRUARY

At Southwold with Lyn and Clare. Yesterday was dull and with intermittent rain but still warm. Clare and I went to the small antique shop in the High Street to buy her birthday present. She chose an enchanting Victorian souvenir of Cambridge, a little circular wooden inkstand with a glass pot and a coloured plaque of King's College Chapel, together with two very heavy square-cut glass inkstands. I found another brown Doulton jug for the kitchen shelf. We had a celebration dinner at the Swan and then went back to the house to review the rough-cut video of *A Certain Justice*.

This was more enjoyable and did less violence to the story than I had feared. The fact remains that it is impossible adequately to adapt a long and complex novel for the small screen in three episodes. Inspector Piers Tarrant has been dropped, with the somewhat risible effect that Dalgliesh and Kate Miskin appear to be the only police officers on the job, evoking the comment from Clare that Scotland Yard was obviously economizing on manpower. This impression is reinforced by the number of interviews which Dalgliesh conducts, not at headquarters, but at any convenient place where he happens to be. But the beginning is very effective, a clever piece of adaptation, and the acting good throughout.

At first I thought that the actress playing Octavia, Venetia's daughter, was too pretty, but she conveyed an impression of vulnerability combined with obstinacy which is effective, and the young man playing the psychopath – an extremely difficult part – is convincing. The trial scene is well done (court scenes seldom fail on television), but the actress playing Venetia moves in court to demonstrate how far a television set is from the witness. I had learned during research that barristers do not move in court and that she would have asked a solicitor to do this for her. As it is, every barrister will note the mistake. Another anomaly is the introduction of Venetia's memorial service. The timescale of the novel is short; indeed the plot depends on this; and in the book there hasn't even been time for the inquest, let alone a cremation and memorial service. But I can see a reason for introducing it. Dalgliesh is present, as are all the barrister suspects, and the camera can range from face to face with the unspoken question: Is this the one? The scene is not true to the book, but if I mildly protest I am sure I shall be met with the usual excuse: it makes good television. On the whole, though, I think this will be regarded as one of the more successful adaptations.

I awoke today to beautiful spring weather. Lyn and I walked round the dunes to Walberswick and met Clare, who had taken the path across the common, at the Harbour Inn. It didn't open for coffee until 12, so we didn't wait but walked back on the narrow path fringing the road and the water meadows and had a drink at the Lord Nelson. We left as darkness fell and I spent the night with Lyn and Clare in Cambridge.

MONDAY, 23RD FEBRUARY

The Prime Minister has exhorted us to show a little more enthusiasm for the Millennium Dome, which he has prophesied will be the envy of the world. This I rather doubt, but I imagine that the Dome Experience will be some kind of repetition of the Diana Experience; once it becomes fashionable to make one's pilgrimage, everyone will want to join in. It can't be allowed to be a failure and if enough money is spent on promotion, it won't be. Perhaps the country will be gripped by Dome mania.

I don't in the least object to a pleasure dome providing a happy day out for all the family, but I do feel antagonistic to the idea that this will be some great cultural experience. If I want to immerse myself in the history of England I have the National Portrait Gallery as well as the V&A and the British Museum, and any passion for scientific achievement can be met by the National Science Museum. For those who want to experience religious emotion, our country's churches, cathedrals and all other places of worship offer a more appropriate place than the spiritual area of the Dome.

I suppose what I most dislike about it is the idea of spending £750 million on a building without first knowing what its purpose will be. If we are celebrating 2,000 years of recorded time, surely something more permanent could have been erected, preferably a modern theatre for opera and dance. Visitors could come up by river – a quarter of the cost of the Dome could subsidize river boats – and there could be restaurants and riverside gardens. Then the Royal Opera House, suitably renovated and with its facilities updated, could be used for smaller operas. I suggested this when I was a member of the Arts Council but I can't remember that it was received with particular enthusiasm.

Hubris has inspired me to celebrate the Dome with a Dome Pome. This is likely to be the only verse included in my diary, which is just as well:

> O Dome gigantic, Dome immense
> Built in defiance of common sense.
> Wide-stretching Dome, O Dome sublime!
> Memorial to recorded time
> How justified will hubris be
> When all the world bows down to thee.
> When millions in awe will scan
> This miracle of modern man.
> For though its shape holds no surprise

There's no denying it has size.
In Greece they'll grit their teeth and foam
In envy of our Wonder Dome,
And crowds will riot in Peru
Demanding that they have one too.
They'll groan from Chad to Montserrat
'How come we never thought of that?'
Italians will weep and swear
'St Peter's dome cannot compare,
Nor all the monuments in Rome
Surpass Great Britain's Wonder Dome.'
And Frenchmen soured with Gallic pride
Will hardly bear to look inside,
The USA will greatly rue it
To think that only Brits could do it,
While millions join the Greenwich queue
From Togoland to Timbuktu.
And God Himself is stricken dumb
To see how clever we've become.

MARCH

I took the 7.30 a.m. bus from Gloucester Green, Oxford, expecting that the M40 would be very busy and the journey take far more than the usual hour. However, the road was clear and I got home in fine style. I made a fuss of Polly-Hodge and fed her, and then took the bus to Marble Arch, walked down Park Lane and joined the Countryside March as it entered Hyde Park. Park Lane was closed, and it was strange to have the road almost entirely to myself. I walked through the barriers to join the marchers and immediately found myself hailed by Margaret Clayton, who was my last Assistant Secretary when I worked at the Home Office. She had retired early and was now working part-time for six days a week and obviously happy. She moved quickly on to join her friends before the march ended on the road just north of the Albert Memorial.

A large barrier slung across the path with the word 'Finish' on it was a slight anticlimax, but I could understand why the organizers had decided against speeches. The marchers are united in their support of the countryside and those who live and work in it, but I doubt whether large landowners and small tenant farmers have a great deal in common, or that all the marchers care greatly about fox-hunting. I wouldn't wish to hunt myself; this is mainly because, even if I were young, strong and able to ride, it wouldn't seem to me an activity worth risking my neck for. But I am sure the fox suffers less from the hounds' jaws at the end of a hunt than by shooting or the horror of poisoning, and it seems irrational to ban hunting while permitting fishing or tolerating the conditions under which our eggs are produced.

It was a wonderfully diverse group of people: a tall corduroy-suited elderly man who looked like the stage stereotype of an irascible colonel striding along alone, groups of the young chatting or singing as they walked, middle-aged ladies who were obviously stalwart

162

upholders of the WI, and agricultural workers who marched with a kind of rugged determination in support of their livelihoods. No one dropped litter.

My walk home along the Bayswater Road was made interesting by the pictures on the park railings. They are an odd mixture. Some of the water-colours, particularly of flowers, have an attractive sponta-neity and freshness and in all I saw three pictures which I would have been reasonably happy to see on my walls. But most are awful, although the non-representational art didn't seem worse than some examples I've seen in prestigious galleries. I suppose it's a matter of taste. I liked the little autobiographies and critical notes and extracts from magazines which are pinned up by some of the paintings. Obviously those painters are managing to make a living, and good luck to them. I would much rather buy a picture from these railings than a reproduction. I did in fact find a very agreeable scene of Dover Cliffs some years ago which I still enjoy.

St David's Day always reminds me of my first day at the Home Office. I was being taken on the usual short induction tour of departments and had arrived in the Home Secretary's private office. James Callaghan was Home Secretary at the time and the outer office was piled high with daffodils sent to him by his constituents. The office was busy and it was hard to reconcile this controlled activity with the overwhelming smell of spring flowers. Thus, incongruously, I began the last stage of my working life as a bureaucrat.

I learned early to cope with parliamentary questions, those regular minor irritants which fell on to the desk in the form of lurid yellow folders. I had to provide background notes about the MP and his preoccupations and the possible reason for the question, provide an answer and then follow up with pages of notes for supplementaries. This was the most difficult part of the exercise. The object was to ensure that the Secretary of State or Minister was never left without a readily accessible answer to any supplementary question that the Member might choose to ask. Apart from the Forensic Science Service and Forensic Pathologists, I was also given responsibility for police vehicles. When I protested I couldn't even drive, my Assistant Secretary said that made me eminently suitable for the task.

By chance my first PQ was from an MP who asked for details of every make of vehicle held by all the police forces in England and Wales. The draft reply I put up said this information would be of no possible public use. My Assistant Secretary gently pointed out that there was a form of words to provide for questions where the cost of obtaining the information would be disproportionate to its use, but that I hadn't hit on it.

I received no period of formal training but occasional miscellaneous advice, the most important being never to use a green biro, since green was the prerogative of Sir Philip Allen, the head of the office.

Despite some initial stress, I enjoyed my time at the Home Office. It is a department where ministers' reputations are more easily lost than gained. The department is inured to receiving a critical press, being seen as draconian, illiberal and dilatory, but I left with a respect for the integrity and intelligence of the senior officers with whom I worked.

It was while I was in the Police Department that I wrote my first work of non-fiction, in co-operation with the Assistant Secretary, Tom Critchley. *The Maul and the Pear Tree* (published in 1971) deals with a series of notorious and brutal murders in Wapping in 1811, referred to usually as the Ratcliffe Highway Murders. The first victims were twenty-four-year-old Timothy Marr, a linen draper on the Highway, his wife Celia, their three-and-a-half-month-old baby son Timothy, and their apprentice boy, James Gowen. It was a Saturday, 7th December 1811, and the shop remained open until eight. A little before midnight, Timothy Marr called to his servant girl, Margaret Jewell, gave her a pound and sent her out to pay the baker's bill and to buy some oysters. She found the baker's shop closed, went to another place to try to buy the oysters but again was unsuccessful. After about twenty minutes she returned home to find the door shut tightly against her and the shop in darkness. Thinking that the family might have gone to bed, she pulled the bell, the jangling seeming unnaturally loud in the quiet street. And listening, she heard a sound that gave her the comforting assurance that Marr or his wife would soon be opening the door. There was a soft tread of footsteps on the stairs. But no one came. The footsteps ceased and again there was silence.

The clanging of the bell and the girl kicking the door aroused the interest of a night watchman and then the neighbour, John Murray. He told the watchman to continue pulling hard at the bell and he would go into his back yard and see if he could rouse the family from the back of the house. The back door was open and he made his way inside by a light from a candle burning on the landing of the first floor.

In the shop he found the first body, the apprentice boy James Gowen, with the bones of his face shattered by blow after blow. With a groan, Murray stumbled towards the door and found his path blocked by the body of Mrs Marr, blood still draining from her battered head. Murray opened the front door and screamed his news incoherently, 'Murder! Murder!' and the small crowd, swollen by the arrival of neighbours, pressed into the shop. The air was loud with groans and cries. They found the body of the child still in its cradle, the side of its mouth laid open with a blow, the left side of the face battered and the throat slit so that the head was almost severed from the body. And behind the counter, lying face downwards, was the body of Timothy Marr.

But that wasn't the end of horror. Twelve days later, and in the next parish, a blameless middle-aged publican, Mr Williamson of the King's Arms in New Gavel Lane, Shadwell, his wife and their maidservant were murdered with equal brutality.

The crimes provoked nationwide panic. The government offered an unprecedented reward for the conviction of the murderers, while there was a vigorous and persistent demand for the reform of the police. The Prime Minister himself speculated on the crimes in the House of Commons while Sheridan made a characteristically witty and trenchant attack on the incompetence of the investigation. De Quincey was powerfully interested in the murders and years later they inspired his essay on 'Murder Considered as One of the Fine Arts'.

Both Tom and I were fascinated by the setting as we were by the investigation of the crime. In 1811 the Port of London was the greatest port in the world. Every year 13,000 vessels from all parts of the world dropped anchor. The great vessels of the East India Company, bulky and formidable as men-of-war, bearing cargoes of tea, drugs, muslin, calicoes, spices and indigo, colliers from Newcastle, whalers from Greenland, coastal vessels, packets, brigs, lighters, barges, ferries and dinghies. The parishioners of Wapping lived their lives against a constant accompaniment of river sounds. It was from the bustling trade of the river that nearly all the inhabitants, rich and poor, drew their life: stevedores, watermen, suppliers of rope and tackle, ships' bakers, marine store dealers, instrument makers, boat builders, laundresses who lived by taking in the sailors' washing, carpenters to repair the ships, rat catchers and the keepers of cheap houses where the seamen lodged.

What was fascinating to me was the investigation. It was extraordinarily incompetent. The various authorities – the river police, the night watchmen, the magistrates of Shadwell and those of Wapping – were more concerned to guard their own reputations and functions than to co-operate effectively. The end of the case was as macabre as the beginning. A young seaman, John Williams, was arrested for the crime but was found dead in prison, apparently by his own hand. His decaying corpse was paraded through the streets of East London to be buried at a crossroads with a stake through its heart. This was an act of public vengeance unique in the history of English criminal law.

The case came to Tom Critchley's attention when he was writing his history of the police in England and Wales, but when he mentioned it to me I remembered that I had read an account in the *Newgate Calendar* and had been very far from convinced of the guilt of John Williams. Accordingly, we sent for as many papers as we could find and started our investigations, arriving at a conclusion which cannot now possibly be proved but which seems far more logical and credible than Williams's guilt. His conviction was certainly expedient. There was a tacit agreement among the authorities that the Ratcliffe Highway affair should be allowed to fade from the public mind. Whether Williams was an accomplice, whether he died by his own hand or was murdered by those who wanted to ensure their own safety, it seems likely that the body which was buried with ignominy at the crossroads of St George's Turnpike was the body of an eighth victim.

MONDAY, 2ND MARCH

The Committee of Management of the Whitbread Literary Awards met at 12 o'clock in Chiswell Street. I was full of a sensible resolution to take the Tube from Notting Hill Gate to the Barbican rather than get embroiled in traffic, but then decided against it and took a cab. I was glad I did when the cabbie drove into the park between tossing daffodils and bright patches of purple crocuses. On the Mall fortress the matted creeper, like a brown tufted rug, was falling from the wall in great swathes.

After the working lunch I travelled from the Barbican to

Westminster and arrived in the House of Lords at about 3.30 for the debate on the report stage of the Teaching and Higher Education Bill. We won a victory on Amendment 50, moved by Emily Blatch, to restore grants, and again on the Amendment providing that English students at Scottish universities shall not be required to pay for the fourth year. At present only Scottish students and those from overseas are exempt. Tessa Blackstone argued that the first year at Scottish universities is the equivalent of an A-level year in the rest of the UK, and that it is reasonable, therefore, for students other than those educated in Scotland to enter at the second year and complete their degree in three years. But it is unjust and, indeed, ridiculous that a student at Edinburgh University who lives in Belfast will pay £4,000 for his course and one from Dublin will pay £3,000, one from Manchester will pay for the extra year but the one from Munich gets it free. Both Lords' Amendments will, of course, be lost in the Commons, but at least the Lower House will have to debate it again.

We were less successful in amending Clause 18 of the Bill designed to reduce the powers of the universities. I wanted very much to speak but lost my chance; by the time I had got the words ready, Tessa Blackstone was on her feet to answer the points made in the debate. I shall have to be much quicker if I am to have a chance of asking a supplementary question.

WEDNESDAY, 4TH MARCH

I had my hair done this morning at 9.15 and then went to Goldsmiths' Hall for the W. H. Smith Literary Award ceremony, which was due to begin at half-past twelve. It is, of course, considerably smaller than the Whitbread or the Booker, but it is usually agreeable since I can be sure of seeing friends. The prize was won by Ted Hughes for his translation of Ovid, the third time this book has been a prizewinner. He wasn't able to be present but had written a short speech which Joanna Mackle delivered. I had the publisher John Murray on my left, who proved to be an entertaining luncheon companion. We talked about the poetry of our youth and happily recited together snatches of verse from old favourites, congratulating ourselves that we were at school before the arrival of political correctness.

Children should be exposed to a large variety of verse and should be encouraged to learn their favourites by heart, not the ones thought suitable for them by teachers or parents. I can remember at a seminar I attended on the teaching of English being shown an anthology issued to schools as suitable for teenagers. Not surprisingly, it included Wordsworth's 'Daffodils'. This is a poem essentially for adults. Children do not often lie upon their couch 'in vacant or in pensive mood' or, if they do, are unlikely to be thinking about flowers and are liable to be rapidly booted off the couch by their parents. One of the consolations of old age is the intense pleasure I now get from nature. It seems that in youth I was too busy confronting life and experience to stand still and gaze. I don't doubt that children should be encouraged in this pleasure, but I doubt whether they will learn it from Wordsworth's 'Daffodils'.

John Murray said that he had compiled a small personal anthology of the poems he had learned by heart in youth and would send me a copy.

WEDNESDAY, 11TH MARCH

Yesterday two young women came to interview me for a Norwegian magazine, one to do the actual interview and the other to take photographs. It was difficult to fit them in and I was only able to spare one hour, but inevitably the photography went over time, as it always does.

Then in the afternoon to the House of Lords for a continuation of the Education Bill, which finished its report stage. I stayed until 11.15 p.m., but after that, knowing I had an early start tomorrow, went home, confident that there would in any case be no further divisions.

This morning I caught a train at Liverpool Street station to Colchester, where I was met and taken to speak at a luncheon in aid of the Essex Autistic Society. The other speaker was Barbara Erskine, who writes Gothic novels set in exciting mood-inducing old houses occasionally peopled by a ghost. She lives, apparently, in just such a house herself and her talk after lunch was mostly about ghosts, including the one which haunts her own house.

She had an interested audience. I have seen no convincing evidence that ghosts exist, but most of us would like to believe that one or two may occasionally put in an appearance. Barbara Erskine seemed quite happy with her obviously benign apparition. Ghosts have no place in detective fiction, which is essentially a rational form. I can still experience a *frisson* when I reread M. R. James, particularly his 'Oh, Whistle, and I'll Come to You, My Lad'. The genre, if one can appropriately use that word, is less popular today; Kingsley Amis has written probably the best modern ghost novel with *The Green Man*. But for me the most terrifying ghost story is Henry James's *The Turn of the Screw*.

I first came to this story in adolescence and found it a more disturbing work even than *Dr Jekyll and Mr Hyde* or *The Picture of Dorian Gray*. I remember that, even then, I attempted to apply to it the rationality of detective fiction and conceived the idea that it was the children, Miles and Flora, who were the evil instigators. Perhaps, I reasoned, they had discovered the love affair between Quint and Miss Jessel and were blackmailing these vulnerable subordinates into obeying their every whim, eventually driving Miss Jessel away to suicide. The ghosts appear, not to reclaim the children, but to warn the new governess. I am loath to relinquish my interpretation, but the plot can't really bear the weight of it; nor am I convinced that the governess was a deluded sexually repressed neurotic. If we accept that the narrator is honest, then we must also accept that the governess is sane since he states that he knew her years after the event, that she was his sister's governess and that he considers her to be the most agreeable woman he had ever known in that position. I think we must also accept that the housekeeper, Mrs Grose, is a reliable witness and that she disliked Quint and saw him as evil. But were the ghosts genuine apparitions or the product of the governess's overwrought imagination? I think we must accept that they were more than a morbid preoccupation with Quint since she sees him on the roof of the house before she knows from Mrs Grose of his existence.

For me the story is about the moral ambiguity of physical beauty and its seductive power to subvert moral judgement. It is also about responsibility, or the lack of it. The uncle is the most irresponsible, using his authority and charm to relieve himself of any involvement in the lives of his small charges. The governess, beguiled both by his attractiveness and his flattering confidence in her, accepts a charge which she must have known was beyond her capabilities, and doesn't even notify him when Miles is expelled from school. She puts her standing with her employer before her duty to the children. Both the governess and Mrs Grose are so enchanted by the Botticelli angelic beauty of Miles and Flora that they find it difficult to believe them capable of wrong-doing, let alone evil. Henry James was right to

make the children exceptionally beautiful, striking at our precon-
ceived notions of the physical manifestations of evil. The wicked
witch is always dark and ugly.

_ And how exactly were the children corrupted? Henry James could
not, of course, be specific. The story is overlaid with such Victorian
preoccupations as childhood sexuality, the ambivalent position of the
governess in the home and in society, and their fascination with the
supernatural. Coming to the story afresh, I am surprised at its
enduring power to puzzle and discomfort. Beside it, James's short
ghost stories – 'Owen Wingrave', 'Sir Edmund Orme' and 'The
Friends of the Friends' – are no more than tales to frighten children.

My visit to Essex was an enjoyable occasion and for a very good
cause which I was glad to be able to help. I feel desperately sorry for
parents with autistic children. It is hard enough to cope with
physical disability but to have a child who is mentally remote,
inaccessible, and may indeed be belligerent and incapable of responding to love, must be very difficult to bear. The day was overcast but
the countryside still looked beautiful seen through a soft mist, the
wayside daffodils sharply yellow against the muted green of the
grass.

SATURDAY, 14TH MARCH

Yesterday I went to Stockport to speak at a dinner organized by the
Patrons' Club of the Altrincham and Sale Conservative Association. I
decided to save them money by travelling standard class, but began to
regret it when the carriage became full and the seats close by were
taken by four young men each carrying four linked cans of beer. They
became increasingly noisy as the journey proceeded and more and
more beer was fetched from the buffet. After that at least three other
passengers began using their mobile phones, so that the hope of a
peaceful journey, with time to look at the countryside (though not
particularly interesting, I admit, on this journey) and to think, was lost.
But then I overheard some of the young men's conversation with a
neighbouring passenger, and realized that they were four squaddies
returning from a tour of duty in Northern Ireland. Immediately the
noise they were making seemed both excusable and, for my part,
supportable.

It was a much more comfortable journey back today, leaving me
plenty of energy to walk down to Kensington High Street to shop. I

went into the Roman Catholic church in Kensington Church Street, feeling the need to light some candles for friends who are ill, and also to rest for a moment and sit quietly. Preparations were being made for a wedding. Already the best man and some of the ushers, wearing morning dress, had arrived, someone was making last-minute re-arrangements to the flowers and there was that quiet determined air of purposeful activity which is surprisingly restful if one is able to sit apart from it. The building for me has no architectural merit, but it is a wonderful staging post on the walk down to the High Street since it is always open and one can sit in solitude without disturbance. I need moments of absolute quiet and stillness, and churches are among the few places where one can find it.

SUNDAY, 15TH MARCH

This morning I went to Mattins at the Chapel Royal, St James's Palace, with Miss Ellen Lowe. I met her two years ago in the local hair-dresser's, but I have seen her fairly frequently since as we usually stand at the same bus-stop on Sunday mornings to go to church. She asked me if I would accompany her one day to the Chapel Royal, and this was the day.

We took a cab, since it conveniently arrived, which made us rather early, so we walked for fifteen minutes in St James's Park. I never get tired of the view from the bridge towards Whitehall, seen this morning through a white flutter of seagulls' wings. A plaque outside the Chapel stated that it was here that Charles I had received communion for the last time before his execution. Before the service I sat quietly, thinking – I hope prayerfully – of that tragic king who paid so dearly for his obstinacy and folly. He now has a day in the revised lectionary, which seems to me entirely right. The Chapel was very full, and I enjoyed the quiet dignity of Mattins, now so seldom heard. The anthem, Parry's 'My Soul, There Is a Country', is one of my favourites. It was helpful to find myself provided with a large Prayer Book I could easily read from a distance, and a comfortable hassock for kneeling.

Afterwards we had lunch together at Il Carretto, an Italian restaurant at Notting Hill Gate, where I enjoyed hearing about Miss Lowe's experience as a nurse at the Middlesex Hospital. Hers has been a life of quiet, determined dedication to a job she obviously loved. The hours were normally long and frequently nurses would stay overtime, as they still do. 'After all,' she said simply, 'if the patient needs you, you can't just walk away.'

To David Hebblethwaite's flat in Powis Square in the evening for supper. The other guest was Sir Derek Pattinson, Secretary-General of the General Synod of the Church of England from 1972 to 1990. It was a good evening but one I had to cut a little short as I needed to be home at half-past ten when son-in-law Peter arrived to spend the night.

THURSDAY, 19TH MARCH

This morning I returned from three happy, if busy, days in Cambridge. On Monday morning I gave the Keynote Speech at a conference on 'Sexing the Liturgy' held at the university's Faculty of Divinity in St John Street. I thought the title a little odd; I associate sexing with chickens. Perhaps 'Liturgy and Gender' would have been more appropriate. It was an interesting three days, and educative for me, but I would have benefited more had the acoustics in the large barrel-roofed hall been better. The sound system seemed to amplify but also to distort, although I accept that my hearing isn't good. The noise level seemed loud but individual words were lost. This made it particularly difficult since some of the young female theologians spoke very quickly, rather as if they were reading a dissertation or thesis and had to get through it in the time. The proceedings will be printed and I shall then have an opportunity to read and, I hope, learn and digest.

I don't suppose anyone was surprised at the stance I took in my Keynote Speech. I reviewed what I saw as the desiderata of liturgy: that it should be intelligible, which didn't necessarily mean that it should be modern and up-to-date; that it should be capable of being spoken aloud in church by priest and people; that it should reflect doctrine; and lastly, but not least important, that it should be written in memorable language. Words in their beauty, their simplicity, their numinous power should be capable of so entering our consciousness that we do not need to remember them, search for them or concentrate on them, but rest confidently on their familiarity to bring us into that hoped-for communion with God which is surely at the heart of prayer and worship.

I went on, perhaps rather late in the talk, to speak about gender and worship. I pointed out that Christianity is both an historical and a patriarchal religion. It was a Jewish patriarch, St Paul, who was chiefly responsible for extending the Judeo-Christian inheritance to non-Jews. Christ Himself taught us to call God 'Abba, Father'. I see a difficulty, at least for myself, in accepting such changes as 'Mother' or 'Sister'. This is surely to substitute one stereotype for another; since God is spirit He can have no gender. Even as a young child I never pictured God as a benevolent Father Christmas sitting in a white nightdress on a heavenly throne.

Between lectures I looked at some of the theological books on sale in the hall. Most seemed to me totally incomprehensible. Obviously doctrinally and philosophically they would be well above my understanding, but it seemed that the sentences themselves were incomprehensible, a string of polysyllabic words strung together from which I could get no meaning. Theology like other professions has its own obscurantism. The problem is surely that theology should impinge on the lives of ordinary non-theologians if it is to have influence. Surely it can sometimes be written in language the intelligent lay man or woman can understand.

One of the women priests to whom I spoke is a hospital chaplain. She said that on a recent visit to the wards she had been accosted by a woman who had said, with extreme anger, 'Don't talk to me about the Church of England! Why did it have to snatch away Princess Di just when she was enjoying her bit of happiness?' I don't know what answer the priest gave; I could think of none appropriate.

After lunch at Trinity I walked and talked in the Fellows' garden with the Professor of Divinity, the happiest time of my visit. Inevitably I thought of George Eliot, pacing between the trees in the same garden with a contemporary writer F. W. H. Myers and pronouncing on the words God, Immortality, Duty. 'How inconceivable was the first, how unbelievable the second, and yet how peremptory and absolute the third.'

I spent the night in the guest room at Peterhouse. This is an eccentric room. It was given to the college by an ex-member, and I suspect that he had something to do with the furnishing. The stairway leading up to the room is a rather disagreeable and violent purplish-red, with an immense coat of arms facing the door. The guest room itself is large, the bed high and curtained with a gold canopy surmounted by two huge crossed keys. The furniture is gilded, and in the bathroom a vast bath has a wide rim as if designed for the bather's friends to sit round comfortably and chat. Four litres of bottled water were provided, suggesting that the extraordinary decorations might induce excessive thirst. But it was a comfortable night.

In the morning, by contrast, I had breakfast in the little parlour, in the oldest part of the college. This is an enchanting room, half-panelled and looking out over the lawns and trees, and with a small combination room next door where senior members of the college can relax and read. It was one of those rooms which promote an atmosphere of tranquil meditative happiness and I wished I could spend the day there and write.

Afterwards two other guests, a speaker at the conference and her husband, and I were shown the Perne Library and able to examine some of the college treasures. These include a very early printed book which was obviously designed to deceive the buyer since the printer's name had been carefully erased. It was beautifully decorated and the print remarkably clear, a fake but still a work of art. The young College Chaplain, Graham Ward, then took me to see the Chapel. The east window, designed by Rubens, is remarkable. Beneath a turbulent sky, a boiling of vivid blue, the figures round the three crosses are crowded together, yet each individual, the two robbers distorted in agony, the figure of Christ, passive and luminous, in the centre of the picture. The window is violent and restless, forcing the viewer to face the reality of what is happening.

SUNDAY, 29TH MARCH

I am writing this just before 11 o'clock at night after what has been an enjoyably fulfilling weekend. It began on Friday with a pub lunch with Bud McLintock. Bud's firm is responsible for the publicity in connection with the Whitbread Awards, one of the most interesting and successful of the literary prizes. She has hopes that the BBC might do a programme about it and we discussed the possibilities. I don't think television has ever managed to cope successfully with literary prizes. Viewers on the whole probably aren't interested in shots of dinner-jacketed guests eating and drinking *en masse*, or in the speeches. But it should be possible to discuss the shortlist in a way that is both interesting and informative. I think viewers and listeners particularly like to hear from the authors themselves – how they get their ideas, how the book began, what are their methods of writing. It will be good if the Whitbread can be given more publicity on the screen.

Jane arrived in the early evening to spend the weekend. She needed to order some blinds for her Oxford house, so we went first to John Lewis and then walked to the Wallace Collection. I hadn't been to the Wallace for over a year, but entered it as I always do with a sense of being received into a private house as a welcome visitor. It is interesting how one's response to some paintings changes while the initial reaction to others is only deepened with every viewing. Titian's air-sea rescue of Andromeda, which once I thought rather fine, now seems to me half-finished and almost slovenly, while I can never view the Guardis without pleasure, and I particularly love the Bonington oils and water-colours. I received more pleasure – and Jane more amusement – from the armour than I expected, particularly the jousting armour. I tried to imagine the sensation of being screwed into this ornate and cunningly hinged accoutrement designed, judging by the bizarre pointed helmets, to terrify as much as to protect. I can see that, once dislodged from the saddle, the jouster would lie helpless, a gigantic up-ended beetle.

We read the notice describing the additions planned as a result of the successful application to the Lottery. There is to be a learning centre and also a coffee house for visitors under a glass canopy in the courtyard. Jane and I disagreed about this. Perhaps because of my age, I am always thankful for a place where I can sit and drink coffee after visiting a museum. Jane dislikes the idea of museums – and in particular galleries – becoming places where people will congregate to meet friends, eat, drink and chat. A purist, she prefers to think that visitors are drawn by one need only: to look at the pictures in comfort and relative solitude. I don't see why they shouldn't, afterwards, be refreshed with a good cup of coffee.

This morning we went to 11 o'clock Mass at All Saints – or it would be more apt to say that that was our intention. Because we hadn't listened to the radio or read the papers in detail, I had completely overlooked putting forward the clock by one hour. We got to the church, as we thought, early and wandered around to kill time, then presented ourselves at the firmly closed door at quarter to twelve, thinking it was quarter to eleven. Opening the door, I saw that the church was very full. My instinct was to leave, but Jane, more robust, was determined that, having decided to go to church, to church she would go, and we were shown to a seat in a side aisle. Afterwards I was very glad that we did go in. I was in time to take communion and

Jane, who is not a believer, greatly enjoyed, as did I, the singing of Byrd's four-part setting of the Mass.

Afterwards we walked to Regent's Park and made our way eventually to the restaurant, where we had a light lunch sitting outside. Although the sun was fitful, the air was warm and moist. Just to breathe, particularly in this green and flower-scented place, was a sensual pleasure.

Each of London's three main public parks has its distinctive ambience. St James's Park is the one I know best, perhaps because I so often walked across it during the years when I worked at the Home Office. Stretching in green and watery beauty between the Palace and Whitehall, St James's has always held for me an air of regal propriety and of high policy tinged with mystery. There have been so many espionage TV series in which bowler-hatted men of power pace magisterially together beside the lake exchanging their dangerous confidences. The very birds seem to know themselves privileged.

Regent's Park is more formally splendid with wide paths leading to Queen Mary's Rose Garden or the zoo; a less intimate park and one for people intent on going somewhere, pausing less often than in other parks to sniff, touch and wonder.

Hyde Park is redolent of high Victoriana (perhaps because of Kensington Palace), peopled with the small ghosts of supervised children sailing their boats on the round pond while beribboned nurses wheel deep-bottomed bassinets between the flowerbeds of Kensington Gardens. The particular pleasure of Hyde Park lies in the vast acres of grass. Here I can walk for miles in untrammelled solitude, the perfect place to be when I am plotting a new novel.

After we reached home, Jane went out again into Holland Park, reluctant to miss the rest of the daylight, while I sat with the Sunday papers. Jane left to catch the bus to Oxford shortly before ten, so now I am sitting alone in that state of indolent tiredness in which the contemplation of sleep becomes more agreeable than making the effort actually to go to bed.

Tomorrow I leave London by the 10 a.m. train from King's Cross to Edinburgh, where I am to give a lecture to the Scottish Medico-Legal Society.

APRIL

Today is the anniversary of my husband's birthday and inevitably it is a day for memory to take hold. It was an unpropitious day to be born, provoking in childhood the inevitable jokes and teasing. Connor would have been seventy-eight today and I am trying to picture him, like me stiffer in his walk, his strong fair hair now a thatch of grey. I know that he was glad to die and I never mourned him in the sense of wishing that it had not happened. I still miss him daily, which means that no day goes by in which he doesn't enter into my mind: a sight which he would have relished, a joke which he would have enjoyed, something seen or read which could be shared with him, the reiteration of familiar gossip, opinions, prejudices, which are part of a marriage. And then there is the success and prosperity in which he never shared and which could have made such a difference to his comfort, and the grandchildren he longed to see but never did.

For much of his last years he was in and out of psychiatric hospitals, chiefly Goodmayes in Essex. It was, indeed still is, one of those impressive and forbidding Victorian edifices which, during my childhood, were called asylums. The word is beautiful, as is its meaning, but it was spoken then always with that mixture of fear and shame associated with the word 'workhouse'. These large communities for the care of the mentally ill have, of course, been largely superseded by community care, which could be described more accurately as the absence of care in a community still largely resentful or frightened of mental illness. Connor was never unhappy in Goodmayes but then, as he said, education at a minor public school and subsequent army service prepared one for anything. For him and for very many, particularly those who could not possibly have survived outside, it was indeed an asylum.

I was living at the time with his parents in Ilford, where my father-in-law was still working as a general practitioner. Every Sunday I

177

would take the bus to the end of Goodmayes Lane and join the straggling stream of dispirited-looking men, women and children trudging up the driveway to the hospital. It was too reminiscent of similar journeys to a similar hospital taken in childhood with my father. All the visitors would be carrying baskets or bags containing the weekly offering of food. I usually carried fruit and a cake baked by my mother-in-law, in addition to cigarettes, any book I thought Connor might enjoy and pocket money to see him through the week. We would meet in one of the large day-rooms smelling as always of inadequately washed bodies and furniture polish. If the weather was fine we would walk in the grounds. The wards were large and barrack-like with small padded side-wards in which patients had occasionally to be incarcerated. Many of the modern drugs had not been developed and patients saw psychiatrists only infrequently. For many of them, the burnt-out schizophrenics, there was in fact little that could be done medically, but here at least they did find an asylum. Sometimes the care might have been a little rough and ready, but on my frequent visits I saw no unkindness – and much compassionate and sensitive caring.

I got to recognize the other visitors, since we went week after week. One, a very large woman, with a son built like a rugby-player and ferocious in mien, took him a cooked meal for each day of the week in a series of heaped metal containers. She confided to me when we walked together up the drive: 'George has been reclassified. He's a voluntary patient now. Mind you, we're not telling him!'

The hospital was a place where eccentricities and bizarre behaviour were tolerated as they rarely are with community care. I went once with Connor to a church service where the chaplain was in no way put out by the fact that a third of the congregation took the high kneeling hassocks and placed them on the pews so that the congregation looked as if it contained a proportion of formidable giants.

Connor, on admission, had decided to call himself Ted, and I got used to hearing him addressed by nurses and patients by that name. For some time he worked in the library but also captained the soccer team. I don't know whether any games were played away, but those on the home ground had their moments of eccentricity. Connor was not pleased when, during one game, the goalkeeper began hearing his voices and stood immobile, eyes raised to heaven, while the ball whizzed past him into goal.

Only those who have lived with the mental illness of someone they love can understand what this entails. One suffers with the patient and for oneself. Another human being who was once a beloved companion can become not only a stranger, but occasionally a malevolent stranger. It is easy sometimes to understand why mental illness was once seen as possession by an evil spirit. But at least I was spared the theory which some psychiatrists subsequently developed: that it was the family members who were ill, the patient who was sane, and that the family, particularly the parents, were responsible for the sickness. This theory is so cruel and wicked – I use the words with care – that it should surely never be put forward unless there is proof of its truth and something can be done about it. The additional burden this placed on parents, already trying to cope with little support with an intolerable burden, was frankly appalling. I suppose it principally arose from the psychiatrists' need to relate emotionally to the patient. But too often it seemed a collusion; parents, in addition to being regarded as the cause of the illness, were denied information about its progress. I know of one case where a schizophrenic son subsequently drowned himself but the hospital at which he was a patient didn't know that he was no longer in his room, since to enter it would have been a violation of his privacy.

The policy of treatment in the community, which began when I was working at the North West Metropolitan Regional Hospital Board and was enthusiastically implemented, has immeasurably increased the burden on families, many of whom live under a pressing cloud of daily anxiety which must at times seem insupportable. When will we learn not to legislate for, or introduce, so-called reforms unless and until we have the will and the means to finance them? Depressing as the old psychiatric hospitals were, at least they provided respite for the family, and control, care and support for the patient. If there is to be community care, there should also be small local in-patient and out-patient facilities to which patients can return in moments of crisis or when they have neglected to take their medication, and to which carers in the community can look for support and help. It might be necessary to have short-term compulsory orders to ensure that patients who won't return to in-patient care voluntarily can be admitted until they are stabilized. But one would hope that these small units – I hate the word, but 'hospital' hardly seems appropriate – can be attractive and welcoming and seen by the patients as true asylums. I suspect that there are many thousands of parents, wives, husbands, children coping with the mentally ill, in circumstances which no one should be asked to endure. It is surprising they are not more vocal, but it is difficult to criticize the system when the system is all you have, and to antagonize it might take away even the inadequate support which you at present receive.

I remember watching with my younger daughter a programme on the television in which a team of psychiatrists and social workers were in session with the family of a schizophrenic boy, indulging in some kind of family therapy. I felt outraged at the intrusion. What exactly, anyway, is a normal family? There can be few in which the relationships are without tension or even occasional acrimony, or in which some unhappiness is not endured. By what right have these outsiders, these experts, come in to meddle in other people's lives when, in reality, they have so little to offer? At least I never had to endure that kind of intrusion. It is an injustice about which, perhaps not surprisingly, I can become vehement.

THURSDAY, 2ND APRIL

I am writing this on the train from Edinburgh to King's Cross, following my address to the Scottish Medico-Legal Society. The carriage is almost empty and I'm enjoying what I like best, a quiet uninterrupted journey. At York a man got in and immediately began using his mobile telephone. I had a horrible fear that this was the end of peace, but he made only the single call. One would like to see carriages set aside for people who want to conduct their business in loud voices throughout a journey, but I am always reluctant to add to prohibitions. Perhaps it's better to have notices asking people to use mobile phones only when standing in the corridor or between compartments. That might get the message over that this is not an acceptable practice.

The first part of this journey is the most exciting; rugged coastline before and after Berwick, the wild sea rolling in over jagged rocks, and the first gorse, bright yellow on the headlands. Then the Tweed, flowing under the last bridge to merge with the sea at Berwick. We are now in calmer country and the weather has changed from dull to rainy; raindrops, like silver tadpoles, weaving and spurting down the panes. The north seems to be painted boldly in dark oils, the south in water-colours. But now the blurred countryside is seen as a pointilliste painting, the fields as yet only smudged with the acid yellow of the rape.

It has been an enjoyable visit. Edinburgh is a splendid city, but one in which a southerner will always feel a stranger, even if – as on this occasion – a welcome stranger. It offers that greatest of city delights, the unexpected glimpse down narrow roadways or cobbled passages of glittering water and far hills.

Grandson James met me off the train yesterday and drove me south to walk on a wide, firm and deserted beach before dropping me at my hotel. This was The Witchery, snuggling down under the castle. It is primarily a restaurant with only two rooms for visitors, one a suite called the Inner Sanctum. This was furnished almost exactly as it would have been for a Victorian visitor and his wife. It looked like a theatre set that was in danger of overpowering the action. Here, artfully arranged, was high Victorian clutter, a large bronze head of the Queen presiding over more artefacts than one would find in a row of antique shops. The nineteenth-century travelling couple would be ushered into a room in which they would feel immediately at home, indeed their luggage is already here: leather suitcases, tartan rugs, an officer's red jacket arranged on a stand. The large sitting-room has tartan rugs as well as a tartan carpet. Both rooms are crowded with family pictures in silver frames, sentimental coloured prints, an open photograph album on a stand, large floral arrangements, innumerable knick-knacks crowding every surface. The bedroom is dominated by a high, wide four-poster bed with a scarlet canopy and eight huge tapestry or embroidered cushions. All this brilliantly arranged re-construction of another age was combined with cleverly concealed modern conveniences: television, fax, telephones, although the eight different taps in the bathroom could be more properly described as a challenge rather than a convenience. I suspect that I shall one day use this room, or one very like it, in a novel. The description of a room can be as revealing of character as dialogue or action.

My lecture was held in the demonstration lecture hall of the School of Medicine, a pleasantly proportioned semi-circular room with high ranked seats and a space in front of the speaker's desk obviously intended to hold a post-mortem table. I was aware of its absence and could picture an autopsy – perhaps on the victims of Burke and Hare – being undertaken under the fascinated gaze of passers-by who had walked in from the street to watch this demonstration of scientific cleverness. After the lecture, which could perhaps be more accurately described as a talk, a small group of us had an excellent dinner at The Witchery. I enjoyed the company very much – forensic pathologists are never dull – and I was seated next to a Procurator Fiscal and was able to discuss some of the differences between Scottish and English law. He is close to the *Juge d'Instruction* in France, and told me that during a police investigation he can ask for any information which he thinks would be helpful, including information on the background of suspects or the defendant. This means that much more is known about the background and details of the case by the time it comes to court than happens in England, probably resulting in a higher level of convictions. We talked about the 'Not Proven' verdict and agreed that Madeleine Smith, the twenty-one-year-old Glasgow architect's daughter tried in 1857 for the murder by arsenic of her lover, Emile L'Angelier, would almost certainly have been found guilty and hanged had she been tried south of the border.

This dinner conversation reminded me of the time during my service in the Home Office when I was concerned with juvenile law and had to come to a conference in Edinburgh to discuss the Scottish panel system as opposed to the English and Welsh juvenile courts. At first I thought there were obvious advantages in dealing with children, particularly younger children, in an informal setting where they face not a juvenile magistrate but a panel of men and women experienced in child care who discuss all the circumstances of the offence with the parents and who arrive at a decision about what should be done. But it later seemed to me, as it still does, that the treatment model has its defects; in particular there is a risk that the juvenile will be deprived of the protection under the law which his elder brother would get if brought before a court on, for example, a charge of grievous bodily harm. The panels at that time had the power to direct that the child could be sent to a special school, and probably still have that power. In other words, a child is deprived of his or her liberty without the order of a court of law. This dichotomy between treatment and control under the law seems to me at the heart of juvenile justice. In the youth courts, for example, the children have legal aid and the services of a defending counsel. This is absolutely right, yet there is the danger that the child may learn from an early age that it is possible to get off if you are represented by someone clever enough to establish reasonable doubt. G. K. Chesterton wrote,

'Children, being honest, love justice; adults, being corrupt, naturally prefer mercy.' What children expect of any legal process is simple. If you have done wrong you will be punished; if you are not guilty, you will be let off. This is hardly commensurate with our present system of criminal justice.

On the journey to Edinburgh, I read the whole of Blake Morrison's remarkable and personal response to the murder of James Bulger by two ten-year-old boys. The paperback is called *As If*. It is a passionate and moving book, the more so because the question 'Why?' was not answered by the court, and could not be answered. The court was convened to answer the two questions, 'Did the boys know right from wrong?' and 'Were they the ones responsible for the taking away and the beating to death of the child?' To these two questions it gave a reply. But we have an insistent need to know why, or at least we need to try to understand an act which in its horror shook all our conceptions about the nature of childhood and of innocence and indeed stretched the definition of evil into a new and terrifying dimension.

I wonder how far very young children do understand right and wrong. They know that certain actions will attract punishment, that they are disapproved of by parents and teachers, and the more sophisticated may know that they are against the law. But how far do they appreciate the nature of evil? I can remember that when I was eight and we were living in Ludlow I went with a school friend called Dora to spend a holiday with her family at Stalybridge in Lancashire. It was the first time I had visited the north, and I was seeing it at a time of depression. I can remember looking down from their council house over the factory chimneys, all without smoke. While I was there we were taken for a treat to a famous amusement park called, I think, Belle Vue, where there was a firework display which was supposed to re-enact the storming of the Bastille. I knew little if anything about the French Revolution, but I remember on my return telling my mother that, during the display, real people's heads were thrown to the crowd. I obviously believed this at the time, yet surely, as an intelligent child (as I think I was) of eight, I must have known that it is wrong to cut off even dead people's heads and throw them to the crowd. A young child's conception of reality is very different from that of an adult. Perhaps that small boy I saw in the juvenile court so many years ago was right after all when he said, 'I knew it was against the law, but I didn't know it was wrong.'

But what those two boys did to James Bulger goes beyond any failure of comprehension, any childish naughtiness, any lack of family care or control. We recoil from using the word evil about any child. But the unanswerable question remains unanswered. Why?

TUESDAY, 14TH APRIL

I spent the long Easter weekend at Southwold with Alixe. As I was expecting Elizabeth Jane Howard, Selina Hastings and a small group of friends from Beccles to arrive for lunch and tea on Easter Sunday, we stocked up on cold meats and smoked salmon.

On Good Friday morning the weather could hardly have been worse. We decided to join a walk of the combined churches from St Edmund's Church to South Green for a service, but by the time we got to St Edmund's the rain had increased to a torrential downpour which became sleet, and then hail. It had been difficult enough to walk, and certainly no one's voice could have been heard in this sheet of ice and water. The new vicar, a cheerful-looking woman, came in from the rain, laughing and shaking her sodden cassock. We waited for a few minutes, but obviously nothing was going to happen, so we departed to seek shelter in the bar of the Swan. We were too early; it didn't open until 11, but we met Nettie de Montmorency at the door and she invited us back to her house on the cliff. We talked, gossiped, drank and looked out over her lawn, which sparkled with hailstones. By the time we left a fitful sun had come out and melted them, and by the late afternoon it was too hot for us to sit comfortably in the conservatory.

I had decided not to write much about politics in what is essentially a record of my personal year, but it would be remiss not to mention the Northern Ireland agreement. I heard the news on the radio at 7 o'clock with a mixture of relief, hope and scepticism. It may not be the end of senseless murder, but perhaps it is the beginning of the end. But the scepticism persists. Sinn Fein/IRA would not have signed unless they believed that this was a significant move towards a united Ireland; the Unionists would not have agreed had they not been convinced that the arrangements set out would strengthen the Union. Both sides cannot be right. The intervention of the Prime Minister at the last minute seems to have been crucial. If the agreement is approved by the people of Ireland and does indeed result in a fair, reasonable and accepted settlement he will deserve all the plaudits he will undoubtedly receive. But there is no great difficulty in achieving at least a temporary peace if one is prepared to propitiate the terrorists. And there is something deeply repugnant about the early release of murderers, some of whose crimes were atrocious even by the standard of murder, and equally repugnant that men of violence should be able to bomb themselves to a conference table. But this, after all, has been the history of the twentieth century and we have long since ceased believing that the meek shall inherit the earth.

SUNDAY, 19TH APRIL

I went very early by bus to Oxford to lunch with Jane and Peter, and to walk with them in Woodstock Park. The park was a delight. We moved slowly since almost every tree offered some particular interest in shape or foliage. The buds of the ash were breaking into their peculiar deformed-looking flowers, the horse-chestnut boughs were heavy with budded clusters which will take another week of sunshine to break into their white candles. We paused at the bridge, its stones warm to the hands, to watch a mother coot nesting in the middle of the lake and feeding her chicks while her mate swam round with lazy insouciance. Once on the pasture we crested a ridge and the palace came suddenly and surprisingly into sight. This is how one should always come across a great house, even one which is familiar: stone, brick, parkland and sky in perfect coherence, which every time strikes the eye afresh.

I felt very sorry for poor John Vanbrugh, bowling up in a coach with his friends to show off his achievement and having admission barred by an irate Duchess of Marlborough. Apparently she never liked the house and would have preferred something altogether more cosily domestic. As I have never yet seen inside Blenheim Palace, I don't know whether or not to sympathize with the first Duchess.

Waiting for Peter to turn the car in the lane outside the park gates, I stood for a moment in complete silence broken only by the note of a single bird and the susurration of the breeze in the wayside grasses. It was one of those moments of happiness and contentment which give reality to death, since however long we have to live, there are never enough springs.

TUESDAY, 21ST APRIL

Yesterday I went to the British Library for the opening by Chris Smith of the galleries which will be open to the public today. St John

Wilson's building was controversial from the first and no doubt will remain so, but the final test will be the use made of it by those with a reader's ticket and by the general public. Certainly there is immense enthusiasm for promoting the Library as a place where everyone interested in books and our heritage can come, see the national treasures, enjoy the facilities and the special exhibitions. The Pearson Gallery and the John Ritblat Gallery, showing some of the greatest treasures of the Library, are examples of the successful use of modern museum display techniques. The material is beautifully organized and displayed. The John Ritblat Gallery is particularly exciting. There, on show, are such treasures as the Lindisfarne Gospels and the Magna Carta. The guest list for the opening was long, but there was no crush in the galleries and I was able to move slowly from case to case and in relative silence. In the Pearson Gallery the display on the development of writing was fascinating. I hope a large number of London schools will be able to visit it. Except for St Pancras Station, this is a seedy and depressing part of London. Perhaps the presence of the Library will do something to rehabilitate the area.

An irritating beginning to today with too many telephone calls and too much to be done before going to Southampton, where I was to conduct a masterclass on 'Writing a Novel' for Meridian Television. The programme went well. We were actually filmed for an hour, which will be cut down to half that time. I was positioned at a desk with the three participants ranged on chairs before me, but this seemed too formal and I moved in front of the desk and perched on it for much of the time. None of the three was a complete amateur; the man was already earning a living as a writer and the two girls had had some success. I had planned for the programme to be more like a discussion between the four of us than a teaching session, and we managed to range through what I described as the five main elements of a novel: the plot, story or narrative; the characterization; the setting; the writing style; and the structure. The audience was drawn from writing groups, who came forward at the end to talk to me and to the other three participants. This is the kind of arts programme which is well worth doing but which should be given more time. Unfortunately ITV scheduling seems now to be fixed rigidly by the full hour or half hour, lacking that flexibility which can accommodate serious discussion.

I have taught creative writing at the University of California at Irvine and at two of the three centres of the Arvon Foundation in the

UK, with which the Poet Laureate Ted Hughes has been closely involved from its beginnings. Obviously you can't make a writer of someone with absolutely no talent, but it is possible to help with technique and, as writing is a lonely business, most people enjoy getting together with other aspirants to share experiences and to give each other encouragement. The Arvon courses, which I strongly support, are remarkably successful in this respect and it always surprises me how a group of people, chosen on a first-come basis, bond together so effectively.

Invariably, when I give a talk after a signing session, there is at least one aspiring novelist in the audience who asks for advice. In the brief time available I can't say much, but there are four principles which I see as important.

The first is to read widely, not in order to copy someone else's style, but to learn to appreciate and recognize good writing and to see how the best writers have achieved their result. Poor writing is, unfortunately, infectious and should be avoided.

Practise writing in whatever form; the craft is learned by practising it, not by talking about it. Some people find that writing courses or local writers' circles are a help, but they are not for everyone.

Increase your vocabulary; the raw material of the writer is words and the more we have available and can use effectively and with confidence the better.

Welcome experience. This means going through life with all senses open: observing, feeling, relating to other people. Nothing that happens to a writer need ever be lost.

Of course what questioners really want is not this somewhat pietistic encouragement, but advice on how to get published. Amateur painters can put their efforts on the wall; a writer never feels that he is a writer until he sees his work in print. Not infrequently I receive letters which seem to suggest that there is some magic way to success or that a publisher will accept a manuscript solely on my recommendation. I can only respond that publishers are business people, not philanthropists, but that they need the seed-corn of new talent, and in my view an aspiring novelist who can tell a story, can write well and can bring the reader into that happy collusion with the writer which is at the heart of fiction, will eventually find a publisher.

MAY

WEDNESDAY, 6TH MAY

The first two weeks of this month are going to be exceptionally busy, leaving little time either for this diary or for the accumulating general correspondence.

On Friday, 1st May, I spoke at the Global Spring Conference of the International Women's Forum at the Park Lane Hotel, Piccadilly, having been asked to do so by Katharine Whitehorn. There were 300 senior women present from this country, the United States, mainland Europe and further afield, to discuss the role of the arts. The session at which I spoke was somewhat pretentiously entitled 'Cultural Vibrancy and Social Cohesion', but the speakers were all very well worth hearing, not surprisingly since they included Janet Suzman, Genista McIntosh, Prue Leith, Rabbi Julia Neuberger and Baroness Symons.

The next day I came to Dorset to attend the Dorset Arts Festival, speaking in the Old Court House in Dorchester. I have given talks at a large variety of venues, but none more interesting. I sat in the huge judge's chair while the audience were disposed about the court in the jury box, the dock and the spectators' galleries. It was a peculiar and sobering experience to be sitting in the very seat the magistrate had occupied when he sentenced the Tolpuddle Martyrs. Before my session began I went down into the cells below the court and then walked in the footsteps of the former accused, negotiating the narrow stairs and finding myself in the dock with the suddenness of a jack-in-the-box. It must have been intimidating for those Tolpuddle men to come from that claustrophobic darkness into the light of the crowded courtroom and to gaze for the first time into the magistrate's eyes on the level of their own. No doubt it was intended to be intimidating.

I spent Saturday and Sunday with Rosemary in her cottage outside Wareham, and then went to Winterborne Houghton to spend two days with Tom and Mary Norman. I had told them that I longed to see cowslips; they were part of my childhood walks in the Shropshire countryside, seen, too, when I cycled as a schoolgirl along the flat roads of the fens, but I rarely come across them now. Tom drove us into West Dorset. We walked along a stony ridge, across two fields and then found ourselves in a sloping meadow leading down to a valley. The field was covered with cowslips, a shivering sea of bright yellow blossom with hardly space to plant a foot between the clumps. It was a warm spring day with some breeze and it seemed that the whole air was delicately and subtly sweet. I had asked to see cowslips and was seeing them in an almost unbelievable abundance.

This morning Tom and Mary drove me to Poole to speak at a luncheon in aid of Dorset Victim Support, held in the old town. This went well, and I am now in the train travelling back to London. I shall be only briefly at home before it is time to go to Oxford on Friday to speak at a conference on 'The Novel and Society' at Rewley House.

TUESDAY, 12TH MAY

On Sunday afternoon I left Heathrow for Paris to promote the French edition of *A Certain Justice*. It was a good day for a flight. The rural landscape passing beneath us looked, as always, like a needlework collage; the hemstitched fields, the silver satin of rivers, the clear linen patches of green and yellow and the tightly knotted woods of dark green wool appeared so cunningly contrived that I half expected the whole design to be drawn up and hung against the blue backcloth of the sky.

I was met at Roissy-Charles-de-Gaulle by Dominique Fusco, whom I have known since my books were first accepted by Librairie Arthème Fayard. As usual, I had been booked into a small and charming hotel, Le Duc de Saint Simon, where I was greeted by the same receptionist. Fayard had filled the elegant sitting-room with magnificent flowers: lilies, clusters of orchids and roses.

France was the last European country to take my books, but Fayard tell me that I am now their highest-selling foreign author.

Fayard had hoped I could stay for longer than two days but it wasn't possible, so I saw nothing of the city and the whole time was taken up with the usual programme of newspaper and radio interviews, all of which took place at the hotel. But it was pleasant to be in Paris, as it always is.

Yesterday a farewell dinner was given for me at her apartment by

Mlle Denise Meunier, the distinguished elderly and academic French-woman who has translated nearly all my novels. The guests jabbered away in French, changing to English when they saw I wasn't with them. I just about held my own but wished, as I always do when in Paris, that I was more fluent in the only foreign language which I have any hope of understanding. It seems ridiculous that I had a French lesson every school day of my five years of secondary education but still can't speak the language with any confidence. Children today are more effectively taught; but then they have television, videos, foreign visits and exchanges and language laboratories. But acquiring foreign languages is a talent as well as a skill. I have met people on my travels who can learn and be fluent in a new language in a matter of months. My paternal grandfather was such a one, but his talent has certainly not been inherited.

FRIDAY, 15TH MAY

I have had three very happy days at Trinity College, Oxford, where on Wednesday I gave the Richard Hillary Memorial Lecture. Like most of my generation, I have a lively memory of first reading his autobiography *The Last Enemy*. Hillary stands for a generation of young men from the university Air Squadrons who fought in the skies over Britain. He was shot down, and on the first occasion was badly burned and disfigured, but managed to persuade the RAF to let him fly again. It was his last flight. An additional tragedy of his death was that he took a fellow airman with him, and one who was married with small children. I can understand that Hillary needed to prove himself by flying again, but the RAF should not have given way to his insistence.

Before the war Hillary was a typically privileged Oxford under-graduate, too handsome for his own good, selfish, arrogant and hedonistic. But the war changed him, as it changed, for good or ill, everyone who took part in it. I am not sure I believe that the poignant final chapter in his book is strictly accurate, but it does show that he had become a writer.

One of the pleasures of Wednesday was meeting the heroine of that book, Denise, now Denise Patterson, a widow. During the war she was engaged to Peter Pease, a friend of Hillary's who was also killed, and it was she who, steadfast in courage and courageous in grief, most helped Hillary through the trauma of his burning. In the book she is described by him as beautiful; she remains beautiful today.

Yesterday and today I gave seminars to some of the English students and postgraduate students. The Master gave a dinner in the Lodge this evening. It was a wonderful night and we were able to stroll on the lawn, glasses in hand. I sat next to George Carman, QC – a guarantee of fascinating conversation. When I was researching *A Certain Justice* I was advised to go to the Law Courts when he was appearing, to learn what cross-examination could be. I did so and he was indeed formidable.

An additional pleasure of three memorable days has been meeting the English tutor Dinah Birch and discussing with her the Victorian novel. I very much hope that we meet and talk again.

SATURDAY, 16TH MAY

I took Nina Bawden and her husband Austen Kark to dinner at the Halcyon Hotel, a small return for the succession of wonderful meals I have enjoyed at their house in Noel Road. It was warm enough to sit outside, which was initially pleasant, but a noisy quartet at an adjoining table made conversation difficult and we asked to be moved inside. An excellent dinner and, as always, the ease and comfort of dear friends.

It was on this day, eight years ago, that I stood with Ruth Rendell and helped knock down a portion of the Berlin Wall. The evidence is a small piece of rubble with one smooth painted surface which rests on a shelf in my bathroom and bears in biro the date, 16/5/90. The colours were a garish purple and red when I hacked the piece away with one of the chisels an enterprising German was hiring out to those who wanted to make their small mark on history. The colours have faded now and the date would have been indecipherable had I not inked over the figures a few months ago. Both Ruth and I had been to Berlin on a previous occasion to lecture for the British Council, and she and her husband Don were anxious to see the Wall coming down.

I still remember clearly my earlier visit, from 1st to 8th December in 1986. Then I stood on one of the high platforms near the Reichstag. The night was very clear and cold, the trees around totally bare. I gazed out over the Wall and the dead floodlit area beyond, imagining the watching eyes and asking myself whether the Wall would come down in my lifetime, or even in the lifetime of my grandchildren. But the city then was one of the most thrilling I have ever visited. The air crackled with a mixture of excitement and tension and no one seemed ever to go to bed. I remember one young West German writer saying that he lived in the most terrifying city on earth and could never bear to leave it. I often remember cities by the quality and distinctiveness of their street lighting: Berlin seemed a city of harsh floodlights. I stood at Checkpoint Charlie, as brightly lit as a film set, and saw in imagination the lonely hero of a Graham Greene or le Carré novel, walking with studied nonchalance along the floodlit road towards the waiting motionless figures.

I can remember what people in Berlin told me, but not their names, nor what they looked like. One, a distinguished film director, told me over dinner that his passion for cinema began as a young boy living in the British-occupied sector. His mother had to work and left him with a minder, and she would take him to the cinema as soon as it opened and leave him there, with such food as she managed to provide, until late at night when the last programme ended and he would be collected and taken home.

Another memory is of leaving my hotel room one morning and seeing a young woman dusting the wainscot in the corridor. When I said 'Good morning', she answered with a Northern English accent. I asked her what had brought her to Berlin, and she said that was a long story, one which she had obviously no intention of elaborating. When I enquired if she enjoyed working in the city, she said that she did and it was much more exciting and better in every way than the last place in which she had worked, which was terribly dull. She added, 'But you won't have heard of it, it was called Berchtesgaden.' It was the first time I realized that the location of Hitler's mountain eyrie meant nothing to a whole new generation.

It gave me the same small shock as I experienced when I first went to Japan to open an exhibition of crime writing in Tokyo. I was told at the hotel that a group of students would very much like to meet me. About a dozen smilingly presented themselves with large gold-edged cards on which they asked me to write a message and sign my name. The message they requested was 'from P. D. James to my fan club at the University of Hiroshima'.

In both 1986 and 1990 I went from the West into East Berlin. On the first occasion I had to submit to the long unsmiling scrutiny of the frontier police. On the second, Ruth, Don and I were greeted with smiles and the hope that we would have a happy day. Were they the same guards?

The *Sunday Times* Hay Festival was held from 22nd to 31st May, and I was sorry that I could only be there for the Friday and Saturday. For non-drivers Hay isn't the easiest town to get to, but I went by train to Newport, a quick and easy journey, and was met by one of the official cars for the beautiful winding drive to Hay.

I stayed, as I always do, with my long-standing friend Joyce Flack in Honey Cottage, Bear Street. I was sad to find her less than well. I had expected this, as I knew that she has a heart condition which may require a pacemaker, and is blind in one eye. This will be corrected when the cataract is dealt with but the eye surgeon is waiting for a decision on the pacemaker. The border between Wales and England actually runs through Hay, but Joyce is in Wales. She says it's odd to hear one surgeon saying, 'We'll have to send you to England for that' when being in England involves walking only a short distance down the road.

I found Joyce as ebullient, determinedly cheerful and courageous as always, but one of the sadnesses of old age is that one seldom hears good news about the health of friends. We talked from time to time about death. Joyce has absolutely no fear of it and is optimistic, if not convinced, that there will be some kind of afterlife, which she looks forward to as an interesting change from Hay-on-Wye. Dear Peggy Causton, with whom I played Scrabble twice a week until she died, also had no fear of death. She was totally without religious faith but said that there was no point in being afraid of death since she wouldn't be there when it happened. None of us, of course, will be there when it happens, but it's being there before it happens that is the worrying part and whether we shall be there with mind intact or imprisoned in some limbo of pain, degradation and dependence.

Hay is a popular festival with writers, as evinced by the glittering variety of novelists, historians, poets and biographers who appeared during the week. I had first thought that Hay wasn't a particularly propitious venue for a literary festival, apart from the difficulty of getting there. There is no large concert hall – indeed no large hall of any kind – insufficient hotels to deal with a large influx of visitors, and success is largely dependent on the weather since all the events take place in tents. But Hay has a distinctive atmosphere of enthusiasm, with warm receptive audiences determined to enjoy everything on offer. The enthusiasm remained unabated some years ago when the rain beat down relentlessly on taut canvas making some speakers almost inaudible, and audiences had to wade gum-booted across sinking planks to get to their seats. This weekend the weather has been wonderful and the hills and woods at their most verdant and shining.

I had two events, the first a discussion with Jill Paton Walsh about her completion of the unfinished Dorothy L. Sayers manuscript, *Thrones, Dominations*, and the second a talk about *A Certain Justice*, including a brief reading. After the first talk Jill and her publisher took me to dinner at the largest hotel. The conversation, concerned with ideas rather than people, was marvellous, the food disappointing.

In the afternoon I went to hear Gitta Sereny talk to Anthony Clare about her new book, *Cries Unheard*, which explores the life of the child murderer Mary Bell. She defended her decision to write the book, rationally and with conviction, and showed herself willing to answer criticism without undue defensiveness. She was also less credulous than I expected in trying to check the veracity of Mary Bell's account of her childhood where this was possible. But I still feel that the book shouldn't have been published, mainly because of the effect of its revelations on Mary Bell's daughter. I also disagree with Gitta Sereny's basic premise. This is that children are born, if not naturally good, at least naturally not disposed to viciousness, so that if things do go badly wrong and a ten-year-old child wilfully kills two small boys, then something must have happened in her life to turn her from innocence into a killer. It must be someone's fault, but not hers. This seems to me both simplistic and contrary to evidence. It is repugnant to think in terms of children being born evil, but some are born with a greater propensity to cruelty and unkindness than are others. Most of us know of children who seem born naturally good in that they are loving, generous and happy; others from an early age seem to take more pleasure from tormenting animals than is normal even with the most destructive child. I also deplore a book which lays the blame on the child's mother when that mother, no longer alive, is unable to defend herself. If bad parenting can produce a monster, then the children of the Wests can have little hope. Such information as we have suggests that they are coping with life. I didn't raise this objection during question time, and afterwards Anthony Clare asked me why not. I said that I felt that audiences had heard enough of my voice and I preferred to listen rather than speak. But I was a little surprised that no one raised the point.

I can never be in Hay-on-Wye, even in summer, without remembering the notorious case of Herbert Rowse Armstrong; but his was a winter crime. Katharine Armstrong died on 22nd February 1921, and it was on 31st December of the same year that her husband Major Armstrong was arrested while in his office clearing up papers at the end of the year. He was at first charged with the attempted murder of a rival solicitor in Hay, Oswald Norman Martin. It was while Armstrong was in custody that his wife's body was exhumed and examined by the Home Office pathologist, Bernard Spilsbury. She had died of arsenical poisoning.

One memorable incident in a classic case was the attempted murder of Martin. Armstrong had invited him to tea and had handed him a scone from the plate with the remark, 'Excuse fingers.' This unorthodox method of providing one's guest with sustenance must have increased Martin's suspicions when, returning home, he was violently ill with sickness and diarrhoea. His doctor sent a sample of his urine to be analysed; it proved to contain arsenic. A very difficult summer then ensued for poor Martin. Police enquiries and the procedures for exhuming Mrs Armstrong's body were slow and in the meantime Martin was ordered to behave naturally with his rival and never under any circumstances to put Armstrong on his guard. This became increasingly difficult as Martin was bombarded by Armstrong with invitations to tea in his office. It must have been a tremendous relief to the poor man when the arrest was finally made.

Another interesting incident took place at the committal proceedings, where the magistrates, unused to committing a prisoner on a charge of murder, had to look to the accused in the dock for advice on the correct procedure.

Reading the account of the trial, it seems to me clear that Armstrong was guilty, but there are still those in Hay, and in particular the owner of Armstrong's house, who believe him innocent. Most poisoners murder, as it were, at a distance, sparing themselves the horror of watching the victim die. Armstrong was in the house while his wife suffered the torments of arsenical poisoning. Could a man be as callously wicked as this and not display his nature in his everyday dealings with other people? Apparently Armstrong never did. He was meek, mild-mannered, a good father to his three children who, in adult life, also believed him innocent. The case still intrigues, largely because the town, particularly in winter, seems so unaltered. The brass plate with Armstrong's name is still inside the solicitor's office he occupied, Martin's office is still opposite, and Armstrong's house still stands, as does the small gaol where he was incarcerated.

Some years ago a television company made a film of the murder and Joyce saw the actor who played Armstrong, looking very like pictures of the man, walking in his 1920s suit up Bear Street. Joyce greeted him and he swept off his hat in salute. She said the moment was uncanny. One can imagine what this little town was like in the 1920s: claustrophobic, remote, everyone knowing the business of everyone else, the same gossip, the same tea parties, the same tennis afternoons at Armstrong's house, where his wife would imperiously call him in to remind him that it was bath night.

There has been a proliferation of local art and literary festivals in recent years and it sometimes seems that no small town is without one. Each has its individual atmosphere and, as a writer, one tends to believe also its different audience, so that one speaks of 'the Cheltenham audience', 'the Edinburgh audience', 'the Hay audience'. Part of this may be imaginary. I doubt whether there is any essential difference. But the audience at Hay-on-Wye does seem particularly enthusiastic and committed, largely, I think, because the festival is small and the tents close together so that there is a sense of shared enjoyment. This closeness can be disconcerting, particularly when a writer is reading a poignant passage and is interrupted by an outburst of enthusiastic clapping, or even by gales of laughter, from an adjoining tent. But this disadvantage is more than outweighed by the convenience of having all the main events on the same site.

I have been thinking about what makes a successful arts festival. Firstly, the organizers should have the co-operation and, ideally, the enthusiasm both of the local authority and of local people. There is never a welcoming atmosphere if residents feel that the festival is not for them, and it is important to have events which they are likely to support. Then there is the question of access; Hay isn't easy to get to, but cars meet the trains at Birmingham and Newport. Organizers should ensure that the writers can get to the festival and that, when there, they are comfortably looked after. Often arrangements are made for them to stay with local people who act as hosts or hostesses. For the gregarious this may be pleasurable, but most writers dislike it. A reading is in effect a public performance, and afterwards most of us need to be quietly alone and not be faced with a dinner party of guests who continue the questioning we have already endured after our session. It helps if the venue is attractive or as beautiful as is Hay-on-Wye, and if there is a reasonable number of good restaurants, but these are of far less importance than the power to attract writers and artists whom people want to hear and see, and the ability to promote that atmosphere of enthusiasm, stimulation and shared enjoyment which marks all the best art and literary festivals.

At nearly every festival I get asked about my novel *The Children of Men*, either during question time or at the line-up for signing. This novel, which is totally different from all my other work, didn't begin with a setting, but with a review I read in the *Sunday Times*. The book reviewed dealt with the dramatic and so far unexplained fall in the fertility rate of western man. Apparently young men today are only half as fertile as were their fathers. The reviewer pointed out that, of the millions of life forms which have inhabited our planet, nearly all have in time died out or were destroyed, as were the dinosaurs. Man's span on earth is as the blinking of an eye.

I began to imagine what the world would be like, and more specifically what England would be like, a quarter of a century after a catastrophic year in which the human race was struck by a universal infertility. For twenty-five years no one would have heard a baby cry or heard a child laugh. This idea for a dystopian novel was not in itself original; a number of novels explore a world in which mankind knows itself to be dying. *The Children of Men* ends on a note of hope, but was traumatic to write, and I was glad at the end to return to the less depressing ambience of classical detective fiction. The novel was not intended to be a Christian fable but that, in fact, was what I wrote. It is also different in technique since the whole story is seen through the eyes of a single character and the structure is linear, the plot moving strongly to its dramatic conclusion.

This is the only one of my novels which has not earned its advance, a depressing and somewhat demeaning thought. But it has produced more correspondence and more controversy, particularly in theological circles, than any other novel I have written.

JUNE

I had a most helpful talk today with Michele Buck, Controller of Drama at United Film and Television Productions, about an irritating complication which has arisen in connection with the televising of a third Cordelia Gray series by Ecosse Films.

For the first time I had decided, after consultations with Carol Heaton and much thought, that Ecosse Films could have the rights to the character so that they could continue to make Cordelia Gray television series, writing original stories. I would have some rights of consultation, but essentially the same thing would happen with Cordelia as happened with Colin Dexter's *Morse*. I had confidence in this decision after seeing their *Mrs Brown*, a film of quality and great sensitivity. I liked the people at Ecosse and felt that I could rely on their integrity and good faith. And the first Cordelia Gray series confirmed my high opinion. The screenplay was true to the book in fact and spirit, was well acted and directed, and Helen Baxendale as Cordelia fulfilled all our expectations.

I was less happy with the second series, the first real test for Ecosse since this was not based on one of my books. There was some good acting but the pace seemed to me too slow with suspense built up which came to nothing, while Cordelia had become ineffectual, dithering and incompetent, willing apparently to see the case solved and the husband of the victim identified as a murderer without a shred of convincing evidence, forensic or otherwise. The police work was incredible, indeed at times risible.

When I was shown the outline to the proposed plot I stressed that in any detective story the finding of the body is a crucial moment, both visually and in terms of character and plot. I suggested that it would be most effective if the body were found by Cordelia. This would have been psychologically as well as visually effective, since she would have had to face for the first time in the television series the reality of the job she was doing. Instead, when the series was shown, we saw neither the body nor its discovery, and Cordelia, when interviewed by the police, didn't even ask how the victim had died. I myself still don't know how she was killed.

And now a fresh complication. I discovered it when sitting under the dryer at my hairdresser's and looking through *Hello!* At the back was an article which stated that Helen Baxendale was pregnant but would continue as Cordelia Gray and the plot 'would accommodate the pregnancy'. When I got home I rang Robert Bernstein, who said that Ecosse couldn't wait to film until after the birth but that they had agreed a plot line. Cordelia would have an affair with an old boyfriend who would then disappear to the United States leaving her, the brave little woman, to cope alone.

In an attempt to salvage what I could, I wrote in April to Ecosse and suggested that Cordelia could have gone on holiday to Italy, met an old lover who was now dying of a brain tumour, and out of compassion and the remembrance of the past, had had a brief affair. Psychologically Cordelia might have thought that her job as a detective was paradoxically making her too remote from real life, too unwilling to take risks, and that for once she was acting with reckless generosity. I still very much disliked the idea of her becoming pregnant, but at least this would make it more believable. I pointed out that a modern, intelligent, responsible young woman does not deprive her child of a father unless that father is vicious or otherwise unsuitable, in which case presumably Cordelia would not have loved him. I even provided in my note of 7th April a page of suggested dialogue. It was a month before a reply came, saying that they were adhering to the original idea.

I then made it plain through my agent that I wished to dissociate myself from the series and, in particular, to have the overall title, *An Unsuitable Job for a Woman*, removed. It was because of this that Ecosse had to go to United Film and Television Productions, for whom they were making the series, and the matter came for the first time to Michele's attention. She totally shares my concern and will do what she can to put matters right, at least as far as the story line is concerned. Robert Bernstein has suggested that we have a meeting, but there is really no point in that. Ecosse have made it abundantly clear that they neither value nor want any input from me and I think I must now concentrate on distancing myself from the series.

Disappointment in the quality of the second series is less important than the way in which Ecosse deliberately kept from me the news about Helen's pregnancy. I can perfectly understand her wish not to make the news public until after the first twelve weeks, but Ecosse, while agreeing to keep her secret, should have made it plain to her that they had an obligation under the contract to tell me as the author, quite apart from the courtesy due between people in a position of trust.

I feel more cheerful now that Michele has taken the matter in hand. But whatever story line is adopted, the damage, as far as I am concerned, can't be repaired, since Cordelia with an illegitimate child is no longer my character. During my January tour of the States I was constantly urged by readers to write another Cordelia Gray story and, before this happened, at least that was an option. I am not at all optimistic that we shall succeed in persuading Ecosse to drop the overall title *An Unsuitable Job for a Woman*. There is, after all, no copyright in titles and I imagine that legally we can't stop them continuing to use it.

The moral here is never let go of the rights to a character; but effectively one always does that with television. It is remarkable how powerful the television companies are and how much control over their work authors lose under the normal television contracts. But most of us are only too happy to have our books televised. The medium is so powerful that inevitably it brings readers in thousands, at least to the paperback editions. And on the whole I have been lucky, first with Anglia Films and now with United Film and Television Productions. When the Anglia film of *Death of an Expert Witness* was made in 1983 it was, as far as I remember, in seven hourly episodes. Today we are lucky to get three. This is due more to financial restrictions than to new methods of direction, although they do play a part. The more leisurely development of plot and character is seldom possible now.

Talking about television with my friends who have also had their works adapted for the small screen, I find we agree on a number of dos and don'ts which it would be useful, but alas impracticable, to include in the contract. Here, in the unlikely event that any television producer or director is interested, are our main points:

1. Don't attempt to televise a novel unless you are really interested in the work. Too often it seems that you are interested only in acquiring the title and the name of the author, and are then happy

to proceed with something which bears very little resemblance to the original work.

2. Novelists accept that television is a visual medium and that things may have to be shown which are otherwise described. But consider first whether the actors could actually communicate in words rather than have everything shown in pictures.

3. Don't fundamentally alter the chief character. With Dalgliesh, the first director decided, as he told me, to bring him downmarket. I had, after all, decided to create a detective who was the son of a Norfolk vicar. That had been my choice and I don't see why television should decide that this was altogether too middle-class for their purposes.

4. Where there is original dialogue, why not use it as far as possible? I was very lucky with the Anglia treatment of *A Taste for Death*, one of the best of the Dalgliesh series. Dame Wendy Hiller took the novel on the set and frequently remarked: 'In the book I say this. Why can't I say it on screen?' It is interesting that writers who are both good and successful, like John Mortimer, seldom alter the original dialogue; *Brideshead Revisited* was almost entirely Waugh. I suspect that adaptors who are less successful can't resist the temptation to have their own words on the screen.

5. As it may be necessary to cut out incidents and characters, what is the point of adding additional ones?

6. Must we always have a car chase? Men may like them (although I can't think why); most women find them boring in the extreme. And if you must have a car chase, must it go on for so long? It need last only as long as it takes us to go and make the tea.

MONDAY, 8TH JUNE

Planning to go to Southwold with Alixe for the weekend, I confidently telephoned a friend, who comes in to feed Polly-Hodge when I am away and who holds a key, but was disconcerted to hear that she was in Gibraltar on holiday – so what to do about Polly-Hodge? I decided to risk taking her. She made some protest when urged into the large wicker basket but was at once silent when the car moved off. We placed the basket on the back seat facing us so that she could both see and hear us. She sat, paws folded inwards, eyes fixed ahead, resolutely resisting the temptation to sleep in case the immense purring creature accompanying us should get out of control.

There were no complaints on the journey until we stopped at a Little Chef on the A12 and decided to have coffee. As soon as we carried her into the café the soft complaining mew began. The waitress at the Little Chef wasn't happy either and explained apologetically that no animals were allowed. We should, of course, have known this, so we took two polystyrene mugs of coffee out to the car. Alixe had decided after our last foray through the East End that she would take the M40 and then the M25 – a longer but, we hoped, swifter route. It worked well both going and coming. We reached Southwold in excellent time for lunch.

There was a sea mist all day on Saturday, the air sweet, soft and warm against the skin. At Blythburgh, looking over the estuary, it was impossible to see if the tide was in as water and sky were an indistinguishable iridescent whiteness. We drove to Snape along the coast road between high banks splattered with red poppies, stopping at Leiston to see the museum, which Alixe hadn't previously visited. It is well arranged, staffed by volunteers and has the charm and interest of all well-kept local museums. It shows the history of the firm of Garrett's, who, at the height of their success, made steam engines and agricultural machinery for home and export and employed as many as 700 local people. I particularly liked the agricultural machinery and the large wooden caravan in which the farm labourers ate and slept while at work on the fields. Alixe was moved most by one of the exhibits from the last war: a tattered Union Jack which had lain on the altar of a crude chapel in a Japanese prisoner-of-war camp, had been placed over the coffins of the many dead, and was at last raised when the camp was liberated. There is always a slight melancholy about these small museums; so many lives lived and lost, a way of life gone forever, each grainy photograph a small *memento mori*.

After the museum we went to the Trading Post, where I bought a Victorian jug and a large Victorian print in its original frame. Some of these prints, although overly sentimental, are beautifully drawn and delicately coloured and seem to have a timeless charm. We loaded it in the back of the car then went on to Snape for lunch at the pub, the Plough and Sail. It was warm enough to eat outside in comfort and we enjoyed roast lamb, perfectly cooked vegetables and sticky toffee pudding fresh from the oven, which was among the best I have ever tasted. I had thought that the sticky toffee pudding at the Ivy could not be bettered, but this was its equal. To eat a cold meal in the fresh air is always agreeable, but to enjoy a well-cooked hot meal is a particular and rarer delight.

After lunch we went to Aldeburgh, parked the car and walked along the beach before returning to Southwold by the coast road. Nettie de Montmorency came at six o'clock to drink red wine and to keep us abreast with local news. We then spent a lazy evening watching a video of *A Room with a View*.

On Sunday to Holy Communion in St Edmund's Parish Church at eight o'clock. I had expected the service to be held in the Lady Chapel with the usual small group of worshippers. Instead there was a substantial congregation in the main body of the church. Most of them, admittedly, were old. I suppose, like myself, they were people who prefer the 1662 liturgy, have an aversion to sermons and prefer to worship early in the day. What one misses, of course, is the music. The rest of the day we spent gardening to good effect, Alixe being particularly adroit at tying up the tangled and top-heavy clematis and training the honeysuckle under the kitchen windows while I more prosaically tackled the weeds between the crevices of the York stone. There was one bright green weed which had encroached like a carpet over a large part of the stones but, because of the recent rain, was quite easy to handle. I could insert a trowel under the edging and then roll it up like a rug, a highly satisfactory procedure that was to show the carefully designed pattern of the stones for the first time.

Later we walked along the promenade towards Walberswick, then back along the beach under a sky rapidly changing from dark blue to black. But the rain held off and, tired, we were able to lie on the pebbles. They are surprisingly comfortable, providing one chooses the right spot where the pebbles are small and can be used rather like a bean-bag, accommodating themselves to jutting bones and curves. It was wonderfully peaceful lying there, looking up at the moving clouds and hearing always the fall and retreating hiss of the waves. I wish I could so order my life that this could happen more often.

Polly-Hodge adjusted remarkably well to the new house. Clare had taken her cat, Charlie, to Southwold and had left a litter tray with a packet of litter in the understairs cupboard. I placed the tray for Polly-Hodge in the conservatory, together with a saucer of water. She drank, and then immediately squatted on the tray, which seemed to me remarkable considering that I have had her for at least ten years and she has never had to use a tray. Then she explored every room in the house, sniffing and obviously defining her territory. Eventually she totally disappeared. We knew that she was upstairs but the most detailed search failed to find her. We even got to the expedient of foolishly opening cupboard doors and drawers which had been shut and which she couldn't possibly have got into. Then Clare phoned and reminded me that Charlie had behaved in just such a way. 'She's in the bathroom,' she said. 'You'll probably find her behind the two wash-basins.' I protested that there was no room behind the two wash-basins, but Clare pointed out that if I lay down flat and looked into the knee-hole between the basins then reached up with my hand, I would find a very narrow slit between the back board and the wall. That is where Charlie had been. I swathed my arm in a towel and then gently inserted it, to be met at once by a hiss and by the appearance of a white furry head. So Polly-Hodge's secret was discovered. She had demonstrated such a degree of ingenuity, not to mention a little malice, that she was thereafter confined to the sitting-room, the kitchen and the conservatory.

Today, Monday, we had an early lunch and were on our way by half-past twelve. The drive back took three hours, not unduly long. Joyce was here to welcome us. Polly-Hodge went to the back bedroom at the top of the house, which she rarely visits, and immediately fell asleep.

WEDNESDAY, 10TH JUNE

This evening Ruth Rendell and I held a conversation on 'The Art of Writing Crime Fiction' at the Royal Geographical Society in aid of the Notting Hill Housing Trust Limegrove Appeal. This was part of a series of literary evenings to raise money for a new centre for West and Central London's homeless people. The Centre will contain forty single bedrooms instead of the usual dormitory accommodation, a doctor's surgery, a subsidized canteen, advice on finding a job and on educational opportunities including computer training, a quiet room for study, showers and a laundry – all the facilities, indeed, to enable homeless young people to rebuild their lives. The facilities will be open during the day to London's rough sleepers, of which there are, I understand, about 2,000 each night. Ruth is one of the Appeal Patrons and gave a brief talk on what it was hoped to achieve before we began speaking.

Ruth and I have taken part in a number of similar events, always for charity. Each event follows the same pattern; we have no chairman and sit together on the platform to talk about our craft, taking it in turns to initiate the conversation. We usually cover the same subjects – how we became writers, why we write crime novels, problems of technique, our differences and similarities – but no conversation follows precisely the same pattern and the level of success depends as much on the response of the audience as it does on us. Tonight was a good evening with a chance to meet a number of friends at the reception before we began. We took questions after the talk and then signed books.

Several people, presumably some of them dealers, came with early editions to be signed. It is dispiriting to see how many of these are now hardly readable with the stuck bindings coming loose and – worse – the paper browning. We are perpetually being reminded of the importance of reading and the written word, yet publishers apparently have given up producing books which will last for more than a few years. I accept that much crime writing is ephemeral, but need it be *so* ephemeral? Before this appalling deterioration in standards, readers could buy a hardback copy of a favourite author in the knowledge that it would be a permanent acquisition for their personal library, to be read and re-read, handled with pleasure and handed down to the next generation. Unless something is done to restore standards we shall have no libraries in future, either national or personal. The reason for the present shoddy productions is, of course, money, but I would have thought that it would pay publishers to bring out at least a limited number of the most important twentieth-century writers in a form which would endure.

I later learned that the evening raised £16,000, enough to build three bedrooms: a remarkable result for a literary evening.

FRIDAY, 12TH JUNE

I am tired, having returned from participating in a session of *Any Questions* at Devizes. As I travelled by train from Paddington to Chippenham where I was to be met, I wondered why I had agreed, for the first time, to take part. I suppose it is an example of my often unwise and sometimes disastrous disposition to say yes to something new which I am far from certain I can carry off successfully. The other guests – if that is the correct word – were Paul Foot, David Puttnam and Bernard Ingham, and we met first at a local hotel for a buffet supper and drink before going on to the venue in the Corn Exchange. Paul Foot and Sir Bernard are old hands at the game; indeed Paul Foot has been taking part, he said, for over thirty years. Nevertheless there is always a sense of slight apprehension before a public performance of any kind, and we would have been happier with a meal after, rather than before, the event.

Over supper Paul Foot and I discussed the Hanratty case and his book on it, published some years ago, in which he seeks to convince the reader that Hanratty was innocent. I said that I had read it but still believed that the verdict was right. Paul said, in that case I couldn't have read the book, but David Puttnam interposed to say that if I said I had read it, then I had. I remember that it was very cleverly argued and certainly raised questions which still remain unanswered. The case is often quoted as demonstrating the differences and the respective merits and demerits of our own accusatorial system of justice and the investigatory system of, for example, France. Under the latter the question would have been addressed as to why a small-time London crook who had never been known to handle guns would be in a field in Slough holding up the lovers Michael Gregsten and Valerie Storie, and why he came to be so far from his normal haunts. The prosecution, naturally, did not address this question and the defence did not do so since they were putting forward the case that he was not there. The explanation I heard later was that he had been hired to frighten the two lovers, but that what had been meant merely as a warning had gone dreadfully wrong and had ended with murder. Then there is the ambiguous part played by Peter Louis Alphon and the fact that the jury were out for nine and a half hours before they returned a verdict of guilty. In some minds a discussion which needed nine and a half hours surely proves that there must have been reasonable doubt. I can't help wondering whether, if Hanratty had been brilliantly defended, a reasonable doubt might not have been established. But none of this affects my own view of his guilt. As the case continues to be controversial it would seem right to exhume the body and establish the truth once and for all by DNA evidence. I find it strange that this hasn't been done.

There was the expected large audience, who were warmed up before we filed on to the platform. The questions were predictable: the recent case of a prisoner released after twenty-three years for a murder which he not only didn't commit, but which was now considered not even to have been murder; how could one deal with the problem of the Balkans; would we employ the Chancellor of the Exchequer to advise on our private finances? I didn't disgrace myself, but nor did I feel at the end that I had said anything either original or useful.

I was driven home with Paul Foot. In the programme he vigorously promoted at length his own preoccupations and seemed rather like a left-wing propagandist who had become permanently stuck in the 1960s. But I found, as so often happens, that I liked him more as I understood him better and we shared the drive to London, if not in agreement, at least in amity.

SUNDAY, 14TH JUNE

I was lucky in the House of Lords draw for tickets to watch yesterday's Trooping the Colour and was particularly pleased about this as I'd hoped to invite Miss Lowe to see the parade with me. The weather forecast was depressing and rain was falling heavily as we joined a queue to go through the security barrier before taking our seats. We were directed to the wrong stand and later had to move, but couldn't have been better placed, in the front row of Stand Five. I had warned my guest to be warmly dressed and this proved very wise advice as, although the rain cleared, it was an exceptionally cold day. The parade took place under grey and lowering skies but no rain fell. The guards marched on wearing short grey cloaks and there was a moment of orchestrated drama when a command was barked out and simultaneously they swept off their cloaks to reveal their scarlet uniforms. The precision of the marching never fails to raise one's spirits and I suspect this must be so even with those who have no sympathy with any military spectacle. But somehow Trooping the Colour lost part of its magic when the Queen substituted a carriage for riding side-saddle to review her guards. The sight of that small figure wearing a summer hat, being slowly paraded like a mascot along the lines of the guards in what I think is a phaeton, looked incongruous and even slightly ludicrous.

Afterwards we went to lunch in the restaurant of the Sainsbury Wing of the National Gallery. It seemed to me a good idea since it gave time for the large crowd to disperse and we were then able to find a cab without too much trouble. I got home in good time to collect my overnight bag and to take the Central Line to Liverpool Street, where I caught the 5 p.m. train to Colchester.

Grey Gowrie had written a few months previously to ask if I would be the speaker at a literary luncheon at the Clare Arts Festival. After ascertaining that he meant Clare, Suffolk, and not Clare in the Republic of Ireland, I agreed – mainly, of course, because Grey had asked. But it proved a happy decision as I enjoyed myself greatly. I was a guest for the night of Countess Benckendorff and felt immediately at home. We had drinks at Cavendish House, were guests at a small dinner party and went early to bed. The weather still continued very unsettled but I was glad to see Cavendish and Clare, the former a particularly lovely village.

Before the luncheon I visited Clare church. It is typical of the best of East Anglian churches, beautifully proportioned, light and airy with the windows and columns closely set and an interesting sixteenth-century lectern. We went up into a galleried pew which I thought at first must have been a Victorian innovation to provide comfort and privacy for the local squire, but is, in fact, much earlier. The parish priest said that the church was considering how best this gallery and the space underneath could be used, perhaps to provide an area for private prayer where people could sit in quiet and be unobserved.

The luncheon was in the old schoolroom. We ate salmon in a very good sauce followed by strawberries and cream and a lemon tart. The service by volunteers, mostly young, was very slow and I found I had transported into Suffolk my London preoccupation with time. When coffee still hadn't appeared at a quarter to three I murmured that guests would find their afternoon gone by the time I had finished speaking; I was assured that they expected their afternoon to be gone and the only worry was whether I would be too late back in London. It was certainly half-past four before the questions were finished and they could have gone on for much longer. One of the visitors was driving back to London and offered me a lift. I was particularly grateful as I had forgotten that the Tube strike had started and I could have been stranded at Liverpool Street.

I had been worried about leaving Polly-Hodge and expected to find her hungry and aggrieved. Happily, although glad to be fed, she seemed reasonably content. I had left her enough to see her through until this afternoon but was later back than I had planned. I expect that, like most of her devious kind, she has a second and secret source of supply for such an emergency.

TUESDAY, 16TH JUNE

This evening I went to the reception and prize-giving of the Society of Authors, which this year was held at the Roof Gardens, Kensington High Street, which I hadn't previously seen. The choice of venue was a happy one as the rain had momentarily ceased and we were able to stroll outside, thus avoiding the congestion and high level of noise which one usually gets at these events. I was surprised at the gardens. There weren't many flowers but a great deal of green, and it seemed amazing that the building could support such a weight of trees, earth and water. The two flamingoes looked rather depressed, as if aware that they were in the wrong place. Michael Palin presented the prizes and made a short, eminently appropriate and very funny speech. Afterwards I was invited by Mark Le Fanu to a small dinner party with Maggie Drabble, Michael Holroyd, Diana Shine, who is shortly, alas, to retire from the Society, and Michael Palin and his wife.

The Society of Authors awards ceremony is a cheerful event, largely because it provides an opportunity for writers to get together. The prizes, except for the Betty Trask Award, are not large and there is no shortlist and no formal dinner where prospective winners have to endure the probing eye of cameras. The Betty Trask Award has, however, always been controversial. It is awarded for a novel of a romantic or traditional nature by a writer under the age of thirty, and one knows perfectly well what Betty Trask, herself a romantic novelist, hoped to achieve. But judges through the years have tended to concentrate on traditional rather than romantic novels and sometimes, I suspect, Betty Trask would be surprised if not a little aggrieved by the choice of book.

WEDNESDAY, 17TH JUNE

Macmillan are planning to reissue two novels by Nicholas Blake, *The Beast Must Die* and *A Tangled Web*, and have asked me to write an introduction suitable for both books. The reissues will be part of a Classic Crime series aimed at bringing back those old favourites which have been allowed to go out of print. I sent off my introduction this afternoon. Nicholas Blake (pseudonym of the poet Cecil Day-Lewis) was one of the writers I most enjoyed during my adolescence but, like Dorothy L. Sayers, he was an innovator of style rather than form. Most of the novels are written within the accepted contemporary conventions of an exciting narrative, a credible and tantalizing mystery and an amateur detective who combines creativity with ratiocination. He based his sleuth, Nigel Strangeways, on his friend the poet W. H. Auden, who was himself a lover of detective fiction and who wrote one of the defining essays on the genre, 'The Guilty Vicarage', published in 1948. In this Auden examines the obstinate appeal of the classical detective story in the light of Christian theology.

In *The Beast Must Die* Nigel Strangeways is married to his second wife, Georgia, a world-famous explorer who contributes her own insights and theories to his cases. It is interesting how many of the 1930s writers who created highly individual detectives married them to successful professional women. Lord Peter Wimsey finally wins popular detective novelist Harriet Vane, although there are differing opinions about whether this wish-fulfilment fantasy on the part of the author was entirely wise. Some readers find Harriet an irritating woman, although she does become more human after marriage. Albert Campion marries Lady Amanda Fitton, whom we are supposed to believe is an aeronautical engineer although we never hear of her with even a spanner, while Ngaio Marsh's Roderick Alleyn is the husband of a famous painter, Troy. At least two of the writers, Dorothy L. Sayers and Ngaio Marsh, were able to make use of their own professional expertise. We can believe that Harriet is a detective novelist and Troy a painter. I think this tendency on the part of women writers to equip their detectives with a successful and distinguished wife is particularly English. Georges Simenon is content to have Mme Maigret happily busy in the kitchen. It is a difficulty I have avoided by keeping Adam Dalgliesh a widower.

SATURDAY, 20TH JUNE

Yesterday to Chatsworth to present the Heywood Hill Literary Prize. It was a perfect day, to the satisfaction of organizers and guests alike as the event is held in the garden. I had Andy collect me at half-past nine to drive me to Derbyshire as I was worried that the one-day strike of maintenance men on the railways might mean a delay on the train. In fact it did, as the train and coach party were late in arriving, but not so late as to put the event seriously out of timing. I hadn't seen Chatsworth before, largely, I suppose, because I don't drive and many of the great houses aren't easily accessible except by car. Superlatives become platitudes in the face of such beauty, such riches of art and architecture and such ordered perfection of nature.

The prize-giving itself was fun. There was a marquee and tables set both inside and on the lawn, and a red-jacketed band played the kind of jolly music one used to hear as a child at the end of piers, adding greatly to the air of slight frivolity. This was not a string quartet affair. It was planned to coincide with the annual party for mayors, so that my first impression was that the local authorities were astonishingly fond of literature. Then there were the literati from London, customers of Heywood Hill, and others who were there presumably because of friendship with the Duke and Duchess or with John Saumarez Smith, who manages the bookshop. So it was a strangely assorted party, but one which went remarkably well, although the mayoral chains sat gently clanking together and there wasn't a great deal of mingling. I envied the confidence which could mix two such discordant groups in the happy assurance that a good time would be had by all, as, indeed, it was.

No one, including me, spoke for too long, which is always an advantage. The two prize-winners were Richard Ollard, whose biography of Pepys I had re-read before travelling, and a writer new to me, Norman Lewis, travel writer, diarist and novelist. He is nearly ninety, and in his speech after the presentation described how, as a boy, he had become enchanted with the written word. He was sent to spend long holidays with three maiden aunts, one an epileptic and subject to constant fits, another who spent the day weeping and a third who was manic. They wouldn't let him out of the house so he watched other children at play from the windows. However, they had a library and he was able to relieve the lonely hours of his imprisonment with reading. From this grew a lasting love of books and his own career as a writer. Of all the reasons given by writers for that first spur to creativity, being imprisoned by mad aunts is the most intriguing.

After lunch guests were able to see the house – particularly the library, where special books had been laid out – or to walk in the park. Then, when the coach had left for the station, I relaxed in the drawing-room until tea was served. I had been invited to stay the night and the room into which I was shown was called 'The View'. It was appropriately named; the view was magnificent. I gazed out of the immense window with its twenty-four panes at the garden and, to the horizon, grasslands, hills, woods, and the summer sky. There were enough books in the room – carefully chosen to suit all possible tastes – to keep one happily reading for a month.

I went to rest before dressing for dinner and picked on Enid Bagnold's autobiography. What a complicated, not entirely likeable, woman she must have been. One passage: 'Who wants to become a writer, and why? Because it is the answer to everything, to why I am here, to uselessness. It's the streaming reason for living; to note, to pin down, to build up, to create, to be astonished at nothing, to cherish the oddities, to let nothing go down the drain, to make something, to make a great flower out of life even if it's a cactus.'

Who wants to become a detective novelist and why? To impose order on terrifying chaos? To bring justice out of injustice? To give the illusion that we live in a moral and comprehensible universe? To make money? To provide a structure within which writer and reader can safely confront terror, violence, death? To show that to some things at least there is an answer? To distance the atavistic fear of cruelty and death? To make a pattern? To explore men and women under the trauma of a police investigation for the ultimate crime? To create a modern morality play in which truth is at least established even if it doesn't prevail? To celebrate justice? To get the better of one's enemies? To gain the illusion of power? To advise and entertain, solace and delight? Because it's the thing one does best?

Bagnold quotes a sentence from Gibbon which caught my eye: 'In that silent vacancy that precedes our birth.' Is our love for the architecture, art and beauty, which links us to the past, part of our need to know where we come from and, by touching, seeing, loving inanimate objects, to give the illusion that we have been here longer than our brief span? It can only work one way, and perhaps that is part of the terror of death. When that final lid is screwed down on us there will be no more vicarious living. But now we stretch out minds, even hands, into the past and gain a spurious immortality. The silent vacancy comes alive.

Tom Stoppard was among the guests and I found in my room the Faber paperback edition of his broadcast plays. They were first broadcast as long ago as 1966 and I can't think why the BBC doesn't let us hear them again. The Corporation must have a wealth of archive. Why is it so neglected? Why do we no longer see on our screens the single play by a distinguished playwright?

Before I began dressing for dinner the telephone rang and the butler said that the Duke wondered whether I would like a glass of champagne. Indeed I would, and he brought it up personally to all his guests. I was thinking how much at home one feels in the private apartments. But how strange to live in a house where every yard walked reveals something fresh of beauty, interest or history, where one glances up to see a Velázquez, a Rubens, a Lawrence, a Frans Hals, a Van Dyck. Some of the Duke's purchases of modern art were resting against the wall, obviously awaiting their right place. It was interesting to see that even the owners of great houses face the problems of we humbler mortals, not knowing what to do with recent acquisitions. I could never get used to living in a house with 175 rooms, 359 doors, nearly 8,000 panes of glass to be cleaned, 56 lavatories and 3,426 feet of passages. It must sometimes seem far more of a responsibility than a pleasure.

After dinner, sitting on the terrace with the other house guests as darkness fell, with the house floodlit and golden behind us, I wished I was standing on a distant hill looking down at it.

This morning, from my bedroom window, looking out over the formal gardens to the river, I could see coloured tents and a large marquee erected for what was apparently to be some kind of flower show, and in the next field a fun-fair with a children's carousel. Small figures moved about with that air of unflurried busyness which is always agreeable to watch. I could have been Glencora, Duchess of Omnium, surveying the preparations for her great summer fête. I almost expected to see the archery targets being set up for the beribboned and crinolined ladies to demonstrate their skills while allowing the gentlemen discreetly to help them pull the bow. But instead the fête burst into bloom with the morning and I watched while, like an accelerated film, shrubs and small trees appeared as if by magic. It was one of those moments when a vivid scene from fiction becomes reality.

After breakfast I went to the shop, which is in the Orangery and, unlike some shops of its kind, actually sells things that one is happy to buy. Andy reappeared with the car at half-past nine, but it was nearly an hour later before we left. We called in at the farm shop and then had a comfortable ride home.

I went down to John Lewis with some Baxter prints which wanted re-framing and to look out samples of wallpaper in the hope that work will actually begin on repairing the house sometime in the next month or so. Then home, a quiet evening writing up the scribbled note for this diary and early to bed.

TUESDAY, 30TH JUNE

I arrived home this evening from a visit to Stockton, where today I received the honorary degree of Doctor of Letters of the University of Durham; this is my sixth honorary degree.

I left London for Darlington yesterday afternoon, was met at the station and driven to my hotel in Stockton in time to change for dinner in the Board Room with the Chancellor, Sir Peter Ustinov, and senior officers of the University. My fellow honorary graduands were the novelist Pat Barker and the actor Richard Griffiths. I hadn't met either of them before, but I admire their work and I greatly enjoyed their company. There was much laughter at the dinner, as one might expect with both Peter Ustinov and Richard Griffiths present, and I thought I detected some competition in wit and a slight professional glint in the eye as they viewed each other across the table.

This morning we got together at the Town Hall to form a procession to the parish church, where the degree ceremony was to take place. It was a long and colourful procession. The English are not given to marching except when in the Forces, and even a formal procession has the air of a leisurely and companionable stroll by people at ease in each other's company and, however bizarrely costumed, not much interested in the reaction of spectators. Apparently last year one of the local onlookers turned to her companion and asked, 'What's all this about, then?', to receive the reply, 'I think it's a Gypsy wedding.'

This was my first visit to Stockton (although not to the North East) and I was impressed by how much is being achieved in one of the UK's poorest regions in terms of deprivation, poverty and unemployment. The Stockton campus, which is an integral part of Durham University, was created in 1992 in purpose-built accommodation on the banks of the River Tees. From the beginning it sought to attract local students, particularly adults and those with no family tradition of higher education. This it is doing with remarkable success: over sixty per cent of entrants to the Stockton campus come from the region, over fifty per cent are mature students coming other than through the traditional A-level route, and the degree results achieved are identical with those of Durham. Even on my brief two-day visit I felt I was being welcomed into a lively community of dedicated and enthusiastic people committed to their vision of what the North East deserves and what it can achieve. For me this has been an educative as well as an enjoyable two days.

JULY

To granddaughter Eleanor and partner Scott for tea and to see their West Hampstead flat. It is small but delightful with light pouring in from large windows and a skylight, and a balcony which now has been made into a small garden. It overlooks the railway, but I never mind the sound of passing trains. When as a child I lived at The Woodlands outside Ludlow, I could hear the trains across the fields when I was in bed, a sound at once comforting, exciting and holding the promise of imagined journeys. On our childhood Sunday walks we would race across the fields at the first intimation of an approaching train, clamber on to a stile and wave at the driver and fireman. Invariably they would wave back. If we were lucky, the fireman might be feeding the furnace and we would glimpse the flaming heart of the monster.

It was on this day, 12th July, in 1988 that Douglas Hurd sent me the letter from the Home Office to ask whether I would be willing for my name to go forward for appointment as a Governor of the BBC. This wasn't altogether unexpected as Duke Hussey, Chairman of the Governors, had telephoned me a few days earlier to get my reaction. His call was totally unexpected but welcome.

My term of five years as Governor, despite the occasional trauma and the persistent realization that I was both less useful and less effective than I had hoped, was one of my most enjoyable periods of public service.

The BBC has had a board of twelve Governors since its inception and the system has on the whole worked well. Governors are appointed by the Queen on the recommendation of the Prime Minister and, as with so much in British public life, the process by which the selection is made remains mysterious. In recent years there has been a pattern. One Governor represents Scotland, one Wales and one Northern Ireland. In addition, there is usually a Governor experienced in finance, one who is a trade unionist, one representing the arts, and an ex-ambassador, who is presumably included to have special regard to the interests of the World Service. The others are usually eminent in their fields. It has always been regarded as an honour to serve as a Governor of the BBC and I certainly so regarded it.

During the five years in which I served, the BBC was chiefly concerned with ensuring the renewal of the Charter. This was a corporate effort involving the enthusiasm and commitment of the Governors, the Director General, Michael Checkland and his successor John Birt, the Board of Management and the staff. Success could certainly not be taken for granted. The BBC had powerful friends and public support but it also had powerful and well-informed enemies who accused the Corporation of extravagance, mismanagement and political bias. It was accepted that there had to be changes, some of which would be painful.

The most traumatic, probably the most controversial, meeting of the Governors was one at a private dinner when it was decided, not at first unanimously, to appoint John Birt to succeed Michael Checkland as Director General. Both the Chairman and Vice-Chairman felt strongly that it was right to make that decision, and at that time. John Birt had served as deputy for five years. He was the obvious candidate; he had both the dedication and the strength required to assist the Governors in making the necessary reforms if the Charter were to be renewed, and to announce the successor to Michael Checkland well in advance of his retirement would avoid months of manoeuvring and speculation which could only be damaging to the BBC. It also seemed pointless to go through the procedure of advertising the post if this were merely a charade to give the impression of transparency.

The appointment of the next Director General will, no doubt, be made in a less controversial manner, which is not to say the choice will be without controversy. But he or she will still be the candidate acceptable to the Chairman. This is inevitable. The relationship between the Chairman and the Director General is vitally important to the BBC. They need to be aware of their special and different responsibilities and the defining limits of those responsibilities. There should be mutual sympathy and respect between them and a clear recognition by both of what is meant by public service broadcasting, a recognition also that their roles are complementary, not collusive.

A question, although it was never raised vociferously during my time as a Governor, is whether the Governors should be chosen in a more open and accountable way, perhaps even elected. I can't see how election could work satisfactorily but it shouldn't be difficult to make the selection process more transparent than it is at present.

There is a dilemma at the heart of the BBC and one which I don't think has been resolved. The Corporation should represent excellence in broadcasting, the standard by which all other broadcasters are happy to be measured. This excellence is sometimes difficult to reconcile with high viewing figures, and the BBC has always been almost morbidly conscious of its share of the market. The fear, largely unspoken, has always been that if the listening and viewing share falls below a critical figure (thirty per cent is often quoted), the licence fee will be in jeopardy since viewers and listeners will argue that it is unfair that they should be compulsorily charged for a service which they rarely use. This leads to a concentration on viewing and listening figures and an insidious temptation to go down-market, which could be fatal to the future of the BBC. If the BBC does not provide something different from, and consistently better than, other broadcasters, it may as well be out in the market place fighting for its audience share like everyone else, and paid for by those who want it.

It seems to me that in the last two years the BBC has concentrated more on market share than on quality. In particular, the reiteration that channels must appeal to the young is a euphemism for going down-market, hardly a compliment to the young. I sometimes feel that, if I covered up the name of the channel in the newspaper listings, it would be difficult to see which programmes have been put out by the BBC. Already it is in danger of becoming just one more broadcaster. We may indeed reach the curious situation where a new broadcaster will come on the scene dedicated to excellence and usurp the high ground once occupied by the BBC.

Whether it is paid for by licence fee or by general taxation, the BBC needs this assured income if it is to continue. My own view is that people will pay for it if it provides quality, even if they watch or listen comparatively rarely. I do not share my elder daughter's enthusiasm for opera, but am happy that I should contribute through taxation to the provision of a major opera house; the fact that I no longer have children or grandchildren at school does not mean that I resent helping to pay for national education.

I came to the BBC as a keen listener and viewer, but as one who was always wary about the subtle dishonesty of much television. It seems to me important always to recognize that every image shown is one which the cameraman has chosen to film and the director, editor or producer has chosen to show. I learned a salutary lesson when I was in the Health Service. There was a shortage in the region of beds for the young chronic sick, who sometimes had to be inappropriately nursed in long-stay geriatric wards. The BBC set out to make a programme about this problem. It showed a very young and pretty patient suffering from MS and, in filming the ward in which she was nursed, concentrated on the most senile, depressing and unattractive of the old people. No mention was made of the fact that the young patient had been offered a place in a young chronic sick centre more than once but preferred to stay where she was because she liked being pampered by some of the elderly patients, enjoyed the excellent facilities of the physiotherapy and occupational therapy departments, and was taken home most weekends by one of the nurses to give her a change of scene. It did not need this programme to reinforce what I suspected; documentary producers all too often decide what point they want to make and then look for the evidence.

I also dislike television programmes which muddle fact and fiction, but usually with the intention of leaving the viewer believing he has seen the truth. *The Monocled Mutineer* and *Tumbledown*, both excellently directed and acted, were examples of this less than honest filming. Only too often protests are met with the excuse, 'But it made good television.' We should ask more often, Was it fair? Was it balanced? Was it true? But it seems to me that the biggest problem for the Governors is that they have least power in the one area which matters most: the making of programmes. The BBC exists for no other purpose than to put out programmes of the highest quality, both on television and on radio. Everything it does should be subordinate to its purpose of excellence in programme-making. Here the Governors have some influence but no real power. By tradition Governors do not preview programmes; the occasion on which this was done with *Real Lives* when Stuart Young was chairman, provoked immense resentment and controversy. Any previewing, and therefore prejudging, of programmes is regarded as impugning the artistic freedom of producers and directors – a suggestion which has always been anathema to the BBC. Programme-making must be left to the experts and they must have the right to fail as well as the satisfaction of succeeding. But all this does mean that Governors are virtually powerless actively to influence artistic excellence, the very task which it is their responsibility to uphold.

The BBC today is not a happy organization. Efficient managerial systems, providing they do not substitute one onerous bureaucracy for another, are important, but less important than the clear acceptance of the ethos and responsibility of public service broadcasting and a climate in which creativity and artistic excellence can flourish.

For a publicly funded organization and one which frequently proclaims its openness, the BBC is extraordinarily secretive. The costs of the central administration are high in relation to those devoted to programme-making and it is difficult to justify the millions spent on outside managerial advice, particularly in the light of the surely adequate salaries now paid to members of the Board of Management. Radio continues to take second place to television and there sometimes seems with radio a somewhat desperate desire for change, as if change in itself were synonymous with progress and improvement. The high cost of equipping the BBC to compete in the international market of digital broadcasting has drained resources from programme-making. The BBC still produces superb programmes but too often they are peaks of excellence in a depressing plateau of trivia.

Much will depend on the talents, energy and vision of the new Director General. Ours is an age obsessed with systems and managerial techniques. What the BBC needs now is someone who can inspire and enthuse human beings, particularly the creative men and women on whom the future depends. Since it seems unlikely that the public will now be prepared to pay a higher licence fee, perhaps the BBC should concentrate on doing less and doing it better.

Before I finished my five-year stint as a Governor I was asked to address my fellow Governors and the Board of Management after dinner at one of our annual residential conferences. Re-reading what I said then, the talk – which, with minor cuts, I attach as Appendix One (page 241) – seems moralistic and even naïve. But what strikes me most forcefully is how old-fashioned it is. I could be speaking of a different age, a different BBC. I find this thought depressing. But the talk still represents what I feel about the purpose and ethics of public service broadcasting and, particularly, about a service which describes itself as the British Broadcasting Corporation.

MONDAY, 13TH JULY

I have just finished reading *The Trial* by Charlotte M. Yonge, which was kindly sent to me by Dinah Birch of Trinity College, Oxford, following our discussion on the Victorian novel. The main interest for me in this somewhat turgid novel is the insight it gives into the domestic and professional lives of middle-class Victorians, and particularly the subservient and restricted role of the women. If the author was intending, at least partially, to write what Trollope in his autobiography described as the novel of sensation, as opposed to the novel of realism, she hasn't succeeded. The murder comes too late, and the story has too little narrative energy to generate either tension or excitement.

With it I have been re-reading *The Duke's Children*, prompted by Dinah's excellent preface to the Penguin edition. I agree with her assessment of Frank Tregear, an admirable young man, no doubt, but one definitely on the make, whose head always rules his heart. We feel none of the sympathy for him that we do for poor Burgo Fitzgerald. I love the Barchester saga and these are books I invariably take with me on long journeys but, for me, *The Duke's Children* is the least successful. Of the young people only Lady Mabel Grex engages my sympathy. Lady Mary Palliser is obstinate and charmless, Lord Silverbridge and his brother no more than amiable nonentities. I found the pert prettiness of the egregiously popular and beautiful American heiress Isabel Boncassen more irritating than appealing. It is obvious that the author was in love with his creation. If Lord Silverbridge had had any sense he would have married Mabel Grex, but the young men in Trollope, seldom worthy of the women who love them, can only be happy with wives who are content to treat them as lords and masters and regard them as young gods. Even the Duke, one of Trollope's most successful and remarkable characters, loses my sympathy when he treats Mrs Finn with ungentlemanly callousness and injustice.

I had planned today to go to Hatfield to have lunch with Clare and visit Lady Salisbury's garden, which is only open on Mondays. However, I had a telephone call from Kay Harper at Swavesey to say that Doris was dying and would like to see me. I caught the 10.15 train from King's Cross, which should have taken just over fifty minutes, but was delayed and diverted because of a defective rail. Doris was semi-conscious but was able to recognize me and when I bent over to kiss her and say 'God bless you', she was able to whisper 'And you too'. She was on one of those merciful continual morphine lines into a vein and was in no pain, although the constant hoarse gurgling in her throat was distressing to hear. But she is fortunate in being nursed to the end at home with Kay's loving care and with nurses and other helpers whom she knows coming in regularly instead of a continual change of agency staff which so many hospital patients have to face. Despite the growth of the hospice movement, which has led the way in the care of the dying, there are still far too many patients who endure unnecessary suffering at the end, or who die among strangers. Doris is dying among those who love her, without pain and, I think, without fear. This is the most any of us can hope for.

TUESDAY, 14TH JULY

I went to the Royal Garden Party, arriving at the Hyde Park Corner gate. This meant I avoided the queues and had a quiet, enjoyable walk through the gardens. The lawn seemed more crowded this year than ever and, being reluctant to join the scrum, I didn't set eyes on any Royal from beginning to end. The Garden Party is wonderful for people-watching, which is its main attraction. I did manage to procure some iced coffee and sandwiches before leaving early. I know that protocol decrees that no one leaves before royalty on occasions when they are present, but I think this can hardly apply to the annual Garden Parties.

Then to the Conservative ward party held in the Cardinal Vaughan School because of the uncertain weather, where I discovered that I was billed as guest of honour and was expected to make a short speech. This I did and returned home in time to see the first instalment of ITV's *A Certain Justice*. The adaptation is skilful and most of the acting admirable, particularly Penny Downie, who plays Venetia Aldridge. It was possible not only to hear what the actors were saying, but to know who the characters were. Admittedly, as author of the book, I had a head start in this, but I get increasingly tired of TV series when one has to wait twenty minutes to sort out the characters and their relationships to each other. If tonight's standard is maintained, this should be a successful adaptation.

Today is Jane's birthday. We don't celebrate birthdays with much enthusiasm in the family except those which mark rites of passage, but I expect she will have the usual quiet and enjoyable dinner with her family. I shall hand over my gift when I am next in Oxford.

Inevitably the anniversary brings back its memories. Before she was born I was living with Clare at White Hall in Chigwell Row, Essex. In June, near the expected birth date, Clare was collected by my parents-in-law and taken to Barry, South Wales, where my father-in-law was stationed, and I went to stay with Dr Lindsey Batten and his family at Lyndhurst Road in Hampstead. Richard Batten had been a contemporary of Connor at Cambridge and at medical school. I had booked in at Queen Charlotte's Hospital in Goldhawk Road, a decision which, considering the length of the journey from Essex, now seems to me somewhat perverse.

While I was at Lyndhurst Road, the doodlebug bombardment began. I can remember gazing with incredulity at my first sight of a flying bomb, which looked more like an aeronautical aberration than a weapon of war. It was shaped like a plump fish, with two stubby wings like fins, and carried at the tail a superstructure from which spurted great tongues of fire. It flew low and the noise was incredibly loud, something between a rattle and a drone. It was the first unmanned terror weapon to hit Britain and was much dreaded, partly because there was a depersonalized malice about those pilotless machines, but chiefly because they were totally indiscriminate. Worst of all was the moment when the engine cut out. The silence then seemed absolute. It felt as if the whole of London was holding its breath. And then, after a few seconds, would come the explosion. I greeted it always with a mixture of relief and shame: relief that it hadn't fallen on me, and shame that, in a sense, I had benefited from someone else's tragedy.

Then labour began, and as I went into Queen Charlotte's the bombardment was almost continuous. Looking back, the morale in the eight-bedded ward was remarkably high. Windows were kept wide open to prevent flying glass. We had our babies in cots by the side of the bed, and when the bombardment began, were instructed to place one of our pillows over the head of the cot. There was, I remember, a shortage of linen and the ward sister seemed as concerned about this as she was about the constant sound of falling bombs and the cacophony above. She would raid the linen cupboard and then secrete fresh sheets and pillowcases in our beds. From time to time a sister from a neighbouring ward would descend on us, turning over pillows and rummaging beneath the blankets before bearing off her trophies in triumph.

Night time was the most difficult to endure with equanimity. All the babies were moved to the basement and our beds were wheeled out into a corridor and placed against the walls. It was felt that this would give us the best chance of survival if the hospital received a direct hit. I can remember lying there silently weeping with that unfocused misery which occasionally follows childbirth and which is made worse by the feeling that one ought to be experiencing great happiness and maternal fulfilment, not this debilitating and un-controllable sadness. My great fear was that the hospital would indeed receive a direct hit and that in the confusion and carnage I would be unable to find my baby. Where exactly had they put the babies? What if the stairs to the basement were blocked? How in the darkness and choked with dust would I find the right cot? What if I were injured and couldn't get to the basement? I can remember praying: 'O Lord, if you will let me out of here alive with my baby I'll never complain again.' It is a prayer which, with uncomfortable persistence, has returned throughout the years to haunt me.

After I was discharged, I went with Jane to join my parents-in-law in Barry. I can remember with what joyous exultation I saw the sea for the first time in years. I stayed for long enough to get strong and then returned to White Hall. Unfortunately this coincided with the bombardment by V-2 rockets. I found them far less frightening than the doodlebugs, partly because there was no warning. The explosive power was much greater, as was the noise of the explosion, but the fact that I could hear it meant that I had survived. There was a system whereby the siren announced an imminent danger warning, but this was ineffective with the V-2s. There seemed no point in trying to take any preventative measures and we all stayed in our beds until the night when a rocket fell at the edge of Hainault Forest. By then we were all so used to the sound of explosives that we woke momentarily and then turned again to sleep. When daylight broke, I felt an unaccustomed coolness in the room and discovered that the windows had been blown out and that Jane was lying in her cot surrounded by shards of glass, any of which could have killed her. Gathering her up and going to the bathroom, I looked up through the non-existent ceiling to the sky. Repairs were carried out with remarkable speed during air raids, but after that night we all moved to the cellar.

The authoritarian and largely misguided baby-rearing doctrines of Dr Truby King were still in vogue, and there were dire warnings about the deplorable results if babies were not fed strictly at four-hourly intervals. But I could hardly let Jane cry at night when the cellar was occupied by the humped bodies of three overworked doctors, the elderly cook, the unmarried housemaid with her small daughter, and Clare. Accordingly Jane had only to whimper to be latched on to a not particularly productive breast, where at least she got comfort if not much sustenance. The cellar door was left ajar for Mrs Price-Watt's elegant pedigree cat who, blessed with an unpronounceable name, was called Poo-Poo. She would hunt at night, bringing her prey to eat on our mattresses so that periods of wakefulness would coincide with the crunching of seemingly innumerable bones and Mrs Price-Watts's plaintive protests.

And then came the morning when Mrs Price-Watts rushed into my part of the house to announce with a mixture of excitement and awe that the invasion of Europe had started. Her eldest son was serving in the RAMC with the airborne forces, so that it was a time of anxiety as well as of huge relief and of expectation. And as the invading armies advanced, so the launch sites of the V-1s and V-2s were overrun and this most disagreeable of bombardments gradually ceased. The children have asked me why I didn't leave Essex and sometimes I wonder myself. But it wouldn't have been easy. Accommodation in safe areas was difficult to find. But I think the main reason was that after four years of war, those of us living in or near London had got used to staying put.

Over twenty years later, when Clare and her husband were in Huntsville, Alabama, I met and walked in the woods with Germans who had been sending off the flying bombs and rockets and who had been recruited by the Americans at the end of the war. Even more ironic was to see a V-2 on display at the local museum, and bearing the label: 'The first intercontinental rocket of the free world.' British visitors at least managed to get the wording changed.

SATURDAY, 18TH JULY

Today I gave the address at the Annual General Meeting of the Jane Austen Society, which was held, as it usually is, in the grounds of Chawton House. I was met at Alton station by Louise Ross and her husband Charles, who kindly drove me to the venue. I had previously met Louise when I spoke at Dartington and it was she who found me my treasured first edition of *Emma*.

The Jane Austen Society, which was founded in 1940 by Dorothy Darnell, then with the prime object of preserving Chawton Cottage, is one of the liveliest of literary societies. The grounds of nearby Chawton House are an appropriate place for the Annual General Meeting since the house was the property of Edward Austen, who was adopted by his wealthy kinsmen, the Knights, and who inherited Chawton with other properties in 1812. Until recently it was still owned by a member of the family but had fallen into disrepair and there was considerable anxiety, locally and among Austen devotees, about its future. At one time it was thought the grounds might become a golf course. The house has now been bought by a wealthy American lady who is restoring it and proposes to use it to house her library of the books of pre-Austen female novelists. It will thus become a study and conference centre and I hope will occasionally also be opened to the general public.

Accompanied by the architect working on the restoration, I was able to see round the house before I gave my talk. Like most Elizabethan manors it strikes one as very dark, with low ceilings, leaded windows and wood-lined walls. The date, 1588, on one of the immense fireplaces identifies the age of the original building. The work of restoration is proving fascinating since the panellings are of different dates and some of the most recent work, once removed, reveals original sixteenth-century wallpaper. Even when restored the house will still be dark and it is hard to imagine these tortuous corridors echoing to the laughter of Jane Austen's numerous nephews and nieces, including the children of Edward Knight, whose wife Mary died at his main property, Godmersham, after giving birth to their eleventh child. I wonder if Jane Austen, hearing the news, remembered the tart sentence in a letter she wrote to her niece Fanny after hearing that a neighbour had given birth to her eighteenth child: 'I would recommend to her and Mr Dee the simple regimen of separate rooms.'

Mary wasn't the only one of Jane Austen's sisters-in-law to die in childbirth and I have no doubt that it was her fear of – indeed repulsion at – the idea of possible yearly pregnancies and the risk of early death which played a part in her refusal of the proposal of Harris Bigg-Wither, which she at first accepted and then rejected next day. I don't think she would have been deterred by the lack of romantic love. If the match were sensible and advantageous and she felt a genuine liking and respect, that would probably have been enough. Perhaps the liking and respect were not sufficiently strong or, more likely, she knew the marriage would be fatal to her art. She seldom wrote or spoke of pregnant women without sympathy, and sometimes a note of disgust. Her books were her children and they were sufficient.

We were fortunate in the weather. A very large marquee had been erected to accommodate about 700 people, some of them from the North American society. I am told the Society always has a sunny summer day for its AGM, but this year hovering dark clouds made it look as if the record was to be broken. There was, in fact, a brief shower at the beginning of my speech but it was no more than a slight inconvenience. The talk – included as Appendix Two (page 250) – was well received, largely, I think, because this audience could catch all the allusions and could no doubt themselves add to the number of clues I had discovered.

After the talk I had a very busy signing session and then went with Louise to join the congregation for Evensong at St Nicholas, Chawton. It was so crowded that we had to stand. The service, largely traditional Prayer Book, included part of a prayer composed by Jane Austen and the hymn 'O for a Closer Walk with God' by her favourite poet, Cowper. Afterwards we visited the two restored gravestones of Jane Austen's mother and her sister Cassandra. I know we should be grateful to Cassandra, who did much while they lived together with their mother at Chawton Cottage to ensure her sister's privacy, to relieve her of some household duties and to give her time for writing, but it is hard to be sympathetic to someone who obviously settled into somewhat forbidding spinsterhood at an early age and who destroyed so many of her sister's letters. I suppose she would argue that the eyes of posterity had no right to see them, but it is still a regret. It's possible that some of them dealt with matters of family money, nearly always controversial, but on which a family like the Austens would particularly wish to be reticent. It was fortunate for Jane Austen that her brother Edward was given away for adoption and subsequently became rich, since it enabled him to provide a home at Chawton Cottage for his sisters and mother, but I suspect he could have provided one earlier and endowed it more generously.

I first read Jane Austen when I was eight or nine years old and attended the Sunday school attached to Ludford church. There was a small cupboard in the hall with a number of books which we children could borrow. Some, like *The Wide, Wide World*, *A Peep Behind the Scenes* and *Jessica's First Prayer* were of depressing piety, but I also discovered there *Little Women* and *Pride and Prejudice*. It seems curious now that the latter should appeal to a child so young, but I was hungry for books and this was one I could both read and to an extent understand, although the irony must have eluded me. Jane Austen has remained my favourite author.

It seems extraordinary, if indeed it is true, that she was once seen as a gently-born, pure-minded spinster, dutiful daughter, compliant sister, affectionate aunt. We don't need the letters to show us a different Jane. There is passion in the novels, even if it is too subtle to be recognized by Charlotte Brontë. And there was passion, too, in her life, if only the passion of what the critic D. W. Harding described as 'regulated hatred'. To me it is far more like controlled resentment. We have to resist the temptation to foist on to her a twentieth-century sensibility; she was hardly deprived by domesticity of a university education or a profession, but she must have known that, however brilliant or successful her brothers, it was she who had genius. And yet, until she could earn from her novels, she was totally without power to control her own life. If her father decided to move to Bath, then Jane moved, neither consulted nor considered. Every penny she had to spend came from her father or a brother. Even Cassandra had the income from the £1,000 left to her by her fiancé. Jane had nothing. No wonder she said, once the money started coming in, that it was the pewter as well as the fame which she relished.

We drove past the cottage on our way to Alton station. It looked spruce, as if it had been recently repointed, and the little village was full of cars. When I first visited Chawton there was a great quietness about the place and it was possible to believe that it looked much as it had in Jane Austen's time. With the bypass the road is certainly quiet and outwardly the changes are small, but I suspect that the television series have led to a large increase in visitors (there were nearly 50,000 last year) so that the cottage will begin to acquire that carefully preserved look of all monuments.

MONDAY, 20TH JULY

Today to Cambridge Crematorium for the funeral of Doris. I arrived much too early, as I usually do, and sat quietly in the garden. Between the ordered rose beds and tended grass was scrubland red with poppies, and beyond it I could see women working in a field, bending between rows of unidentifiable crops. I wondered how much they were paid for such back-breaking work and who got most of the profit, the grower or the supermarket.

I arrived from the station by taxi. Drawing up at the crematorium, the taxi driver said, 'I believe in God, but all the rest is crap. If God did send His son to earth, assuming He had a son, I don't see why we think He came as a human. It's just our vanity. It's making ourselves too important to think God would bother to make His son look like us. He'd be much more likely to make Him an eagle.' I felt unable to argue this interesting theological point.

As Doris was an unbeliever, the service – if that is the appropriate word – was humanist. It was ably and sensitively conducted by a woman humanist who had obviously taken considerable trouble to make it appropriate to Doris's life and interests and who had visited Doris to discuss with her what she would like. All Doris's friends took part, either with a reading or a personal reminiscence. I have been to other non-religious funerals which have been less successful. All ceremonies, even the simplest, need preparation. We may believe that we go into the darkness like animals but we still have a human need to celebrate with love and dignity this final rite of passage.

My mother's ashes are buried somewhere in this crematorium garden, although 'ashes' has always seemed a ridiculously anodyne word for what is essentially the packaged grit of crushed bones. She died in Chesterton Hospital after an old age made unhappy by Parkinson's disease and unrelievable mental anguish. That final misery left me wondering, as it still does, why those who live good lives relying on the support and comfort of their religious faith should be denied its solace at the end. My father, who was then living in a small and damp flat close to Poole Harbour, arrived for the cremation wearing his boating clothes, not from any lack of respect but because I don't think it occurred to him that it would be appropriate to change. After the service – although that is too dignified a word for the cold impersonalities of this preliminary to hygienic disposal – he walked round the garden surveying the shrubs with a gardener's eye, before finally saying, 'This one looks healthy', and deciding that the ashes should be sprinkled beneath it. I have no hope of identifying it now.

His own death was more merciful. He had been admitted to a

residential home overlooking Oulton Broad, where he settled very happily and might have enjoyed a peaceful decade or two if he hadn't taken it upon himself to scythe the lawn. He was found dead among the tall grass and wild flowers on a warm June afternoon. The doctor said that he had suffered a major heart attack and had almost certainly died instantly and without pain. Perhaps I, who am like him in so many ways, will be equally fortunate.

SUNDAY, 26TH JULY

I read moving but distressingly frank extracts in *The Times* from a book written by John Bayley about living with his wife Iris Murdoch now that she is suffering from Alzheimer's. I had never thought that anything either reassuring or optimistic could be said about this terrible disease, which nearly all old people dread, but John Bayley writes that, so far from diminishing his marriage, it has brought him and his wife even closer. Personally I would feel that closeness had been bought at far too high a price. Other people's marriages are, of course, always mysterious, perhaps even to the partners themselves. I was surprised by John Bayley writing that one thing which had originally attracted him to his wife was the mistaken belief that she lacked sexual appeal to other men. How could this have been possible? I have always thought her very lovely. I don't know her well, and on the few occasions when we did meet, felt myself inhibited by the knowledge of her infinitely superior intelligence.

I can remember one summer when she and her husband drove me from Oxford to Penelope and Jack Lively's garden party at Great Rollright. All the way she asked about my children and grand-children, rather as if a family were a strange phenomenon of which she had no knowledge and of which she wished, as a novelist, to inform herself. I felt that she had a genuine interest in me and my family but this, I think, was part of her special grace. Another occasion, strong in memory, is when we were both guests at Grand Night at the Middle Temple. Before the procession into the Great Hall, Iris and I were in the women's cloakroom. It was an occasion for dressing up and I had done my best. I saw that Iris was studying herself in the mirror, but without any apparent interest in her image. She was wearing shoes remarkably like carpet slippers, a dirndl skirt in flowered cotton such as one might have worn on a beach, what was obviously one of her husband's striped shirts, a black velvet jacket and magnificent amber beads. She looked absolutely wonderful. I don't know how interested she was in dress but her taste, although erratic, produced a highly individual result.

One Christmas we were both invited to read a lesson at a service of carols and lessons held at St Martin-in-the-Fields Church in aid of a book trade charity. I found myself sitting beside her in the front row, placed in order ready to mount into the high pulpit when our time came to read. Iris asked me, 'Are you a Christian?' I began my usual confused reply to this question. I said that I regarded myself as one and was a communicant member of the Church of England, although I had difficulty with some theological doctrines and could hardly claim to be a good Christian. Iris said simply, 'Oh I'm a Christian. I don't think I believe in God and I don't believe Jesus Christ was divine, but I am a Christian. I nearly became a Buddhist, but then I said to myself, "Don't be foolish, Iris. You're a member of the Church of England."' Can I really have remembered that conversation accurately?

Now she inhabits some private world, partly accessible, apparently, to her husband but which no other person is able to enter. One wonders whether it is a world of some contentment; one surely can't use the word happiness. I hope that she doesn't know what has happened to her. That would be the final cruelty. It seems to me in my spiritual naïvety that these diseases which destroy personality always raise uncomfortable questions about the nature of the soul.

And should John Bayley have written this book? Until it is published one can't be sure. But judging from extracts in *The Times* I think that he was wrong. The biography is a testament of love and perhaps writing it helped him to bear an almost intolerable daily burden. But would the Iris Murdoch of the novels and the philosophy have wanted these intimate and sometimes demeaning details made public? I think not. The great tragedy of Alzheimer's disease, and the reason why we dread it, is that it leaves us with no defence, not even against those who love us.

THURSDAY, 30TH JULY
This evening I was the guest of Sir Brian Shaw, Chairman of the Port of London Authority, and his wife at dinner on the PLA launch *Royal Nore*. Brian and Pennie called for me, their arrival coinciding with a downpour which drenched Brian and myself, although we were under an umbrella, and even penetrated the car when the door was

opened. I was last a guest on the *Royal Nore* five years ago, and on that occasion we were driven south of the river to cross Tower Bridge. Unfortunately it had jammed when we arrived and we had to be picked up by the launch farther upriver at Westminster Pier.

I seem to be a Jonah on these occasions as tonight we were held up for fifteen minutes on the Embankment because of an accident. Eventually the police directed traffic on the other side of the road into a single file and allowed cars on the left-hand side to cross the reservation and pass the scene. The ambulance had departed and all one could see were pieces of motor-cycle strewn across the road. I suppose few of us pass the scene of a serious accident without much the same thought; the skeleton fingers reach out momentarily to twitch at our clothes and we face our own mortality and, worse, that of those we love. We think, too, of that unknown wife or mother now happily oblivious to the police appearance on the doorstep which will change her life forever. I said a brief silent prayer for those concerned, and then the car moved on. Those seconds of sympathy for the unknown victim wouldn't, as I knew, overshadow a happy evening.

One of the sadnesses of old age is that few experiences ever match the exhilarating excitement of youth, but being on the Thames, particularly at night, can still kindle in me that mixture of awe, wonder and delight which I used to feel as a child when I saw the river. The launch is named after the lightship *Nore*, which marked the former seaward limit of the Port of London Authority, and renamed *Royal Nore*, after the Queen embarked for her River Progress at the time of her Silver Jubilee. The launch is, in fact, used as the royal barge when the Queen travels by the Thames. The journeys must be speedier, and presumably more comfortable, than when Henry VIII was rowed in his glorious royal barge from Westminster to visit his Chancellor, Thomas More, at Chelsea.

We sailed – perhaps an inappropriate verb for a motor launch – upstream as far as Chelsea, then turned and went downstream to the Thames Barrier. The weather was changeable, sudden heavy squalls battering on the roof of the cabin and a turbulent sky which brightened into layers of dark grey and pale azure blue tinted with the red of the setting sun. It was getting dark by the time we reached the Barrier and, for me, one of the most splendid sights of the evening was when the launch turned and we saw through the huge shell-like hoods of the Barrier the gleaming pencil of Canary Wharf.

Captain Peter Steen gave us during dinner a brief talk about the Barrier and afterwards kindly let me have a brochure about its building and functioning. The engineering of the flood barrier is simple. There is a series of movable gates positioned across the river, each gate pivoted and supported between concrete piers which house the operating machinery and control equipment. The walls of the Barrier can be sealed when necessary, and when they are not in use the gates rest out of sight in concrete sills in the river bed. If there is risk of a dangerously high tidal surge, then the gates swing up through about 90 degrees from the river bed to form a continuous steel wall facing downriver.

The Barrier is one of the most exciting constructions of our age. On each pier, gleaming hoods of stainless steel conceal the equipment. These hoods are lined with timber and Captain Steen said that the interior was for him almost as beautiful as the roof. The beauty for me resides not only in the power and size, but in that perfect marriage of function and form. Surely few large modern sculptures can compare with the Barrier and yet we give honour to our artists and architects and few of us, if any, know the names of the engineers responsible for the Barrier. Before its completion the risk to London of severe flooding was very real. In his diary of 7th December 1663, Pepys wrote: 'There was last night the greatest tide that ever was remembered in England to have been in this River, all Whitehall having been drowned', and in 1236 the river overflowed, 'and in the great Palace of Westminster men did row with wherries in the midst of the Hall'. During my lifetime the last flood in Central London was in 1928, when fourteen people drowned, but I remember with great clarity the disastrous flooding of the East Coast and Thames Estuary in 1953, when 300 people lost their lives.

From the Barrier we saw the Royal Naval College at Greenwich floodlit. Admiral Sir John Brigstocke, who was one of my fellow guests, told me that the Trinity School of Music was to have half the accommodation, the Painted Hall will be preserved by the Maritime Museum and some of the accommodation will go to Greenwich University. I suppose there could be no justification for retaining the Royal Naval College for the Navy, but I felt a sadness that so much history and tradition will be lost.

As we approached the glittering floodlit wonder of Tower Bridge the helmsman asked if I would like to steer the launch through. He said that the wheel reacted very much like the wheel of a car. I pointed out that I didn't in fact drive, but he seemed prepared to take the risk although, obviously, he stood very close to my shoulder. There was no other traffic on the river and we sailed through with great ease before I relinquished the wheel to more expert hands as the launch was brought alongside Tower Bridge Pier.

I first met Sir Brian Shaw when I was researching my novel *Original Sin*. We were both guests at a Grand Night at Gray's Inn, of which he is a member, and I sat beside him at dinner. He asked what I was writing and I explained that I was researching a new novel, which was to be set in the publishing world but on the River Thames. I wanted the Thames to run like a dark, somewhat sinister stream, bearing its weight of history and linking characters, setting and incidents in the book. He very kindly offered to help with the research by letting me explore the river from one of the PLA launches. This I was able to do and learned a great deal from his officers about the history of the river.

During this research occurred one of those coincidences which seem to feature with every book I write. I visited the headquarters of the River Police at Wapping, which is the earliest police station in the United Kingdom and has its own small but extremely interesting museum. I was able to read newspaper reports of the greatest of all Thames tragedies, when in 1878 the paddle-steamer *Princess Alice*, returning loaded from a trip to Sheerness, was mown down by a collier and 640 people drowned. The passengers had mostly been poor Londoners enjoying with their families an inexpensive trip to the seaside. The mass drowning in the darkness must have been horrific. I used this incident in my book when one of the characters, Frances Peverell, deeply unhappy in her private life and worried about the future of the family firm, stands at her window overlooking the river and seems to hear above the cries of the gulls the screams of those drowning Victorians and, looking down at the dark river splattered with light, imagines the pale upward faces of the drowned children torn from their mothers' arms, floating like frail petals on the tide.

I wrote the passage on my return home from Wapping as I often do when images and atmosphere are fresh in mind. Then I went to spend the evening with my elderly friend Peggy Causton in her flat on Kensington High Street. She was crippled with bad arthritis and house-bound, and each week we would spend at least one evening, and sometimes two, playing Scrabble. Peggy was one of the few really good people I have known and I miss her. On that evening she gave me a tattered leather-bound book bearing the title *Memorandum Book*. She said it was found among her sister's effects but had nothing to do with her family and, as it was Victorian and she knew my fascination with the Victorian age, she thought it would be of interest. I have it still and it is, in fact, the memorandum book of a Sergeant of Marines. His name apparently was Westell, judging by the number of entries for the Westell family, and his initial W. It is a curious record in which the purchase of a black silk handkerchief for five shillings and sixpence receives as bold an entry as that of his marriage and the birth of his children. He was much interested in home remedies, and one for bowel complaints was probably effective and would be as useful today if one could get hold of the laudanum: 'Rhubarb – one pennyworth, magnesia – one pennyworth, peppermint essence – one pennyworth, Laudanum – one pennyworth'. There are notes on the movements of the ships, the number of dead at the battle of Alma, and odd facts which caught his imagination, such as the entry for 3rd August 1842, that children under eight years of age would not be admitted to the British Museum. But when I first opened the book, it fell open at the following entry: 'Wednesday, 3rd September '78. My son James was Drowned in the *Princess Alice* which sank. The poor fellow was found on the evening of 7th September '78 and buried at St Thomas Church on the evening of 9th September '78.'

FRIDAY, 31ST JULY

Tonight to a party at the Ritz given by George Carman, QC. I knew only about four people there of a mixed company of senior lawyers and judges spiced with well-known faces from television and the media. Robin Day was being his usual rumbustious and argument-ative self. He and I engaged in a conversation with Lord Alexander about the recent decision of the Appeal Court to quash the conviction of Derek Bentley. Bob supported it, Robin stoutly defended Judge Goddard.

I'm not sure how valid it is virtually to retry cases so long after the event and to apply contemporary standards of justice, morality and compassion to those operating some forty-seven years earlier, and I have an uncomfortable feeling that, had I been a member of the jury, I too would have found Bentley guilty. He was certainly engaged with

Craig on a joint criminal enterprise. The knuckle-duster with which he was armed, as Lord Goddard had great satisfaction in pointing out to the jury, was a formidable weapon and I find it hard to believe that he didn't know his accomplice was armed. But I would certainly have made a very strong recommendation for mercy as I believe the jury did. The central injustice of this case surely rests on the fact that Bentley was hanged while Craig, who actually fired the shot, could not, because of his age, receive the death sentence. Had Bentley also been sent to prison and later released to live, as Craig has done, an unmomentous life, we should hardly have heard of this case. The carrying out of the death sentence, not the verdict, was the abomination, and for that the Home Secretary, David Maxwell-Fyfe, and not the trial judge, was responsible. Lord Goddard and the jury expected Bentley to be reprieved. But if one is criticizing Lord Goddard, what of the three Appeal Judges who heard Bentley's appeal? If it is the verdict not the sentence which is the essential injustice, surely they bear a considerable part of the responsibility.

But this can't be the only case in which a judge's summing-up has been seen as prejudicial to the accused. A far more grievous case in my opinion is that of Edith Thompson, who was half-carried in a state of insensibility to the scaffold in 1923 and hanged for her alleged participation in the murder of her husband. Edith Thompson was a fantasist, almost the prototype of that dangerous species. She was married to a dull, worthy husband, Percy Thompson, and lived an equally dull and worthy life in the eastern suburb of Ilford. She took a lover, a P&O liner steward, Frederick Bywaters, eight years younger than herself and, in an obvious and somewhat desperate attempt to keep him, wrote him passionate letters in which she described her attempts to kill her husband by grinding up light bulbs and putting the pieces of glass in his food. There was absolutely no evidence that this had ever happened, as pathologist Bernard Spilsbury attested at her trial. The murder took place on 3rd October 1922 when Edith Thompson and her husband were walking home after an evening at the theatre in London. Bywaters sprang out and stabbed Thompson to death while Edith Thompson perpetually cried, 'Don't! Oh don't!'

Bywaters had kept her letters and, had these been destroyed or not admitted in evidence, it is probable that Edith Thompson would have lived to an old age. As it was, they were damning and the judge made the most of them. Edith Thompson was effectively hanged for adultery not for murder. But although the case has always left an unpleasant stain on British justice, no relation ever campaigned for a pardon or for the conviction to be quashed.

And what about Ruth Ellis, the last woman in England to be hanged? She was executed on 13th July 1955 for shooting her lover David Blakely shortly after she had suffered a miscarriage. A verdict of manslaughter would surely have been more just. If we are to retry the past, how shall we select the cases? By the apparent injustice of the original sentence or by family and public pressure? And at what year do we stop?

The judge in the case of Major Armstrong of Hay-on-Wye was also biased to some extent against the prisoner. As he was leaving the box after cross-examination, the judge, Mr Justice Darling, intervened and began to question him closely about the way the arsenic found in his possession had been divided up into twenty small packets. Armstrong was claiming that the arsenic was to kill dandelions in the lawn. Why then did he not merely sprinkle the weedkiller directly round each root? Armstrong was unable to give a convincing explanation and merely said feebly that it seemed the most convenient way of doing it at the time. It is possible, though not probable, that without this intervention Armstrong might have gone free.

On the other hand there are instances of judges being sympathetic to the defendant and yet not influencing the jury towards an acquittal. William Herbert Wallace, sentenced to death on 25th April 1931 for the murder of his wife, is an example. This time Mr Justice Wright summed up favourably to Wallace, pointing out what he described as 'the loops and doubts' of evidence that was entirely circumstantial. But after only an hour's absence the jury returned a verdict of guilty. The Court of Criminal Appeal subsequently quashed the verdict on the grounds that it was unsafe having regard to the evidence. This has remained one of the most fascinating cases in English law and still remains a mystery. My own view is that Wallace was innocent.

The Prime Minister and Cherie Blair were at the party and said how much they enjoy my books, which is, of course, always disarming to a writer. He looked much younger than he does on television, and modestly vulnerable – an impression which is surely fifty per cent misleading. In our group around him was a woman professor of Law from America who used the opportunity to badger him about the defects of the proposed no-win, no-pay rule in cases which would

previously have attracted legal aid. She said she would submit a
paper and he promised to read it. I was told that the Lord Chancellor
was expected but did not arrive; he would have been a more suitable
candidate for her arguments.

I continue to find Tony Blair puzzling. The problem is that I still
have no idea what drives him and his government. What are the
principles, if any, on which he operates? What aim has he beyond the
strong intention of winning a second term? Beneath the charm and
conviviality, and apparent vulnerability and the humour, what has he
of force, intelligence and commitment? I believe he has conscience
and sensitivity, qualities which, in a politician, are not always helpful
in a crisis. I was left wondering whether he has the emotional and
physical resilience to meet disaster if and when it comes. But the
likeability will prove a great asset and not only in Britain. It is a rare
enough quality in a politician. Admittedly it didn't help John Major;
but no country is governable with a majority of one.

AUGUST

SUNDAY, 2ND AUGUST

Tomorrow I shall be seventy-eight and, by the time this fragment of autobiography is published, I shall be within sight of my eightieth birthday. If seventy-seven is a time to be in earnest, eighty is a time to recognize old age, accepting with such fortitude as one can muster its inevitable pains, inconvenience and indignities and rejoicing in its few compensations.

Looking back at what I've written in the last twelve months has reinforced my conviction that I could never have sustained the daily chore of writing a diary. The one I've produced is incomplete, with more omitted than has been recorded. I still find scraps of writing which were obviously scribbled at the end of the day and intended for the diary. These notes of books read, people met, family occasions, talks and lectures given are now indecipherable and I can't pretend that it matters. But at least I have an imperfect record of one year and of the life of which it was part.

Youth is the time for certainties. In old age we realize how little we can be sure of, how little we have learned, how little – perhaps – we have changed. But looking back on my life I do know myself to be greatly blessed. I have met with little malice and much encouragement and kindness. I am sustained by the magnificent irrationality of faith. I have two daughters who have been a joy to me since the day of their birth, sons-in-law whom I respect and greatly love, and five grandchildren whose doings are a source of continued interest and amazement. I go into old age with the companionship of loving friends even though we all know that we can't expect to travel the whole way together. And I have my work. I shall continue to write detective stories as long as I can write well and I hope I shall recognize when it is time to stop. It gives pleasure to me and to thousands of readers. No other justification is needed.

The cells of my body must have renewed themselves countless

238

times since that eleven-year-old walked round Ludlow Castle carrying so carefully the letter which would open to her the delights and opportunities of a high-school education. I inhabit a different body, but I can reach back over nearly seventy years and recognize her as myself. Then I walked in hope – and I do so still.

Address to the BBC Governors and Board of Management
on Thursday 17th June 1993

When it was suggested to me as a retiring Governor that I should give the after-dinner speech today, and when I was foolish enough to let Michael persuade me, my first thought was that I would talk about what these five years have meant to me personally, what I have learned from them, and perhaps what I would say to a newly appointed Governor if he or she asked for my advice. But we all know about the last five years. Most of you here have experienced them with me. We know about the successes, the failures, the triumphs, the occasional disasters, what has been attempted and what has been achieved. We now have our document, 'Extending Choice', and our response to the Green Paper. We are well placed to fight the battle for the renewal of the Charter. Probably at no time since its foundation has the BBC been clearer about where it should go and how it proposes to get there. So I thought that I would look at the Corporation from a somewhat wider perspective, from that of someone for whom the BBC has been a vital part of life for nearly seventy years, in peace and in war. Despite the vast expansion and the many changes, is it still essentially the same BBC? Do I recognize in the BBC of today the BBC of my childhood, my youth and my middle age?

It is easy for some of us, particularly the old, to enjoy a nostalgic regret for the past and make frequent references to so-called Reithian values while overlooking the vast social and political changes which have occurred since the last war. We owe much to our founding father, but I very much doubt whether he would have made a successful Director General today. His job in size was roughly equivalent to that of the Controller of Radio Four. He operated a monopoly without competition and with an assured income. The BBC served a largely cohesive United Kingdom which, although there were great inequalities of wealth and opportunity, had a common heritage derived from the Judeo-Christian tradition of Western Europe, and common allegiances; a nation which was patriotic, monarchist, more accepting than today of authority, both spiritual and temporal, and affirming moral principles which, although they might not always be followed, were seldom publicly questioned. In that very different world John Reith set out to give people what he thought was good for them whether or not they actually wanted it (and most of us did want it), and he did so from a position of unchallenged authority. As with many moral crusaders his private life did not always bear close scrutiny, but in those days he was unlikely to find himself pilloried in the tabloids. From this lofty eminence what, I wonder, would he say if he were with us tonight?

He would surely be gratified that the BBC is acknowledged as the finest broadcasting service in the world and that it is still regarded in this country and, indeed, in all countries where it is received, with trust, affection and respect. He would see a developing World Service trusted as is no other international broadcaster, an immense asset to Britain's reputation, casting light into some very dark corners of our turbulent world.

If he were to read our document, 'Extending Choice', and our response to the Green Paper, he would be amazed and, I hope, impressed both by the huge expansion of the BBC as a public service broadcaster and by the care and thought that has gone into these documents. But he might also say: 'Yes, you are to extend choice, to provide a comprehensive service, to listen to your viewers and listeners, to define and separate the functions of the Governors and the management, to be more cost-effective. But where is the great statement of moral principle for which you stand? Do you any longer see yourselves as a force for the good of individuals and the nation, claiming to embody certain fundamental values, some of which, I am glad to see, are still carved on the wall of Broadcasting House?' I wonder, if that wall were bare and we here today were asked to choose an inscription, what words would we have the confidence to carve? Extending choice? Surely not only that.

There have, from time to time, been attempts to define the moral ethos of the BBC. In 1965 Hugh Carleton Greene said that although the BBC in general is impartial, there are certain matters about which it does not pretend to be impartial, and he named racialism and what he called extreme forms of political belief. Racialism is, of course, the sin against the Holy Ghost, and he might just as reasonably have mentioned cruelty and intolerance, of which racialism is a particularly ugly manifestation. In 1987 Dick Marriott, Assistant Director of Radio, attempted to define 'extreme forms of political belief' and said that the BBC would not offer a platform for anti-Semitism or for Fascism. And in 1968, in the pamphlet 'Broadcasting and the Public Mood', the BBC went further and solemnly affirmed that it could not be neutral about moral values and that therefore we declared that hatred and intolerance and cruelty are bad, and that love and kindness and truthfulness are good. Well, none of us, I think, would disagree about that. Like the Bishop, we are all against sin. But does this mean that the BBC has a responsibility actively to promote kindness and truthfulness and love? And if the Corporation has this moral duty, from what authority is it derived? What are its limits? Is there a corporate code of morality and where in the organization is it located? Or is the BBC entitled to say: 'We are in the business of making the best programmes for the widest audience and making them honestly, economically and fairly. That is sufficient moral dimension for any organization. Our corporate ethics are set out clearly in our "Producer's Guidelines". We have no obligation to promote democracy or to make people better citizens; that is for parents, schools, religious leaders and the Government, if it has the will and the ability.' And if we do accept that certain generally accepted ethical values should be promoted, how in fact is this to be done? By a form of internal censorship? By the careful promulgation of guidelines and their periodical revision? By influence? By example? But all moral values are ultimately personal values and they depend not on Corporation edicts and guidelines but on each individual broadcaster, and can only be inculcated by parents, by schools, by churches, synagogues and mosques, from moral philosophers and the great humanists. All these influences are less strong than they were and many young people today grow up without encountering any of them. No great institution can be uninfluenced by the ethos of the community it serves. Is it our prime responsibility to improve society or merely to reflect it? Are we, nation and BBC alike, in danger of living off our moral capital?

We do not at present live in a gentle, considerate or good-mannered world. In particular, sections of our Press are increasingly malicious, peevish, ill-tempered and cruel. Are we in some danger of becoming contaminated by this rancorous and destructive ethos? As the Chairman said in his Goodman Lecture, the BBC can surely inherit a gentler world. In particular, political interviewers should avoid that arrogance which betrays itself in bad manners and rudeness. Ministers of the Crown should be respected for the office they hold, whatever their political party, even if one cannot always afford them personal respect. As Brian Walden and Sir Robin Day have shown, it is possible to question leading politicians persistently, closely, rigorously and indeed with ultimately devastating effect, and at the same time remain courteous. Rudeness and arrogance are in any case self-defeating and unprofessional. They antagonize the audience and transfer sympathy to the victim. Senior politicians should come to their interview with some trepidation, knowing that no specious reasoning, no evasions, no attempts to dominate and control the discussion will go unchallenged, but also in the confidence that they will be treated with respect and courtesy because this is the BBC.

This, of course, leads me to the BBC's moral responsibility to the institutions of the State. There are those who would say that we have no such responsibility, the job of broadcasters is constantly to criticize and question. Only thus can democracy flourish in an age when newspapers are owned by fewer and fewer people, and individual MPs under the discipline of the Whips are less and less effective in criticizing the actions of the party in power. Does the BBC, because it is the British Broadcasting Corporation, publicly funded, have a responsibility towards the State, and what precisely do we mean by that word? For one man, Lord Annan, the answer is plain. The State, in his eyes, is quite different from the Government, and different again from what we call the Establishment, and the BBC does, indeed, have a responsibility towards it, as do we all. Speaking to a BBC Seminar on Impartiality held in November 1988, he said:

> The State is the legal expression of the nation, repository of sovereignty, sole source of legal cohesion, source of authority of the armed forces, agent of law, that which demands our loyalty because it defines and sustains our rights through the laws of the country and alone can defend us from invasion or anarchy.

One response to this confident affirmation would, of course, be that the State, its power made manifest through its institutions of monarchy, parliament, law, the armed forces, is as likely to be tyrannous, oppressive and vexatious as beneficent and that it is the job of the BBC constantly to challenge its powerful agencies. There is a very real philosophical and ethical dilemma here which bears both on the ethos of public service broadcasting and on the independence of the BBC. Today the pillars of the State, which in my childhood seemed so strong, so impervious to the erosion of time and changing climate, so firm against tyranny and the hurricanes of social and international unrest, are dangerously cracking: the monarchy; the church; parliamentary democracy; the City. Our attitude to trade unions has changed. In my childhood they seemed less organizations for bargaining with employers than moral crusaders for a fairer and different society. But if the great pillars of State are cracking, is it for the BBC to shore them up, and if so, by what authority? Was the 1977 Annan Report on the future of broadcasting right when it stated:

Statements which discredit not merely the politician, but the whole concept of government, without which a society cannot exist, destroy public confidence in the nation in a peculiarly poisonous way.

Perhaps this is a warning we should all heed, broadcasters and newspapers alike, before the poison gets into the national bloodstream.

We need to be constantly aware of the difference between criticism – fair, just and indeed necessary in a vigorous democracy – and that iconoclastic impulse to pull down and destroy, often most strongly urged by those least able to build up and create. This, of course, applies too to the BBC. If through folly, or the malice of its enemies, or lack of public commitment, the BBC is allowed to wither, it will never again be strong and vital. Once destroyed, it can never be recreated. All great institutions which have evolved, slowly and patiently adapting to changing needs and times, embody the wisdom and experience of decades and sometimes centuries, wisdom and experience which should not be lightly cast aside. Most of us, whatever our discontents, know that we are exceptionally privileged to be citizens of this United Kingdom. Patriotism is an unpopular, unfashionable virtue, but there is much for which we have to be grateful and to celebrate in our national life; our freedom, our laws, our language and culture, the beauty and variety of the land, and surely it is right that the BBC should be as ready to celebrate and help support what is good as it is to criticize and bring down what is bad.

The BBC should be courageous. It has over the decades demonstrated that it can stand up fearlessly to successive governments. The

BBC's independence from government is vital. If we lose that we may as well close down, and it would be better for the country if we did close down. But I don't think that, for most of the time, it requires very much courage to stand up to a government, particularly a government which is discredited or weak. In a democracy there are many ready enough to do that. It takes rather more courage to stand up to a Robert Maxwell and that too we have done. It may take greater courage still to stand out against certain fashionable shibboleths which are strongly advocated by powerful and articulate interests, whether of the left or the right, whether permissive or repressive. I hope, for example, that the pernicious linguistic fascism, politically correct language, does not take a hold in this country as it has in universities in the United States, but if it does, the BBC must resist it. We must continue vigorously to promote the fuller participation of women and the ethnic minorities but resist the positive discrimination that some powerful influences would like, and without setting quotas, which are patronizing and offensive both to women and to the minorities concerned. We must be courageous in acknowledging when things have gone wrong and in putting them right.

The Pilkington Committee in its report of 1960 said that one of the functions of the Governors was to see that the executive did not, to the detriment of the purposes of broadcasting, give way to pressures simply because they can make themselves felt. Increasingly they are making themselves felt. One has only to attend one of our public meetings to see how often people are attending, not in their own right, but as representatives of a particular interest. But it would be a pity if, in our anxiety to serve minority groups, we see the public as a collection of diverse and often mutually exclusive groups, less human beings than categories: women, gays, blacks, the disabled. Perhaps we oldies should get in on the act. *The Last of the Summer Wine, Waiting for God* and *One Foot in the Grave* would be at risk for a start. Of course we must take account of these interests and be sensitive to the needs of minorities and, in particular, to the way they are portrayed on our screens. But we have, after all, a common humanity and a common citizenship and the things that unite us are far stronger than those which divide us. And there is one pressure group to which I think we do occasionally pay too much deference: the educated, London-based, liberal and permissive middle-class, the so-called chattering classes whose ethos has dominated so much of British life.

Although their liberal credentials are impeccable they are not necessarily typical of the rest of England, still less are they of the United Kingdom. There is not only life, but intellectual life, cultural life, vigorous life north of Watford and we have a responsibility to show it in all its richness and variety.

The battle for fair, accurate and balanced reporting of news has been won although we still need to be vigilant to ensure that we do not fudge the line between reporting the news and comment and to be mindful of the need to illumine and explain as well as to report. Balance in documentaries is less easy to achieve. There is always the temptation for producers to decide what it is they want to show and then go out to film the evidence for it. Balance in drama is more often criticized and more difficult to achieve. We need to respect the integrity of the creative imagination, to encourage experiment and innovation, to allow dramatists the freedom occasionally to fail without which all drama will be timid, unimaginative and blandly conformist. Some of our best dramatists are strongly committed politically and this is inevitably reflected in their work. But some drama praised as courageous or subversive is, in fact, neither of these things. It is comparatively easy to write a powerful play about the horrors of war. Plenty of writers can do that for you. It is less easy to examine how, without war, you can deal with a Hitler, a Galtieri or a Saddam Hussein. It is easy to make programmes criticizing the police and judiciary (and there is plenty to criticize), more difficult to explore how in a democracy we can hold that precarious but vital balance between personal freedom and good public order. It is easy to show security forces in Northern Ireland in a bad light. Film-makers do not have to face the dilemma of acting within the law when your enemy has a gun and is acting outside it.

I won't spend time speaking of those familiar friends, gratuitous violence, explicit sexual scenes and bad language. We have the Producer's Guidelines, which are admirable statements of policy, although easier to promulgate than to enforce, and do we always have the will to enforce them? We have during the last five years spent a great deal of time in seminars discussing these issues, issues which are not as clear-cut or as simple as they apparently seem to Mrs Whitehouse or to the proponents of greater licence. I would only say that standards elsewhere, particularly in the tabloids and with some of our broadcasting competitors, are falling and are likely to fall still further in the scramble for readers and viewers. The BBC needs to be particularly sensitive in a deteriorating climate to ensure that our own standards don't, at first almost imperceptibly, begin to slide.

The relationship between the BBC and the people it serves at home and abroad is one of trust. That trust has been built up over decades but it could be destroyed in twelve months. It is for us to see that it is not betrayed. The principles, more often understood than publicly articulated, for which the BBC has stood for nearly seventy years and on which this trust is founded, are threatened by more than the pressures of the competition, declining standards of taste and decency or fashionable moral relativism. I personally think – and some of you may agree – that the likely outcome of the present negotiations will be the renewal of the Charter but a freezing of, perhaps even a reduction in, the licence fee. If this happens we shall have to look for additional sources of income if our present services are to be maintained and if there is to be any hope of fulfilling the promises implied in 'Extending Choice'. This increased commercialism will have its dangers. We shall need to be very careful and selective of the organizations and products with which we become associated if we are not to jeopardize both the independence and the integrity of the BBC.

Honesty, kindness and courtesy, humility, justice and fair-dealing, a refusal to exploit the vulnerable or betray a trust, courage. We know what we mean by these words. They transcend differences in religious belief and depend on no religious belief. They have down the centuries governed the lives of good and civilized men and women. They are as necessary to the BBC as are good programmes, efficiency, economy, communication. I believe that it is because the BBC stands for values that transcend systems, accounting and managerial efficiency, important as these are, that talented, hard-working men and women – some of the most talented in this room here tonight – work for it with such dedication and often at financial cost. Those who serve the BBC in the next ten years as Governors, members of the Board of Management, channel controllers or programme-makers, may well determine the future of public service broadcasting. It is a huge responsibility and I believe that it is also a moral responsibility and that we should not be afraid of that word or of the values which it embodies.

I have throughout this talk used the word 'we', but at the end of next month I shall return to what I have been for seventy years, one of your listening public. I am immensely grateful for the privilege of having served as a BBC Governor, although I am only too aware that I could, and should, have done more. I am grateful to you all, fellow Governors and members of the Board of Management, for what you have taught me, for what you have given me with such generosity: encouragement, support, comradeship, friendship. I shall miss you greatly. Thank you for listening to me with such patience. Good luck to you all in the vital task ahead.

*Emma Considered as a Detective Story: Jane Austen Society AGM
Chawton, Saturday 18th July 1998*

It is both a privilege and a pleasure to give this talk at the Annual
General Meeting of the Jane Austen Society, although I accepted the
invitation with some trepidation; there is nothing I can say about Jane
Austen which will, I feel, be new to this audience of her devotees. I
shall crave your indulgence before I begin. It is also a particular
pleasure to be speaking at Chawton, where in Chawton Cottage Jane
Austen lived for the last eight years of her tragically short life. The five
years preceding the move to Chawton were unsettled with constant
changes of residence and were artistically unproductive with her
writing virtually at a stop. It could be argued, therefore, that, without
this unpretentious final home in which she found that mixture of rural
peace, ordered domestic routine and mild stimulation which best
suited her character and her art, we might never have been given the
greatest of her novels.

My title this afternoon is '*Emma* Considered as a Detective Story'. It
may seem presumptuous as well as a little eccentric to consider one of
the greatest novels written in the English language with reference to
the conventions of popular genre fiction. Apart from this presump-
tion, the detective story is, after all, usually concerned with murder
and there is no crime in *Emma* if we except the despoiling of Mrs
Weston's turkey houses; few orthodox detective novels are so rural,
so peaceable, so remote in spirit from the crime and violence of Jane
Austen's own age or of ours. But the detective story does not require
murder; Dorothy L. Sayers's *Gaudy Night* is an example. What it does
require is a mystery, facts which are hidden from the reader but
which he or she should be able to discover by logical deduction from
clues inserted in the novel with deceptive cunning but essential
fairness. It is about evaluating evidence, whether of events or of
character. It is concerned with bringing order out of disorder and
restoring peace and tranquillity to a world temporarily disrupted by
the intrusion of alien influences.

Emma, most faultlessly constructed of all Jane Austen's novels, is a story in which peace and reconciliation are produced out of discord, mysteries are elucidated and facts previously misinterpreted are at last seen in their true light. But there are other interesting parallels with the traditional detective story. The genre is often at its most effective when the setting is self-contained and the people are forced into a sometimes unwilling proximity. Here in *Emma* we have a self-contained rural community in which virtually all the characters in the book either live in or near the village of Highbury or, like Frank Churchill, are concerned with it. Only Mrs Elton comes in as a stranger when she marries the vicar. We know them all completely in the sense that we can imagine what they would say and how they would behave when we are not there. We know intimately the life of Highbury: the Crown Inn where the gentlemen congregate to conduct their business or play whist, and where the ball is held; Mrs Ford's shop and what she sells; the vicarage and the lane to it; the Bates's apartment; Mrs Goddard's school; the shrubberies of Hartfield and the strawberry-beds of Donwell Abbey. The scene is set.

Against this self-contained background is played out the drama of Emma, handsome, clever and rich, whose energy and powers of mind are fatefully under-used so that she occupies herself in disastrous interference in the lives of others. Emma, in her zeal to manipulate and control, misinterprets facts, emotions, situations, relationships, and it is a fair guess that the nineteenth-century reader and the modern reader, coming to the novel for the first time, would be seduced by Jane Austen's cleverness in inducing us to share Emma's misconceptions and misunderstandings. At the end of the book, of course, chastened and penitent, she recognizes not only the truths of other people, but the truth of her own heart, and marries the one man who, loving her from her childhood, brings her from destructive imaginings to happy reality.

What then are the mysteries in *Emma*? All of them centre on a human relationship. There is Frank Churchill's secret engagement to Jane Fairfax. There is the hidden truth of Mr Knightley's love for Emma and Emma's growing love for him. There is Emma's misjudgement of Mr Elton's matrimonial intentions. There is the lesser mystery, or perhaps more accurately described as a misunderstanding, centred on Emma's interfering and injudicious attempts to find a husband for her protégée Harriet, culminating in her horrified belief that Mr

Knightley is in love with Harriet and actually means to marry her.

But the central truth cunningly concealed at the heart of the novel is, of course, the engagement of Frank Churchill to Jane Fairfax. We share the lively interest in Highbury in seeing Mr Weston's long-expected son, and we may perhaps agree with Mr Knightley that the young man certainly should have come earlier to pay his respects to his father's new bride, poor Miss Taylor that was, as Mr Woodhouse would say. But it isn't until Jane Fairfax comes to Highbury to stay with her grandmother and aunt, the Bateses, that Frank Churchill manages to free himself from his demanding stepmother and comes to visit his father. We should have spotted that clue. Mr Weston brings him at once to see Emma but after sitting together for a short time they part; Mr Weston has business at the Crown about his hay and a great many errands for Mrs Weston to perform. Frank does not accompany him, but goes instead to visit Mrs Bates and Miss Bates. It would perhaps be rather more natural if he stayed with his father, or went directly home to his stepmother, but at the Bates's he will, of course, find Jane Fairfax, the main motive for his coming to Highbury. His excuse for the visit is that they had met at Weymouth, but it is perhaps a little surprising that he should place Miss Fairfax and her relations so high on his visiting list. And when there he stays much longer than a morning courtesy visit in those more formal days would normally demand. Next day he says to Emma:

'Ten minutes would have been all that was necessary, perhaps all that was proper, and I had told my father I should certainly be at home before him – but there was no getting away, no pause, and to my utter astonishment I found ... that I had been actually sitting with them very nearly three-quarters of an hour.'

Emma asks how Miss Fairfax was looking and, mischievously and cunningly, Frank pretends not to admire her complexion:

'Miss Fairfax is naturally so pale, as almost always to give the appearance of ill-health – A most deplorable want of complexion.'

We are seduced into believing from the outset that Frank Churchill is no admirer of Miss Fairfax's beauty. It is when Frank, Mrs Weston and Emma are strolling together in Highbury that Emma asks the question which Frank must have known was inevitable, but which he must also have dreaded. Emma asks: 'Did you see her often at

Weymouth? Were you often in the same society?' Frank has only seen Miss Fairfax in the presence of her grandmother or aunt and they have had no opportunity to discuss privately what their story will be. It is a tricky situation for Frank, and this is how Jane Austen deals with it:

At this moment they were approaching Ford's, and he hastily exclaimed: 'Ha! This must be the very shop that everybody attends every day of their lives, as my father informs me . . . If it be not inconvenient to you, pray let us go in, that I may prove myself to belong to the place, to be a true citizen of Highbury. I must buy something at Ford's.'

The diversion gives him time to think, but he knows that the question has to be answered. A little later he voluntarily returns to it and cleverly suggests that Emma should address it to Miss Fairfax, saying:

'It is always the lady's right to decide on the degree of acquaintance. Miss Fairfax must already have given her account. I shall not commit myself by claiming more than she may chuse to allow.'

Miss Fairfax has *not* given her account and, reticent and secretive, nor will she.

It is during this walk together that Frank asks Emma's opinion of Jane Fairfax as a musician and the next day we have one of the strongest, perhaps most obvious, clues to the true relationship between Jane and Frank. Frank Churchill goes to London to get his hair cut. The excuse is, of course, not sensible, and he hardly troubles to make it credible; he would not have come to visit his new stepmother with his hair uncut. But he is of course going to London to purchase and arrange for the delivery of the pianoforte to Mrs Bates's house. It is not a grand pianoforte but a solid square one, suitable for the smallness of the sitting-room, which he has now seen for himself. We first hear of its arrival when Frank Churchill, with Emma and the rest of her Highbury friends, is attending the dinner party at the Coles's. Here Frank colludes with Emma in her suggestion that the pianoforte comes not from Colonel Campbell, which is the general opinion, but from Mr Dixon, who has married Miss Campbell but who is in love with Jane. And Frank, pretending to be convinced, finally admits that 'I can see it in no other light than as an offering of love.' It is, indeed, an offering of love. The clue here could not be stated more plainly. It is at the same Coles's dinner party that Emma detects Frank gazing fixedly across the room at his love, and when Emma notices this, he recollects himself and claims he cannot take his eyes away from Jane's outré hairstyle. That Jane herself very well knows who sent the pianoforte is apparent to us from her embarrassment when it is referred to, an embarrassment which Emma attributes to Jane's guilty love for her friend's husband.

> Mrs Weston, kind-hearted and musical, was particularly interested by the circumstance, and Emma could not help being amused at her perseverance in dwelling on the subject; and having so much to ask and to say as to tone, touch, and pedal, totally unsuspicious of that wish of saying as little about it as possible, which she [Emma] plainly read in the fair heroine's countenance.

Next day Emma and Harriet are walking to Highbury to buy ribbons in Ford's when, looking down the Randalls road, they see Mrs Weston and her son-in-law. Frank is, of course, again calling on Jane Fairfax. Mrs Weston says:

> 'My companion tells me that I absolutely promised Miss Bates last night, that I would come this morning. I was not aware of it myself. I did not know that I had fixed a day, but I am going now.'

Mrs Weston, of course, had not fixed a day, but Frank cannot wait to see his love again, and no doubt to see the pianoforte. He makes some little demur at the visit, but he obviously has every intention of accompanying Mrs Weston to the Bates's and not being diverted to Randalls.

One of the strongest clues to the secret engagement is the amount of time Frank Churchill spends with the Bateses. Apart from being almost the first house at which he calls, he manages to devise opportunities of being with Jane on every possible occasion. When the ball at the Crown is mooted and the Westons and Emma are examining the possibilities of the room there, it is he who suggests that Miss Bates should be invited to join them. Mrs Weston understandably is unconvinced the garrulous and too obliging Miss Bates will be able to offer any real assistance, but she is sent for and brings Jane with her, as Frank very well knew that she would.

Then comes that moment, disagreeable to Emma but devastating to Jane, when Frank Churchill is called back to Enscombe. Here he calls on the Bateses *before* he comes to say goodbye to Emma. He almost tells Emma his secret, imagining that her quick wit has probably already divined it. The conversation is as follows. Emma says:

'Not five minutes to spare even for your friends, Miss Fairfax and Miss Bates? How unlucky! Miss Bates's powerful, argumentative mind might have strengthened yours.'

'Yes – I *have* called there; passing the door I thought it better. It was a right thing to do. I went in for three minutes, and was detained by Miss Bates's being absent. She was out; and I felt it impossible not to wait till she came in . . . It was better to pay my visit, then.' He hesitated, got up and walked to a window. 'In short', said he, 'perhaps, Miss Woodhouse – I think you can hardly be quite without suspicion.'

He looked at her, as if wanting to read her thoughts. She hardly knew what to say. It seemed like the forerunner of something absolutely serious, which she did not wish. Forcing herself to speak, therefore, in the hope of putting it by, she calmly said:

'You were quite in the right; it was most natural to pay your visit, then . . .'

She heard him sigh. It was natural for him to feel that he had *cause* to sigh. He could not believe her to be encouraging him.

Emma, deluded as ever, is, of course, half-expecting a proposal, or at least a declaration of love. In reality Frank Churchill, suspecting that Emma has guessed his secret, has got very close to telling her that he is engaged to Jane Fairfax. A careful reading of the passage shows clearly that what he is about to confide is related not to Hartfield, but to his visit to the Bates's.

So Frank Churchill departs, to the distress of Highbury and, no doubt, the satisfaction of Mr Knightley, and we come to the clue of Jane Fairfax and the letters. We do not hear of her going out to the post office to collect her personal mail until Frank Churchill is no longer at Highbury. We learn that Jane is receiving letters, which she prefers to collect herself, at the dinner party which Emma gives for Mr Elton and his new bride, when Mr John Knightley, sitting next to Jane, expresses the hope that she did not venture too far that morning during the wet weather. He says:

'The post office has a great charm at one period of our lives. When you have lived to my age, you will begin to think letters are never worth going through the rain for.'

Immediately the kind Mrs Weston expresses concern that Miss Fairfax has been out in the rain and the officious Mrs Elton pesters her with offers that her servants can fetch the mail. Jane, of course, is quietly adamant. In the early nineteenth century young men and young women did not correspond unless they were engaged, and for Frank Churchill to be known to be corresponding with Jane Fairfax would be fatal to their secret.

And it is, of course, one of these letters which puts them in danger again once Frank has returned. This is in Chapter 5 of the third volume of the novel, where Emma, Harriet and Mr Knightley, taking an evening walk, fall in with Mr and Mrs Weston, Frank Churchill, Miss Bates and Jane Fairfax. Emma invites them all back to Hartfield, and they are turning into the grounds when Mr Perry passes on horse-back and the gentlemen speak of his horse. We then have this conversation:

'By the bye', said Frank Churchill to Mrs Weston presently, 'what became of Mr Perry's plan of setting up his carriage?'

Mrs Weston looked surprised, and said, 'I did not know that he ever had any such plan.'

'Nay, I had it from you. You wrote me word of it three months ago.'

'Me! Impossible!'

Frank, obviously embarrassed, suggests that he must have dreamed of Mr Perry's carriage and attempts to change the conversation by suggesting that Miss Smith walks as if she were tired. But he cannot so easily rid himself of the subject. Miss Bates confirms that there was indeed such an idea for Mrs Perry herself had mentioned it to Mrs Bates. She said:

'Jane, don't you remember grandmamma's telling us of it when we got home? I forget where we had been walking to – very likely to Randalls; yes, I think it was to Randalls ... I never mentioned it to a soul that I know of ... Extraordinary dream indeed!'

It was at that moment, when they were entering the hall, that Mr Knightley glances at Jane. He sees confusion suppressed or laughed away in Frank Churchill's face, who seems determined to capture Jane's eye, but Jane passes between them into the hall and looks at neither. The John Knightleys and their children are at Hartfield at this time and a little later all the company sit themselves round a circular table to play with the children's alphabets, forming words for each other. Frank Churchill places a word before Miss Fairfax. She discovers it, and with a faint smile pushes it away, leaving the letters to be immediately mixed up with the others. But Harriet picks it up and, with the help of Mr Knightley, rearranges the letters to form the word 'blunder'. Harriet exultingly proclaims it and there is a blush on Jane's cheek. It is indeed a blunder. Who else could have conveyed to Frank the news of Mr Perry's proposal to set up a carriage but Jane Fairfax.

And there are, of course, other clues. If we wonder why Frank Churchill should suddenly have remembered his obligation to his father and his father's bride, we may ask ourselves why Jane Fairfax is content to remain so long at Highbury when she has a standing invitation from Colonel and Mrs Campbell to join them in Ireland with the Dixons. Frank, of course, attempts to explain this, at least to Emma, by their joint collusion in the idea that Jane cannot be with the Dixons since she has seduced Mr Dixon's affections from his bride. But this doesn't prevent Emma from finding it strange that Jane should wish to stay at Highbury. As she says to Frank Churchill:

'I'm sure there must be a particular cause for her chusing to come to Highbury instead of going with the Campbells to Ireland. Here, she must be leading a life of privation and penance; there it would have been all enjoyment. As to the pretence of trying her native air, I look upon that as a mere excuse ... What can anybody's native air do for them in the months of January, February and March?'

But Jane, of course, cannot bear to leave Highbury. Frank Churchill could not possibly visit her either in London or in Ireland, but he had every excuse for coming regularly to Highbury whenever he could obtain Mrs Churchill's consent.

And then there is the telling incident at the Donwell Abbey strawberry-picking. Jane is monopolized by Mrs Elton and officiously urged to take the desirable situation as governess which Mrs Elton has procured for her. Frank Churchill has promised to ride over from Richmond and is eagerly awaited, but still has not arrived. And then Jane, in obvious distress, tells Emma that she must walk home, refuses the use of the Hartfield carriage and sets off alone. Fifteen minutes later Frank Churchill arrives and for the first time Emma, and we, see him in a serious bad temper: deploring the heat, almost wishing he hadn't come, saying he's too hot to eat, and announcing that he's tired of England and proposes, as soon as his aunt is well enough, to go abroad. But surely Frank Churchill, arriving fifteen minutes after Jane Fairfax left, must have met her on the road. He admits as much, but doesn't even mention her name. He says:

'You will all be going soon, I suppose; the whole party breaking up. I met *one* as I came – Madness in such weather! Absolute madness!'

It doesn't occur to Emma, nor did it to me when I first read the novel, that Frank Churchill's bad temper is the result of that encounter on the road with a distressed and reproachful Jane.

Jane can bear it no longer. She breaks off the engagement and becomes ill. Emma feels real compassion, but her efforts at help, and even her arrowroot, are spurned. Jane is consumed with jealousy and distress. But then, of course, all ends happily. Mrs Churchill, who was never admitted by anyone to be seriously ill, justifies her hypochondria by dying. Frank Churchill has no difficulty in obtaining the easy-going Mr Churchill's consent to his marriage, and returns triumphantly to Highbury to claim his bride.

The news of the engagement is initially greeted with great distress by the Westons, who were completely taken in by Frank's attentions to Emma. But when they realize that Emma's heart is untouched, they are reconciled, as is the whole of Highbury. But it is surprising that the engagement should cause such widespread astonishment. The clues to the truth were there for them to deduce as they are for us. But only the perceptive Mr Knightley suspected the truth.

The reader has small excuse for misinterpreting Mr Elton's matrimonial aspirations, but here Emma is particularly obtuse. Mr Elton's visits to Hartfield are to commend himself to her, not because he knows he will find Harriet there. His tender sighings over Harriet's portrait, painted by Emma, and the care he takes to convey the precious consignment to London for framing, is because he aspires to the artist not the sitter. The conundrum he writes and sends anonymously is obviously meant for Emma, and even Emma is struck by the incongruity of ascribing bright eyes and a ready wit to her friend. Mr Elton has no intention of missing Mrs Weston's dinner party just because Harriet Smith is ill. And there is the evidence of character, as important in well-written detective stories as it is in *Emma*, and always the most telling of clues. Mr Elton is the last person to court a penniless and illegitimate girl. As Mr Knightley tells Emma:

'Elton is a very good sort of man and a very respectable vicar of Highbury, but not at all likely to make an imprudent match. He knows the value of a good income as well as anybody. Elton may talk sentimentally, but he will act rationally.'

But Emma's final misunderstanding, that Mr Knightley seriously wishes to marry Harriet, was perhaps fortunate. It was only when she was faced with this appalling possibility that Emma admitted the truth. Mr Knightley must marry no one but herself. When we come to consider Mr Knightley and his love for Emma – and he tells her at the end of the book that he has loved her since she was thirteen – the strongest clue is undoubtedly the amount of time he spends at Hartfield. He does, in fact, visit Emma and her father daily, sitting with them in the evenings, and this can hardly be for the lively pleasure of Mr Woodhouse's company.

And Mr Knightley is always genuinely interested in every aspect of Emma's welfare, even her reading list and her handwriting. He takes the trouble to correct her when he thinks her wrong and to praise her when she does right, but he does it always as an equal, not as a patronizing superior or with avuncular condescension. He respects her intelligence as well as admiring her beauty and to that beauty he is certainly not impervious. As he says to Mrs Weston, 'I love to look at her', and we can picture him as he sits, night after night, in the drawing-room at Hartfield enduring the tedium of Mr Woodhouse's conversation and the fire which Mr Woodhouse's tender habits require on almost every evening of the year, resting his eyes on Emma's lovely face before walking home to the coolness and solitude of Donwell Abbey.

The second and perhaps the strongest clue is, of course, his unreasonable jealousy of Frank Churchill. The announcement that Frank is at last to visit his father and his father's new wife causes a general flutter of anticipation in Highbury which Emma shares. Mr Knightley must be aware that the Westons hope that Emma and Frank will fall in love. Mr Knightley betrays jealous disapproval of the young man even before his arrival. When Frank Churchill defers his first visit because of pressure from Enscombe, no one is more censorious than Mr Knightley.

'There is one thing, Emma, which a man can always do if he chuses, and that is, his duty; not by manoeuvring and finessing, but by vigour and resolution.'

Emma argues vigorously that without being acquainted with Enscombe and Mrs Churchill's temper they should not be too hard on Frank Churchill, and accuses Mr Knightley of being determined to think ill of him.

'Me! Not at all,' replies Mr Knightley, rather displeased, 'I do not want to think ill of him. I should be as ready to acknowledge his merits as any other man, but I hear of none, except what are merely personal, that he is well grown and good-looking, with smooth, plausible manners.'

Their argument continues, and when Emma points out that her love for Mr and Mrs Weston gives her a decided prejudice in Frank Churchill's favour, Mr Knightley says crossly, 'He is a person I never think of from one month's end to another', a somewhat surprising assertion since he has obviously been giving a great deal of thought to Mr Churchill's defects of character and behaviour and has spent the last half-hour vigorously arguing about him.

And when Frank Churchill does at last arrive – a day early, which is a little inconsiderate of him bearing in mind Mrs Weston's desire to have everything at Randalls perfect for his arrival – only Mr Knightley doesn't join in the general praise of him throughout the parishes of Donwell and Highbury. Hearing about his trip to London to have his hair cut, he comments, 'Hum! Just the trifling silly fellow I took him for.' He even criticizes his handwriting. 'I do not admire it. It wants strength. It is like a woman's writing.' And Mr Knightley is alone in disliking the prospect of the ball at the Crown where, of course, Miss Woodhouse and Mr Frank Churchill will undoubtedly shine. Mr Knightley, the normally fair-minded and judicious Mr Knightley, can't say a good word for Frank Churchill until, at the end of the novel, 'Emma is his Emma by hand and word' and we read:

> If he could have thought of Frank Churchill then, he might have deemed him a very good sort of fellow.

And if Mr Knightley is constantly in Emma's company, continually concerned with her welfare and her conduct, he is certainly seldom out of Emma's mind. Every male character is judged against him. Much as she liked Mr Weston's open manners and friendliness to all,

> she felt, that to be the favourite and intimate of a man who had so many intimates and confidantes, was not the very first distinction in the scale of vanity ... General benevolence, but not general friendship, made a man what he ought to be. – She could fancy such a man.

It is of course a precise description of Mr Knightley. And when Emma, accompanied by Harriet, pays a wedding visit to the newly married Eltons, there is another clue given with great subtlety. Mrs Elton says:

> '"My friend Knightley" had been so often mentioned that I was really impatient to see him; and I must do my *caro sposo* the justice to say that he need not be ashamed of his friend. Knightley is quite the gentleman. I like him very much. Decidedly, I think, a very gentleman-like man.'

Emma can hardly contain her indignation until they have left the house:

> 'Insufferable woman!' was her immediate exclamation. 'Worse than I had supposed. Absolutely insufferable! Knightley! – I could not have believed it. Knightley! – never seen him in her life before, and call him Knightley! – and to discover that he is a gentleman! A little upstart, vulgar being, with her Mr E, and her *caro sposo*, and her resources, and all her airs of pert pretension and under-bred finery. Actually to discover that Mr Knightley is a gentleman! I doubt whether he will return the compliment, and discover her to be a lady.'

She then wonders what Frank Churchill would say about it if he were here and adds:

'Always the first person to be thought of! How I catch myself out! Frank Churchill comes as regularly into my mind!'

But she hasn't, of course, been thinking of Frank Churchill. It has been Mr Knightley who came first into her mind, Mr Knightley of whom she constantly thinks.

When I discussed this talk with my daughter Jane, she reminded me of another example of Emma's preoccupation with Mr Knightley, which she described as 'the clue of the spruce beer'. Harriet is demonstrating her total recovery from her infatuation with Mr Elton by destroying in front of Emma her 'most precious treasures'; the court plaister which Mr Elton had worn on his cut finger and the end of an old pencil which Mr Elton had used to make a note in his pocket-book about Mr Knightley's recipe for brewing spruce beer. 'I do remember it', cried Emma; 'I perfectly remember it. Talking about spruce beer. Oh! yes – Mr Knightley and I both saying we liked it, and Mr Elton's seeming resolved to learn to like it too. I perfectly remember it. Mr Knightley was standing just here, was not he? I have an idea he was standing just here.'

And then there is her passionate argument with Mrs Weston when her old governess suggests, after the ball, that Mr Knightley might wish to marry Jane Fairfax. Emma, of course, has convinced herself that her dislike of Mr Knightley marrying anybody is based on her wish that her nephew, Henry, shall eventually inherit the Donwell property.

'Mr Knightley and Jane Fairfax!' she exclaims. 'Dear Mrs Weston, how could you think of such a thing? – Mr Knightley! – Mr Knightley must not marry! You would not have little Henry cut out from Donwell?'

Then, a little later:

'I am sure he has not the least idea of it. Do not put it into his head. Why should he marry? He is as happy as possible by himself; with his farm, and his sheep, and his library, and all the parish to manage ... he has no occasion to marry, either to fill up his time or his heart.'

And the argument continues with Emma increasing in virulence against the idea. As Mrs Weston says:

'If Mr Knightley really wished to marry, you would not have him refrain on Henry's account, a boy of six years old, who knows nothing of the matter?'

We may suspect that Emma's vehemence has very little to do with little Henry and his inheritance. Later Emma cannot resist a delicate hint to Mr Knightley about his admiration for Jane Fairfax, and is told:

'That will never be . . . Miss Fairfax, I dare say, would not have me if I were to ask her, and I am very sure I shall never ask her.'

Emma compliments him on his lack of vanity and Jane Austen writes:

He seemed hardly to hear her; he was thoughtful – and in a manner which shewed him not pleased, soon afterwards said: 'So you have been settling that I should marry Jane Fairfax?'

'No, indeed I have not. You have scolded me too much for match-making for me to presume to take such a liberty with you. What I said just now, meant nothing . . . Oh! no, upon my word, I have not the smallest wish for your marrying Jane Fairfax, or Jane anybody. You would not come and sit with us in this comfortable way, if you were married.'

Here again there is a subtle clue. Why should Mr Knightley be so displeased at the suggestion he might be interested in Jane Fairfax, the beautiful, accomplished and elegant Jane? Surely it is not the gossip which has displeased him; Highbury lives by gossip. No, it is the thought that Emma can discuss the prospect of his marrying another woman with such apparent equanimity.

Then there is the long-deferred ball at the Crown, one of the most brilliant chapters in the book and one in which there are clues to all the relationships as well as the incident which gives rise to further misunderstanding when Mr Knightley dances with Harriet and she first imagines that she is in love with him. The evening is packed with interesting little incidents. There is the moment when Mrs Elton says to her husband:

'Oh! you have found us out at last, have you, in our seclusion? – I was this moment telling Jane, I thought you would begin to be impatient for tidings of us.'

'Jane!' – repeated Frank Churchill, with a look of surprise and displeasure. – 'That is easy – but Miss Fairfax does not disapprove it, I suppose.'

Emma asks in a whisper:

'How do you like Mrs Elton?'

'Not at all.'

'You are ungrateful.'

'Ungrateful! – What do you mean?' Then changing from a frown to a smile – 'No, do not tell me! – I do not want to know what you mean. – Where is my father? – When are we to begin dancing?'

Emma could hardly understand him; he seemed in an odd humour.

Emma is referring to Mrs Elton's recent praise of Frank to his father. 'A very fine young man indeed, Mr Weston. A very handsome young man, and his manners are precisely what I like.' Frank, of course, thinks that Emma is referring to Mrs Elton's condescending kindness to his secret love.

Mrs Elton, as the bride, opens the ball with Mr Weston, with Frank Churchill and Emma following. But even when she is dancing with Mr Churchill Emma's eyes and thoughts are with Mr Knightley. Jane Austen writes:

He could not have appeared to greater advantage perhaps anywhere, than where he had placed himself. His tall, firm, upright figure, among the bulky forms and stooping shoulders of the elderly men, was such as Emma felt must draw everybody's eyes; and, excepting her own partner, there was not one among the whole row of young men who could be compared with him. – He moved a few steps nearer, and those few steps were enough to prove in how gentlemanlike a manner, with what natural grace, he must have danced, would he but take the trouble.

He does later take the trouble, when he leads out Harriet to the set after she has been disgracefully snubbed by Mr Elton. But, at the end of the chapter, he dances with Emma.

'Whom are you going to dance with?' asks Mr Knightley.

She hesitated a moment and then replied, 'With you, if you will ask me.'

'Will you?' said he, offering his hand.

'Indeed I will. You have shown that you can dance, and you know we are not really so much brother and sister as to make it at all improper.'

'Brother and sister! no, indeed!'

Those few words surely tell us all we need to know about Mr Knightley's feelings for Emma.

There is one moment of physical intimacy between Mr Knightley and Emma which should in its delicacy and, for me, its erotic charge, tell us that they are in love. Mr Knightley, obviously convinced that Emma and Frank Churchill will soon be engaged, unexpectedly determines to go and stay with his brother and Emma's sister, and comes to Hartfield to take his leave. He cannot bear to be in Highbury when the engagement is announced. Emma has just returned from visiting Miss Bates to try to make amends for her deplorable unkindness at the Box Hill picnic. Learning from Mr Woodhouse where Emma has been, Mr Knightley looks at her 'with a glow of regard, as if his eyes received the truth from hers, and all that had passed of good in her feelings were at once caught and honoured'. Jane Austen writes:

> She was warmly gratified – and in another moment still more so, by a little movement of more than common friendliness on his part. – He took her hand; – whether she had not herself made the first motion, she could not say – she might, perhaps, have rather offered it – but he took her hand, pressed it, and certainly was on the point of carrying it to his lips – when from some fancy or other, he suddenly let it go ... The intention, however, was indubitable ... nothing became him more. – It was with him of so simple, yet so dignified a nature.

It is one of the most touching moments in the novel.

All detective stories have that final chapter or chapters in which the clues are explained, misunderstandings resolved, errors corrected and the truth at last revealed. Jane Austen does this in three ways. Mrs Weston visits her daughter-in-law-to-be, then calls at Hartfield to explain to Emma the full story of Jane Fairfax's ill-begun but now prosperous love from Jane's point of view. We have Emma's musings as she recalls with remorse her humiliating errors of understanding and offences against good taste. And we have Frank Churchill's long explanatory, self-justifying letter to his step-mother, which Mrs Weston, of course, shares with Emma. This device of explaining the mystery in epistolary form is not uncommon in detective fiction. In Frank's letter the significance of all the moves in this game of love and misunderstanding are clearly explained. Jane Fairfax's increasing unhappiness at the deception she was practising, his own sanguine expectations that somehow all would come right, his deliberate courting of Emma to divert attention while he was convinced that Emma herself was indifferent to him and, indeed, shared his secret, the quarrel with Jane Fairfax after the strawberry-picking and her letter breaking off the engagement. I suspect that when, as a girl, I first read *Emma* I was left wondering why I hadn't seen it all myself.

And did they indeed live happily ever after? Mr Woodhouse is made so miserable by Emma's engagement that he can only be reconciled to the marriage by their suggestion that Mr Knightley should live at Hartfield. As Mr Elton says, 'rather he than me'. G. B. Stern, in a book entitled *More Talk of Jane Austen* published in 1950, looks ahead for seven years and suggests that indeed there were great strains on the marriage when Mr Knightley was required continually to suffer Mr Woodhouse's companionship while his and Emma's children were at Donwell Abbey. G. B. Stern gets over the difficulty by conveniently killing off Mr John Knightley so that Isabella can return to her father's house. Emma takes her rightful place at Donwell Abbey.

Well, that is all conjecture and, as Frank Churchill says, 'Sometimes one conjectures right, and sometimes one conjectures wrong'. I think that I shall choose to believe the author when she tells us so plainly at the end of *Emma*,

> the wishes, the hopes, the confidence, the predictions of the small band of true friends who witnessed the ceremony were fully answered in the perfect happiness of the union.

INDEX

INDEX

ff

Faber and Faber is one of the great independent publishing houses. We were established in 1929 by Geoffrey Faber with T. S. Eliot as one of our first editors. We are proud to publish award-winning fiction and non-fiction, as well as an unrivalled list of poets and playwrights. Among our list of writers we have five Booker Prize winners and twelve Nobel Laureates, and we continue to seek out the most exciting and innovative writers at work today.

Find out more about our authors and books
faber.co.uk

Read our blog for insight and opinion on books and the arts
thethoughtfox.co.uk

Follow news and conversation
twitter.com/faberbooks

Watch readings and interviews
youtube.com/faberandfaber

Connect with other readers
facebook.com/faberandfaber

Explore our archive
flickr.com/faberandfaber